The Arnold and Caroline Rose Monograph Series
of the American Sociological Association

The costs of regime survival

This comparative study of two republics – Guyana in South America, and Trinidad and Tobago in the Caribbean – examines the conditions which determine regime survival in less developed countries. Given the prevailing structure of political and economic organization typical of these countries, and of the web of international relations of which they are a part, political survival can very often depend on a leader's willingness to serve the interests of a small, but politically strategic minority. In both Guyana and Trinidad post-independence leaders made politically expedient decisions that foreclosed policy choices consistent with the satisfaction of collective needs. As a result both countries experienced a series of political and economic crises.

Professor Hintzen looks at the functioning of political elites and the strategies employed, such as ethnic mobilization, to gain and maintain control of the state. He argues that political and economic development can only be adequately advanced by the resolution of the conflict between regime survival and the satisfaction of collective needs. If these collective needs are to be met, equitable mass participation in the domestic political process must be guaranteed. He also sees a need for a shift in the international relations of less developed countries to alliances with politically neutral powers rather than with those who aim to satisfy their own interests.

This book, unique in its in-depth comparative study of Guyana and Trinidad, will be of interest to all scholars, students and policy-makers concerned with aspects of political and economic development in the third world.

The Rose Monograph Series was established in 1968 in honor of the distinguished sociologists Arnold and Caroline Rose whose bequest makes the Series possible. The sole criterion for publication in the Series is that a manuscript contribute to knowledge in the discipline of sociology in a systematic and substantial manner. All areas of the discipline and all established and promising modes of inquiry are equally eligible for consideration. The Rose Monograph Series is an official publication of the American Sociological Assocation.

Editor: Ernest Q. Campbell

Editorial Board:
Andrew Cherlin
Daniel Chirot
Phillips Cutright
Kai Erikson

Glenn Firebaugh
Virginia Hiday
Teresa Sullivan
Jonathan Turner

The Editor and Board of Editors gratefully acknowledge the contributions of Professor John D. Stephens of Northwestern University and Professor Richard Tardanico of Facultad Latinoamericana de Ciencias Sociales, San Jose, Costa Rica as expert reviewers of this book in manuscript.

For other titles in the series see p. 239.

The costs of regime survival
Racial mobilization, elite domination and control of the state in Guyana and Trinidad

Percy C. Hintzen
Afro-American Studies
University of California, Berkeley

Cambridge University Press
Cambridge
New York New Rochelle
Melbourne Sydney

CAMBRIDGE UNIVERSITY PRESS
Cambridge, New York, Melbourne, Madrid, Cape Town, Singapore, São Paulo

Cambridge University Press
The Edinburgh Building, Cambridge CB2 8RU, UK

Published in the United States of America by Cambridge University Press, New York

www.cambridge.org
Information on this title: www.cambridge.org/9780521363785

© Cambridge University Press 1989

This publication is in copyright. Subject to statutory exception
and to the provisions of relevant collective licensing agreements,
no reproduction of any part may take place without the written
permission of Cambridge University Press.

First published 1989
First paperback edition 2006

A catalogue record for this publication is available from the British Library

ISBN 978-0-521-36378-5 hardback
ISBN 978-0-521-03014-4 paperback

Transferred to digital printing 2008

To Vera Hintzen, my mother

Contents

	Acknowledgements	Page ix
1	**Regime survival and control of the post-colonial state**	1
	Introduction	1
	The setting	2
	The colonial bureaucracy, political mobilization, and control of the state	4
	Strategies for regime survival	10
	The international conditions of regime survival	13
	Mini-state vulnerability	14
	Conditions for autonomy in economic decision-making	16
	Class divisions and political support	17
	Factors preventing class mobilization	20
	Race and class in Guyana and Trinidad	20
2	**Mobilization for control of the state in Guyana and Trinidad**	28
	Nationalism and class mobilization: the initial phase	28
	Nationalist mobilization in Guyana	32
	Incremental nationalism, communal politics and class interests	37
	Metropolitan interests and the transfer of power	51
	Intra-class contentions and control of the state	55
	Summary	56
3	**Maintaining control of the state: strategies for regime survival in Guyana and Trinidad**	57
	Ideology and regime survival in Guyana and Trinidad	58
	PNM ideology and sectoral interests in Trinidad	58
	PNC ideology and sectoral interests in Guyana	63
	Clientelism and control of the state	70
	Coercion and control in regime power	77
	Conclusion	100

viii   Contents

4	Elite support and control of the state: race, ideology, and clientelism	103
	Methodology	105
	Sectoral and institutional background of leaders	106
	Distribution of wealth among leaders	109
	Ideological consensus and party support among the leaders	111
	Racial, ideological, and clientelistic support among Trinidadian leaders	116
	Bases of party support among Guyanese leaders	119
	Conclusion	124
5	**Regime survival and state control of the economy**	126
	Economic policy and regime survival in Trinidad	132
	Economic policy and regime survival in Guyana	151
	Conclusion	163
6	**The political and economic costs of regime survival**	165
	Regime survival and the maintenance of social order and stability	168
	Regime survival and self-sustaining development	175
	Regime survival versus equity and social security functions	193
	Regime survival and civil and political rights in Guyana and Trinidad	197
	Regime survival and collective needs in Guyana and Trinidad	198
7	**Collective needs versus the demands of powerful actors in less developed countries**	200
	International actors	200
	Governmental actors	201
	International organizations	204
	International business	206
	International actors and collective needs	207
	Domestic actors	208
	Regime survival and the link between domestic and international actors	211
	Conclusion	214
	Appendix	216
	Bibliography	219
	Index	233

Acknowledgements

A study of this sort, by its very nature, leaves the researcher with a list of indebtedness too long to mention. My selectiveness is in no way meant to imply that the contributions of those not identified by name were any less important than those so acknowledged.

This book emerged out of research conducted for my Ph.D. dissertation which was funded by the Ford Foundation and by a Shell Companies Foundation Incorporated Grant administered by the Sociology Department of Yale University. Subsequent phases of the project were funded by the Afro-American Studies Department of the University of California, Berkeley where I teach and by the Institute of International Studies and the Center for Latin American Studies, both at Berkeley, with which I am affiliated.

I will be eternally grateful for the encouragement, assistance, and unfailing support that I have received over the years from Professors Wendell Bell, Leo A. Despres, Cynthia Enloe, and Michael Smith. Professor Ralph Premdas contributed significantly to my thinking. His friendship is well appreciated.

The Sociology Department at the University of Guyana and the Faculty of Social Sciences at the University of the West Indies, St Augustine provided me with full access to university resources and a local institutional affiliation that gave me an entrée to persons and places which I would not otherwise have had.

I owe a special debt of gratitude to the Guyanese and Trinidadian leaders who, over the years between 1977 and 1985, were willing to take time off from extremely busy schedules and from their tasks of running nationally important institutions to agree to answer a hodge-podge of questions ranging from their personal habits and lifestyles to issues of international import. I hope that this study makes some (hopefully major) contribution to the solution of the problems they face as national leaders attempting to make their societies better places in which to live.

I would like to make special mention of Winston DeSilva in Trinidad and Edwin France in Guyana for making the frustrating task of a researcher bearable, pleasant and enjoyable. Cheryl Pittman's efforts in typing the manuscript and patiently retyping the numerous and constant revisions went way beyond the call of duty. I am truly grateful.

In a way, this book is a selfish endeavor, addressing the hopes, fears and concerns of my own family for the future. My wife, Joan, and my daughter, Candace, are both Trinidadians. My younger son, Kai, is a Guyanese. And my older son, Ian, is an American citizen by birth. It is our fervent hope that the writing of the book will contribute to the betterment of the three societies which we collectively represent. The flaws and errors in the book are entirely of my own making.

1. Regime survival and control of the post-colonial state

Introduction

There is a most serious dilemma facing political leaders engaged in the process of formulating and implementing national policy in less developed countries (LDCs). It emerges out of a conflict between the prerequisites for satisfying the collective needs of society on the one hand and the imperative of servicing the power, security, exploitative, and accumulative interests of metropolitan actors and their local allies, dependents, and clients on the other. The conflict pertains to conditions for political survival.

In an ideal world, the survival of political leaders should be linked to their effectiveness in promoting the generalized interests of the entire population and the developmental interests of society as a whole. Unfortunately, political survival in LDCs can depend on a leader's willingness to acquiesce to politically strategic international and domestic actors whose sole interests rest with their own wealth, power, and prestige. Such actors are intertwined in a web of international alliances. More often than not, the positions of power and influence of the small local minority among them derive from a willingness to protect and promote the economic, political, and security interests of metropolitan allies, partners, associates, and employers. In return, these local actors are provided with resources which allow them to dictate, determine and influence national policy if not directly to control the state.

Political leaders in LDCs are faced with the need to mobilize mass support without threatening the interests of these powerful and strategic actors. To do so, many come to depend upon their ability to appeal successfully to subjective sentiments. The politicization of communal or nationalist identity can serve to effectively separate decisions by mass constituents on which leader to support from any assessments of that leader's commitment to satisfying their own objective needs. For the mass population, political support comes to be based upon subjective identity rather than upon an evaluation of the program and performance of the political leadership. As a result, the political, economic, social, and cultural interests of the majority can be easily swept aside in a wave of subjective sentimentality. These interests are then bartered for control of the state by political leaders acting in the interest of a powerful minority.

Mobilization rooted in subjective identity can prove more effective than other forms of mobilization (such as those based on objective appeals to class and economic interest group) in ensuring that political leaders gain and retain control of the state in an LDC. It allows political leaders to retain mass support while, at the same time, providing guarantees of protection to elite and metropolitan interests. With mass support determined by subjective appeal, the conflict between elite and mass interests becomes depoliticized. This, perhaps, explains the pervasiveness of communal and nationalist politics in less developed countries.

The above arguments lead to one of the major theses of this study: that, in the light of the prevailing structure of political and economic organization typical of LDCs and of the web of international relations of which they are part, regime survival can come at the cost of the satisfaction of the collective needs of society. Among the latter are included social order and stability, self-sustaining economic development, equity in the allocation of valued ends, the social security of all members of society, and civil and political rights. The chances of political leaders gaining and retaining control of the state need not depend upon their willingness and ability to ensure that collective needs are met. These leaders may be able to employ successfully a "mobilizing idiom" based upon subjective appeal to gain and retain popular support. They might also be able to rely directly upon the resources of powerful and strategic actors to circumvent mass participation in the political process. Either strategy allows acquiescence to the demands of powerful domestic and metropolitan actors without jeopardizing political survival. Once in power, leaders enjoy exclusive access to the resources of the state. These can be used to co-opt support through political patronage and for coercion and control employed in repressing political dissent and circumventing mass participation.

The setting

Guyana and Trinidad and Tobago (hereafter Trinidad) are two former British colonies in the Anglophone Caribbean. Both are multi-racial with large black and East Indian populations. In Trinidad slightly over 56 percent of the population is either of black or mixed racial origin while close to 40 percent is East Indian. In Guyana the black and mixed groups comprise around 42 percent and the East Indians slightly over 51 percent of the population. Both countries contain small groups of whites (in Guyana, Portuguese) and Chinese (less than 2 percent for each group) while Guyana has a small remnant of the indigenous group of Amerindians (4 percent).[1]

Trinidad was granted its independence by Britain in 1962 and Guyana in 1966. Given the combined strength of the black and mixed population in Trinidad, majoritarianism and racial politics favored a black political party which relied on communal mobilization to gain control of the state. In Guyana the party which eventually assumed exclusive control of the post-colonial state was brought to power by relying not only upon mobilization of the black and mixed masses but, perhaps more importantly, upon the fact of black domination and preeminence in the colonial and post-colonial state bureaucracy, including its armed branches.[2]

It was only during the 1950s, however, that an appeal to racial sentiment became a central feature of mass political mobilization in Guyana and Trinidad. In both countries, nationalist mobilization had its roots in trade union agitation against colonial and expatriate employers (for Trinidad see Ryan 1972: 28–45; Oxaal 1968: 80–95; for Guyana see Chase 1964; Lutchman 1970). Political leaders rode the backs of mass economic dissatisfaction during the first half of the century to press for political change. They called for more representative government, for the sharing of colonial power, and for a shift of political control away from the colonial office and its representatives to local decision-making bodies (Ryan 1972: 28–45; Oxaal 1968: 80–95).

In the 1950s, however, during a "tutelary" period, acknowledged to be one of preparation for eventual independence, mass politics (which was up to that time directed against colonial intransigence to political reform) fell victim to race as the new "idiom" of popular mobilization.

The immediate question that is raised by an examination of the political histories of these two societies concerns the conditions under which members of aggregate communal categories become available for political mobilization and the consequences of such a pattern of mass politics for the political economy of a less developed country.

[1] These figures are for 1970 and are reported in the *Population Census of the Commonwealth Caribbean 1970*. The mixed population comprises mostly descendents of black–white (colored) and black–East Indian unions. Most identify politically, socially, and culturally with the blacks except the very light-skinned among them who are closer to the white population.
[2] For the post-Second World War history of politics in the two countries see, for Guyana, Despres 1966; Burnham 1970; Greene 1974; Hintzen 1981; Newman 1964; Sims 1966; Smith 1962; Manley 1979. For Trinidad see James 1962; Oxaal 1968; Ryan 1972; Williams 1962; Bahadoorsingh 1968.

4   *Control of the post-colonial state*

The colonial bureaucracy, political mobilization, and control of the state

One way to understand patterns of mobilization in colonial and post-colonial third world societies is through an analytical focus on the state. Such a focus has warrant because of the nature of colonial society and its post-colonial political legacy. Whilst creating and sustaining the conditions for systematic economic and political underdevelopment,[3] the paradox of colonialism is that it transferred to the colonies, in the form of a bureaucratic administrative structure, the most modern system of political and economic domination and control. This structure of organization, considered to be "technically the most highly developed means of power in the hands of the man who controls it" (Weber 1964: 232 and 196–244) became the fulcrum of colonial occupation (Greenberg 1980: 387–91). Its pervasiveness was manifest particularly in "colonies of exploitation" where, even more so than in "settler colonies" the role of bureaucratic administration came to be one of facilitating exploitation "in the interest of a foreign power" or of the relegation of the colony "to a market for foreign surplus commodities."[4]

Bureaucratization in the colonies came without an accompanying system of "checks and balances" such as a representative "open" democratic political system, parliamentary and executive control over the administrative apparatus, constitutionality and the rule of law, and an independent judiciary. As a result, the colonial bureaucracy was taken in a direction diametrically opposed to the Weberian ideal type (see Weber 1964: 196–8): i.e., it was rarely guided by the principle of "equality under the law." Rather, its preeminent, and oftentimes only, function came to be the protection and promotion of the interests of a small group of colonizers and the metropolitan concerns associated with them or which they represented. Under such conditions, bureaucracy can become "a power instrument of the first order" to be used exclusively for domination and control. This is particularly true when the "distribution of economic and social power" is so highly skewed as to produce a clearly dominant group (Weber 1964: 228–30). This was its precise function in the colonies.

Hence, the colonial bureaucracy became an instrument of both class and racial domination. Initially, power was ascriptive and the political system racially closed (Kuper 1971: 7–26; Greenberg 1980: 16; Smith 1971: 27–64). Any attempt by the colonized masses to have their demands met was

---

[3] This is the argument of dependency theorists. See Amin 1976; Beckford 1972; Bodenheimer 1971; Cockroft, Frank and Johnson 1970; Dos Santos 1970; Frank 1969; Furtado 1964.
[4] Adam 1971: 30–1. The distinction between "settler" and "exploitation" colonies is also made by Maurier 1949 and Hunter 1965.

guaranteed success only through the type of mass mobilization that so disrupted colonial order as to place metropolitan interests in jeopardy. Colonial response to such mobilization took two forms. More familiar was a gradual process of localization. This began with the recruitment into quasi-representative political institutions of a local proto-elite which usually was sympathetic to colonial interests. This elite was provided with nominal participation in decision-making deliberations. The process ended with the transfer of control of the state apparatus to an indigenous educated elite at independence. It was usually accompanied by the recruitment of locals into the colonial bureaucracy at increasingly higher levels of authority and by a greater participation of locals in domestic business and the professions. Oftentimes, however, there was strong colonial resistance (including the resistance of settler groups) to the relinquishing of political control to local political leaders and this led to the development of "insurgent nationalism" (Saul 1973: 379–80).

Whether the nationalist movement was incremental or insurgent, it was forced to depend on mass mobilization because of the closed and exclusive nature of the colonial power structure. Popular access to political decision-making was rarely present. Hence, mass popular mobilization directed against the colonizers came to be the only means of securing changes in colonial policies and practice that were consistent with the interests of the colonized. In its insurgent form, the aim of popular mobilization came to be the securing of absolute and immediate control of the colonial state. Alternatively, when the colonial authorities responded to nationalist demands by granting locals incremental and *de facto* access to political decision-making, there was usually a willingness to accept a tutelary period of transition to full independence.

In their efforts at mobilization, the aspirations of indigenous political leaders are best served if they are able to exploit patterns of social organization that make sense within the existing context and that relate to the reality of colonial social structure (Cohen 1969: 23–4; Lewis 1968: 387 415). In a typical colonial society, there is a rigid and impenetrable boundary separating the colonizer and colonized. This boundary remains impermeable to the upwardly mobile because the colonizer enjoys almost absolute political power and exclusive economic domination. It is supported by a system of institutionalized behavior which reinforces the status and cultural distinctions between the colonizer and the colonized. To this is added the racial distinctiveness of the colonizer. Given the above, the ideology of nationalism directed against the colonial aggressor becomes a powerful mobilizing idiom (see Chaliand 1978: 178–84). Nationalism becomes particularly appealing to the masses in the face of economic crises that prove threatening to their already precarious existence.

This entrenched equilibrium changes, however, when the colonial regime becomes committed to transferring control of the state to local politicians. With such a commitment, nationalist mobilization can lose much of its meaning. Since the issue of colonial control is settled, or about to be settled, the colonizers may no longer serve as rallying points for mass political action. This can jeopardize the mass appeal of nationalist leaders, particuarly against counter-claims to political power from elites who may or may not have been part of the nationalist effort. They are forced to look for new organizing idioms better suited to domestic political contentions.

In most instances, the organization of colonial society rendered social and economic boundaries more or less coterminous with those of race, culture, religion, language, tribe, or other manifest communal distinctions. These communal segments were generally differentially incorporated into the various strata of colonial society. Because of selected communal recruitment into the middle classes, communal segmentation can become even more pronounced as the colonized population becomes upwardly mobile. Thus, an appeal by leaders to segmental loyalty can prove dramatically successful since such loyalty is usually reinforced by socio-economic factors. As a result, political ethnicity can become the basis of mass mobilization. The most successful political leaders are typically those who are able to "define the situation" in communal terms.[5]

Political mobilization for domestic (as opposed to anti-colonial) political contentions need not inevitably take on a communal character. It does so under peculiar conditions created by colonialism itself. Because of a pattern of differential incorporation into colonial society, communal groups can develop conflicting socio-economic interests. This is quite obvious when the white colonizing group is compared with the non-white indigenous or migrant colonized groups. When the colonized communal groups occupy different areas of the country, or are associated with exclusive and distinctive socio-economic activity, the political task of unifying them under a nationalist banner becomes well nigh impossible. Members of one group will hardly support the mobilization efforts of another when the collective demands of one are seen to be anathema to the interests of the other. Under such conditions, appeals for cross-communal mobilization can hardly succeed.

[5] For two comprehensive overviews of ethnic politics see Young 1976; and Enloe 1973. The emergence of political ethnicity and its development in a specific case, that of Hausa migrants in Ibadan, Nigeria, is discussed by Abner Cohen 1969. For another of the many scholars who propose ethnicity as a "political" response to conditions of modernization see Adam 1971: 21–2.

Communal politics emerges within the context of domestic contentions for power. The group of political leaders which emerges to challenge colonial authority is not monolithic. Its members have different ideological positions and are identified with different interests. There is intense competition among them in their quest to gain control of the post-colonial state. The forging of communal alliances with the masses offers one of the most effective means of ensuring a mass following. It is for this reason that some Marxian analysts of colonial society dismiss communal mobilization as rooted in "false consciousness," seeing it as a consequence of the development of an ideology of domination by an ascendant bourgeoisie.[6] Other such analysts admit to the ontological status of communal organization while continuing to attribute motives of class domination to those who orchestrate its politicization.[7] Thus, communal political organization has much to do with the conflicting socio-economic interests of groups differentially incorporated into colonial society and with the competition for control of the state among political leaders representing different interests and holding different ideological positions in communally divided societies.

The argument, thus far, is that political ethnicity becomes particularly important when the issue of colonial control is resolved and when the country is in the tutelary phase prior to independence. This is because of a shift, during this phase, away from anti-colonial mobilization to competition among local political leaders for control of the post-colonial state. An appeal to communal identity can serve to guarantee mass support to competing political leaders when it is employed as an idiom of mass mobilization.

Mass support is only one of the political preconditions that must be satisfied if a political leader is to be assured of control of the post-colonial state. A way must also be found to assuage or neutralize strategic political actors with whom that leader is not aligned. Included among the former are powerful domestic interest groups, strategic sectors of the local elite, and powerful international actors. All of these are capable of using the formidable resources available to them to prevent a political leader from gaining control of the state. Likewise, they are able to make the task of retaining power impossible for leaders who have managed to gain such control. They have the wherewithal to mount or support mobilization efforts against leaders to whom they are opposed or, in the case where the errant leadership already controls the state, to undertake efforts aimed at destabilizing the political economy and disrupting social order.

[6] See, for example, Mafeje 1971; Post 1972. This view is summarized by Kasfir 1979: 368–9.
[7] See for example, Greenberg 1980: especially 405–10ff. See also Magubane 1979. Magubane, however, takes a more reductionist position by giving primacy to motives of class domination in his explanation of racial categorization.

8   Control of the post-colonial state

The capacity to assuage and neutralize powerful and strategic actors is very much enhanced if the state bureaucratic apparatus is not weakened in the transfer of control of the state to a national political leadership. Elite actors were almost exclusively dependent upon the colonial state for their positions of power, influence, and privilege and for the furthering and protecting of their economic interests. The colonial state also served as an agency of reconciliation in the face of inter-elite conflict and competition. Thus the colonial state was viewed as legitimate and the decisions of state-controlling colonial officials considered binding by powerful interest groups and their elite representatives. The omnipotence of the colonial state and the power of those who controlled it were rooted in the colonial bureaucratic apparatus that protected and preserved colonial hegemony. The colonial bureaucracy was also the major instrument used to organize society in the service of colonial interests.

But the colonial bureaucratic state can become undermined by nationalist mobilization and by the break-up of the hegemonic colonial system that buttressed colonial political domination. Strategic resources provided by the metropolitan colonial power normally become less available as independence approaches and as local elites gain political control. For most purposes such resources are withdrawn with the granting of political independence. Without access to these or alternative resources, the new leaders might find their efforts to perform effective state functions severely restricted.

Diminished effectiveness can be complicated by new conflicts. New nationalist definitions of state interests and policy and a new nationalist agenda normally produce a fracturing of the old relationship between the colonial state and many of the privileged sectors of the society. Where there was convergence of interests under colonialism there might be antagonism and conflict in the relationship between the state and elite segments of the population in the immediate post-colonial nationalist period. The result is that the legitimacy of the post-colonial state might come to be questioned by powerful segments of the population which had previously enjoyed privileged relations with colonial government. The weakening of the state bureaucratic apparatus by the withdrawal of colonial resources renders it less capable of functioning as an instrument of power and domination. The new political leaders must therefore seek new ways to accommodate these powerful actors by offering new guarantees of protection or they must devise new methods to secure their compliance to state decision-making, and, in the final analysis, to ensure their neutralization. Without such guarantees or in the absence of new effective methods of control, regime survival would be placed in severe jeopardy.

There are other problems that threaten the survival of a post-colonial regime. Once it assumes power it needs to seek the means to demobilize politically organized groups which have rallied behind its political opponents; otherwise these groups may continue to disrupt socio-political order by mounting persistent challenges to its authority and by engaging in anti-regime activities. At the very least, the state-controlling elite must make efforts to render anti-regime mobilization ineffectual. At the same time, the regime has to seek ways of holding on to its mass support.

The problems of demobilizing the opposition and maintaining mass support become considerably complicated when race, ethnicity, tribe, and/or other sectarian alignments form the basis of political organization. In the campaign for control of the state, objective interests might be rendered unimportant. However, once political leaders with a communal base of support gain power, they are popularly perceived to be mandated to favor their own communal followers in their programs and policies. To do otherwise would be to risk losing much of the support upon which their power is based. Nonetheless, giving in to communal demands can make the task of running the state all but impossible and can render the regime's hold on state power tenuous. This is so for a number of reasons. A regime is compelled to cater to the interests of those powerful actors that it cannot neutralize. In addition, it has to ensure that resources are allocated in such a way that at least a minimal level of state functions are performed. In doing both, it usually has to act against the interest of its mass followers while allocating state resources in ways that visibly benefit other communal groups. This leads to what political scientist Zolberg (1971: 624–5) has observed as an inevitable conflict between the demands of a regime's racial supporters and the performance of state functions. The conflict poses particularly acute political problems for a communal regime. Efforts to accommodate elite interests and to perform state functions effectively can easily lead to what anthropologist R. S. Milne (1981: 184) calls "outbidding." This is defined as "the act of making offers or promises to an ethnic group by an opposition party which is able to offer more than the government because, unlike the government, it is not under obligation to reach compromises" with other groups. In effect, outbidding represents a bid to gain control of a regime's communal supporters by leaders within the same communal group who are disaffected with its current political leadership. These disaffected leaders exploit the disenchantment and frustrations of the regime's communal supporters over programs and policies which favor other groups at their own expense. Outbidding thus represents an effort to use the regime's popular base by opponents bent on ousting it from political office.

When successful, it can pose one of the most profound challenges to regime survival.

Thus, three fundamental and immediate needs face a post-independence regime: (*i*) *the need to satisfy or neutralize powerful local and international actors*, (*ii*) *the need to demobilize or co-opt the organized opposition, and* (*iii*) *the need to retain one's own mass support and to prevent outbidding*. These needs combined constitute the conditions of regime survival, at least in the immediate post-colonial period. In their efforts to meet these conditions, regimes may be forced to sacrifice the collective needs of society. It is the consequences for society of making such a sacrifice that I term the costs of regime survival.

Strategies for regime survival

Ideology

There are many mechanisms available to political leaders to be used for gaining and retaining control of the state. One is ideology. I would like, here, to make a distinction between "pure ideology" and "practical ideology". The former refers to a systematic and internally coherent "world view" held by leaders and their supporters. It is quite fixed and inflexible and does not allow many degrees of freedom to employ different strategies for survival. This is not the case with pragmatic or "practical" ideology. The latter is defined as a socio-political program for the organization of the state presented by leaders as a means of communicating to politically strategic actors, both local and international, that their interests will be furthered and protected in regime policy (see Schurmann 1968: 17–104). Naturally, the constituent elements (and therefore the very character) of such an ideology can be constantly changed over time to suit changing circumstances. Such changes occur in spite of vehement denials or charges of ideological inconsistency and vacillation. Swings in the "content" or definition of their ideological positions have become quite typical of third world leaders as they struggle to respond to changes in the international and national arenas that affect their own chances of gaining or maintaining political power and influence (see Hintzen and Premdas 1983). Such swings can be interpreted as attempts to gain and maintain the support of powerful domestic and international actors who possess strategic resources and to appease actual or potential strategic opponents. For a regime already in control of the state, changes in practical ideology contribute to its survival by allowing it to respond to changes in the domestic and international environments that pose potential threats to its power and authority.

Patronage

To underwrite their survival, third world regimes also have available to them the resources of the state to be used for the distribution of patronage in exchange for support. With such resources, clientelistic ties can be developed with strategic elites and, through them, with those whose interests the latter represent. Mass support can also be generated and maintained through patronage allocations. Similarly, support from strategic groups such as the military, the civil service and other branches of the state bureaucracy can be guaranteed. Leaders of groups opposed to the regime can also be co-opted through the use of patronage. Such co-optation can prove most effective in demobilizing the latter's supporters since their leaders are no longer willing to engage in and support their own anti-regime efforts (see Hintzen 1983).

Control

The chances for regime survival can also be considerably enhanced when state control is strengthened and when activities under the domain of the state bureaucratic apparatus are expanded. As activities previously outside the sphere of influence of the state come under its control, resources associated with them are no longer available for use by those opposed to the regime. A particularly pertinent example of this is nationalization of the economy when the state takes over assets and engages in activities that were previously the preserve of the private sector. In the process, the private sector becomes miniaturized and international business becomes considerably weakened. Without control of the economy and lacking domestic sources of income, elites in the private sector become politically enfeebled. Another example of strategic state expansion is when the regime effectively deactivates the trade union movement – a major base for lower- and middle-class mobilization. The methods employed may be indirect as, for example, when the political executive gains control of trade union organization by placing its agents in effective positions of leadership. They may also be direct using, for example, effective legislation of state participation in bargaining, and the mandating of state arbitration of industrial disputes.

The political executive can also seek to assume full control of political activity. In this regard, the one-party state is exemplary in its ability effectively to demobilize and to regiment the members of groups which might either challenge regime power or compromise state autonomy. So, too, is the principle of party paramountcy which can be employed to reconstruct the ruling party for the service of statism (Holmquist 1979). What party paramountcy accomplishes is the removal of those mobilizing agents who control local party organization. They are replaced by state bureaucratic elites acting on behalf of and in the name of the party. In this way, power becomes centralized under the political executive which employs the state bureaucratic apparatus as an instrument of control. The effect is the demobilization and regimentation of those engaged in party-political activities to which the principle of paramountcy refers. In a similar manner, the regime can accomplish the demobilization and regimentation of every organization and activity that the state manages to penetrate and control. While demobilization brings an end to anti-regime activities, regimentation serves the purpose of organizing activities in support of the regime and consistent with its policies and programs.

Coercion

A regime also has at its disposal the entire coercive apparatus of the state to be employed against the political opposition, dissident groups, elite contenders for power, and disenchanted segments of the population that choose to engage in any form of behavior with political implications. While coercion is most efficient when used only as a temporary measure in a crisis (however ongoing), it can prove the most effective of the strategies employed by a regime to ensure its survival (see Hintzen and Premdas 1982: 337–54).

International realignment

Finally, when the threat to survival appears at the international level, a regime can seek alternative suppliers for those resources which it obtains in international exchanges and upon which its survival depends. These include guaranteed and preferential markets for the country's products, raw resources, industrial goods, consumer products, grants, aid, skilled personnel, weapons, and guarantees of defense against powerful international aggressors.

A typical regime in a less developed country employs a combination of the strategies discussed above to remain in power. Failure to employ these strategies successfully might easily spell political disaster given the fragile social, economic, and political order of LDCs and their vulnerability to actions by the various sectors to which such strategies are directed.

The international conditions of regime survival

The web of international economic, political, and even cultural relations within which developing countries find themselves place almost insurmountable barriers in the path of post-colonial regimes. Powerful international actors participate as interest groups in the local political economy and need to be accommodated, co-opted, or controlled in the manner discussed in the previous section. The fear of political and economic retaliation from these powerful actors is ever present, fed by the knowledge of the devastating effects on the political economy and on socio-political order that such retaliations can produce. Moreover, international actors are free to use their formidable and abundant resources to mount and support local and international mobilization efforts against the regime in power.

Irrespective of the behavior of international actors, the international structure of relations delimits the boundaries that circumscribe sociopolitical and economic stability. Most post-colonial third world states, because of the particular character of their international dependency, are extremely vulnerable to externally originated economic fluctuations. Their planners and policy makers have little control over the elements which govern national economic success or failure.[8] A fall in demand for any of their exports and an accompanying fall in prices can cause immediate economic disarray. A significant increase in the price of any one of their major imports can send costs of living skyrocketing and wreak havoc on balance of payments. This is much more the case for general inflation. A third world state finds itself powerless to meliorate and control the effects of inflationary spirals because these pertain to factors outside of the local economy. Efforts to control the economy, therefore, boil down to "timing, sequencing, and manipulation in an unending effort to perceive or create and, in any case, to exploit a multiplicity of little openings and opportunities" (Best 1971: 30).

Little wonder, then, that there is a major thrust by third world regimes aimed at control of the economy. There is the hope that economic control brings with it the ability to prevent the interminable economic crises that affect regime power. Such crises provide ammunition for anti-regime dissent and feed the fires of political violence and anti-government mobilization.

---

[8] For example, during periods of international inflationary crises governments of the developed countries have, time and again, demonstrated their capacities to exercise control over their own economies in their efforts to achieve economic turnabout. The structures of third world economies prevent planners from taking effective countermeasures and render economic controls unworkable. Demas (1978: 242) lists the developmental difficulties with which small states are faced and locates as their causes the pattern of undiversified and specialized production which typifies their economic structures.

Mini-state vulnerability

Both Guyana and Trinidad are mini-states (countries which are small in physical size and population), the economies of which are almost totally dependent upon export earnings from a very small number of products. This places particularly severe limitations on efforts at economic control. The economies of mini-states have been called "terminal" by West Indian economist Lloyd Best (1968) because of the existing structure of the international economy within which they participate and because of the nature of their internal domestic demand. A terminal economic structure is characterized by a number of interrelated factors. First, the international economic environment plays a much greater role in economic affairs than it does in those of the highly industrialized countries. This is even more true for mini-states whose economies are exclusively, and almost totally, tied to foreign trade.[9] Secondly, like most third world states, terminal economies rely upon importation for almost all of their consumer needs. Thirdly, they depend, for the most part, upon the revenues and upon the business and economic activities generated by the production of a very small number of goods, usually primary commodities, for export.[10] They have little leverage over the prices that their products command on the international market – especially when the volume of production is limited by small size.[11] The economic success of their export-oriented productive concerns depends, in most instances, upon negotiated prices and quotas and upon preferential tariffs and marketing arrangements agreed upon by the industrialized countries with which they do business. In many instances, access to markets for their products is controlled by the international corporations which own

---

[9] See Bairoch (1975: 198) who suggests that there is a considerable difference in the importance of foreign trade for the developed countries at the point of developmental take-off as compared with the developing countries at a similar stage of development.

[10] More recently, in countries which emphasize private investment, there has been an industrial upsurge geared towards production especially of consumer goods for markets in Western industrialized economies. Such production – which includes textiles, clothing, and telecommunications equipment – is usually labor-intensive within the context of an industrialized economy even though relatively capital intensive in a labor surplus economy. Low labor costs in developing countries make the location of these industries in the third world highly profitable.

[11] Brewster (1971: 205–7) discusses the conditions associated with economies that have a high dependence on export earnings and the economic implications of being "price takers" rather than "price fixers." Industries operating in industrialized countries have a great degree of control over their prices. They can fluctuate output, or their governments can effectively intervene to fix prices when these industries are threatened. This is not the case in export-dependent third world economies, especially when the volume of output is small compared to total world production. In these states, economic planners have no control over externally located markets.

Control of the post-colonial state 15

their major productive enterprises. In addition, terminal economies lack the capacities and facilities for production of industrial goods.

Mini-states with terminal economic structures experience a particular type of dependence which is fundamentally different in nature, character, and structure from that of the industrialized countries. Most countries of the world (with the possible exception of China) are vulnerable to economic conditions existing, and economic decisions made, outside their borders. However, industrialized nations have the capacity to respond to, to control, and to manage potentially disruptive conditions and events occurring and existing in areas outside their direct jurisdiction. In the small terminal economies such a capacity is nonexistent, as it is for most third world countries with the possible exception of the major oil-producing states among them. Export-oriented economies with a limited productive base are extremely susceptible to economic decision-making in countries with which they conduct their trade and to conditions in the international market affecting any single one of their products.

This is compounded by the dependence of most third world countries upon high-priced suppliers in the industrialized West for capital, technology, skilled personnel and industrial equipment. The purchase of these essential resources is a serious economic drain and undermines efforts at the accumulation of economic surplus for developmental investments (see Thomas 1974: 91-3; and Muller 1979).

Because of these economic conditions, state-controlling elites are forced to compromise the political and economic autonomy of the third world mini-states which they lead. Their political economies thus become vulnerable to manipulation at all levels. This is especially evident in the relations between the governments of host countries and the multinational firms that own and operate local subsidiaries. The international resources controlled by these firms can be far in excess of those available to governments of small states which, typically, have little of the capital and find themselves without the technology and skills necessary for running local productive operations. By contrast, many multinational firms have the capacity to shift operations to other countries when conditions prove unfavorable, and to absorb easily the losses sustained in such a shift. In small countries where major economic activities are usually undertaken by a small number of productive enterprises, the loss of any one of these can have disastrous consequences.

Given these sets of circumstances, governments of small states can find themselves with no alternative but to acquiesce to the demands of these companies, however outrageous such demands may be and whatever the effects upon long-term developmental prospects (the identical point is made by Ryan 1971: 196). To refuse would be to risk economic chaos and political turmoil. In many cases these firms eventually dictate the terms of the country's economic policy.

There are political constraints placed upon leaders of third world ministates as a result of dependence upon the industrial nations for capital, technology, skilled personnel, capital equipment and other types of economic resources. Private investors are quite reluctant to do business in a country that is not overtly capitalist and pro-Western unless it has natural resources that can be exploited for enormous profit. Private financial institutions may be unwilling to advance capital and provide foreign exchange to a country where Western investors are absent. Similarly, unless a country's resources are highly strategic to Western interests, bilateral and multilateral economic assistance from the West can come tied to political and ideological considerations – namely, a regime's expressed willingness to align with and protect the interests of donor countries. Given that the supply of critical economic resources comes primarily from the industrialized West or from agencies under Western control, the choice may very well be between explicit alignment with the West or economic and political chaos.

More directly, dependence upon bilaterally negotiated prices and quotas and upon preferential tariffs and marketing arrangements leaves small third world states at the mercy of the industrial nations with which they trade. States that act in ways that are perceived to run counter to the interests of the countries in which they market their products run the risk of economic retaliation. This can come in the form of cancellations of preferential arrangements, of the raising of tariff barriers, or of outright banning of their exports. All these have the effect of cutting off access of a country's products to markets in which they had previously enjoyed preferential status. The exports of such products constitute the major ingredient in the economies of most third world countries. Because of this, many small states are forced to acquiesce to the political and economic demands of the industrial countries with which they trade.

Conditions for autonomy in economic decision-making

A third world state has considerably more opportunity to act in its own self-interest when it has the wherewithal, internally, to run major economic enterprises and when these enterprises produce large volumes of strategic resources upon which industrial economies depend. Under these circumstances leaders are able to dictate the terms – economic, political, or otherwise – under which their country's products will be supplied to the international community. Ultimately, these leaders are free to undertake, if they wish, a program of national control of the economy without the fear of economic retaliation, without the worry of securing markets for the country's products, and without the concern of being able to run local industries effectively.

There are factors related to the role that local subsidiaries play in the international structure of operations of their parent company which can render state decision-making less vulnerable to the dictates of transnationals. When the operations of local subsidiaries are indispensable to the international operations of their parent firms, or when a considerable proportion of the company's international profits is derived from these subsidiaries, the bargaining power of the host country is increased. State-controlling elites can exercise more control over their operations. They can insist that in their operations the multinationals cater for local developmental needs and for the needs of the local population.[12]

The economic conditions which favor greater state autonomy and control and which offer the best protection against externally directed attempts at "destabilization" are more likely to be present in the larger third world states. This is especially true for those countries with large reserves of strategic minerals (the OPEC countries are a good example). Mini-states are less likely to be producing strategic resources in large enough quantities, if at all, so that disruption of production would threaten the economic stability of industrialized nations. They are therefore much more open to retaliatory economic, political, and military action.

Class divisions and political support

The term "class" is used in this study to mean an aggregated socio-economic category with common objective interests which, when acted upon, can produce unified political action of one form or another.

In societies such as Trinidad and Guyana, aggregated socio-economic categories can be divided into the following:

(a) An upper class of large businessmen and large planters.
(b) An upper middle class of professionals, owners of medium-sized businesses, college level educators, corporate managers, senior bureaucrats in the public sector and leaders of voluntary organizations.
(c) A lower middle class of small businessmen, primary and secondary

[12] For a discussion of the options available to mineral-dependent developing countries pursuing their own development in developing strategies to deal with transnational corporations see Stephens 1987. See also Moran 1974.

school teachers, white-collar workers (in private business, in civil administration, and in the parastatals), skilled workers, and owners of medium-sized farms.
(d) A rural lower class of small peasants, agricultural laborers, seasonal and short-term migrant laborers and the rural unemployed. An urban lower class of unskilled and semi-skilled urban laborers and the substantial number of urban unemployed. (These categorizations of class are a modified version of those presented by Stone 1973.)

The lower classes

In the process of political mobilization, members of each of the class categories listed above bring with them different strategic resources to be used by political leaders vying for control of the state. The lower classes are important for sheer numbers. In Trinidad, for example, figures for 1970 indicate that over 76 percent of the labor force was employed in typically lower-class occupations as unskilled and semi-skilled urban and rural workers, both employed and unemployed. Professional and technical workers were 9·7 percent of the total labor force, administrative and managerial workers were 1·2 percent, clerical workers were 10·6 percent, and farmers, farming managers and supervisors were 2·5 percent, making a total of 24 percent of the working population located in the upper- and middle-level occupations (Chernick 1978:274). Similarly, for Guyana approximately 75 percent of the labor force, during the early 1970s, had lower-class occupations while professional and technical workers were 6·5 percent, administrators and managers 0·7 percent, and clerical workers 6·5 percent of the total labor force. Of the income-earning population 6 percent were farm owners and farm managers (Chernick 1978:269 and 274). Thus, through the sheer weight of numbers and proportionate size of the total population, mobilization of the lower classes can become a powerful weapon in the arsenal of political leaders bent on capturing and maintaining control of the state and of regimes attempting to expand and fortify such control.

The lower middle class

The lower middle class comprises the lower level of the petit bourgeoisie who provide critical manpower in strategic sectors of the economy such as the civil, security, and skilled service sector, both private and public. To these are added the own-account peasant farmers. Members of this class are generally highly organized in voluntary associations such as trade unions. When such associations become politicized, the successful mobilization of their members can wreak havoc with socio-political order. These associations thus constitute a powerful political weapon to be used by political leaders attempting to gain and maintain control of the state. Leaders lacking a support base among the lower middle class might find it essential to co-opt elite representatives of its various associations and organizations and to seek to control and regiment its political activities. Otherwise, they may find it difficult to gain power or to maintain socio-political order when they do.

The upper middle class

The upper echelons of the petit bourgeoisie comprise members of the upper middle class who control resources critical enough to make them the logical "inheritors" of colonial power. It is mainly from within this socio-economic category that contenders for control of the state emerge. The patterns of political alignments within it are critical in determining which sets of competing political elites will eventually control the state and which sets of interests will be given privileged treatment. These interests pertain to the institutional bases and patterns of international alliances of competing factions within the class and the relationship of political leaders with these factions. The leaders of the upper middle class have resources which can be mobilized in support of and against a political elite, enhancing or effectively blocking the latter's chances for gaining control of the state. In predicting the chances for socio-political stability (and hence the chances for the regime maintaining its power position) one needs to know the nature and strength of support for and opposition to the regime within this upper middle class. Typically, political leaders are representatives of one or the other of these competing upper-middle-class factions who have developed intra- and inter-class alliances and an institutional base for popular mobilization.

The upper class

The relationship between the upper class and political mobilization is rooted in the former's control of the economy and upon the international resources its members have at their disposal. These resources can be used in support of one political contender against another or in a generalized campaign against "undesirable" political leaders. They can be used to mount mobilization efforts against a regime or to create and sustain conditions where mobilization becomes likely. They can also be used in support of a regime and to create and maintain conditions which are highly favorable to the

20 *Control of the post-colonial state*

continued tenure of that regime. For these reasons, members of the upper class must either be accommodated, neutralized or demobilized by the regime; otherwise the population has to be mobilized to withstand their retaliatory action.

The regime's ideology is pitched to class categories as a means of mobilizing support by appealing to objective interests. Such interests can override other considerations in determining political support. This might be true when the ideological position of a political elite proves highly appealing to members of the communal opposition because of its potential and actual beneficial effects upon their objective interests. These members may become reluctant to oppose such an elite solely on communal grounds. They may even become transformed into active supporters of this elite despite the latter's identification with a group perceived as communal opponents.

Factors preventing class mobilization

There are factors that act, over and above objective interests, to determine the nature of political mobilization and support within class categories. Communalism, nationalism, economic sectoral affiliation, patterns of voluntary organization and the like can act to preempt unified class mobilization. All are capable of undermining the objective interests of a class category particularly as a basis for political mobilization.

Thus, both subjective (communal and nationalist) and objective (class) interests converge in the strategies of political leaders to gain and retain control of the state. Some analysts have argued that an appeal to both subjective and objective interests can be "of equal fundamental importance within the same political situation" (Kasfir 1979: 378). Radical or populist political leaders might appeal to the objective interests of the lower classes when seeking to combat challenges mounted by middle- and upper-class groups. Other leaders, irrespective of ideology, might employ communal-mobilization as a counter to political opponents mobilized on the basis of their own subjective appeal to the masses. A third set might combine both class and communal appeals for mobilization against opponents and actors distinctively identified with each, such as white international capitalist investors in the economy.

Race and class in Guyana and Trinidad

In Guyana and Trinidad the most important, visible, and salient dimension of political cleavage is race (for Guyana see Despres 1966, 1967; Premdas

Control of the post-colonial state   21

1977; Milne 1977; J. E. Greene 1972, 1974; for Trinidad see Ryan 1972; J. E. Greene 1971; Stone 1972; Bahadoorsingh 1968, 1971). In both countries the intensity of communal sentiments has prevented the emergence of an interracial political alliance among the lower classes despite a common experience of severe and extreme economic hardship.[13]

The racial divisions in Trinidad and Guyana were cast out of the needs of plantation production. Several groups emerged, of different relative size, with different socio-economic interests, and occupying different power positions in the society.

Whites: By the end of the nineteenth century, the foundation had been laid for the structure of race relations in the two countries as it is manifest today. At the apex of power, privilege, prestige, status, and wealth was a small dominant group of European planters, administrators, and businessmen. This group was almost exclusively English in Guyana. In Trinidad, a more numerous French-speaking white creole population, together with a small number of Spanish-speaking settlers, were as prestigious, as wealthy and had as much status (even though not as much political power) as the English sugar planters and political administrators.

The group of French and Spanish creoles in Trinidad came closest to a local landed aristocracy. As merchants and planters, the members of this group were at the apex of white society in nineteenth-century Trinidad in spite of the greater political power of the British. Unlike the latter, who considered themselves colonial expatriates, the French and Spanish creoles developed a special pride in their Trinidadian identity. Their presence in the colony attracted other European settlers including Scotsmen and new Spanish settlers from Venezuela. In addition, many of the Englishmen who came after Britain captured the colony from Spain were encouraged by the presence of this group of creoles to make the colony their permanent home.

Unlike the British planters in the two colonies, the Trinidadian creole

[13] For a general discussion of the "instrumental" basis of racial mobilization see De Vos and Romanucci-Ross 1975; Enloe 1973: Chapter 7; and De Vos 1975. Enloe (1973: Chapter 9) discusses the conditions and forms of racially rooted political mobilization. Leo Despres (1975) explains the persistence of racial politics in terms of strategies for resource competition in resource-deficient environments, implying that an increase in the resources available to a country can lessen, if not eliminate all together, racially based political fragmentation. He discusses this proposition with specific reference to Guyana. Milne (1977) compares different developmental strategies adopted by Guyana versus Malaysia in the two countries' efforts to prevent programs for income redistribution and development from affecting social integration. Manley (1979) points to the success Guyana has achieved in this regard. In a conflicting view, Premdas (1978, 1980) shows how these very strategies adopted by Guyana have further impeded efforts at political and racial integration.

22   *Control of the post-colonial state*

whites were never entirely dependent upon sugar production. They were major producers, marketers, and financiers in lucrative coffee and cocoa industries. When Trinidad's small petroleum industry got under way in 1910, many creoles poured capital into spin-off services created by the new industry. Thus, the group's continued economic success was assured over the years in the wake of the growth in importance of cocoa, coffee, and citrus for export, and especially by the development of the country's petroleum industry. Later in the century, members of the local white population became the major beneficiaries of a phenomenal growth in manufacturing, construction, commerce, and local finance in the economy of the country.[14]

The business sector of the creole white population in Trinidad has become organized within a powerful Chamber of Commerce dominated by white businessmen, and around several exclusive clubs which protect and further the economic interest of the group. Further, the social identity of the white population and its social cohesiveness has been cemented through religious organization around the powerful Roman Catholic Church to which most members of that population belong. Wealth, social prestige, and institutional organization have combined to give the white group political influence way in excess of its small number.

Beginning in the last decade of the nineteenth century, sugar plantations in both colonies began to shift away from small planter-owned operations to larger, more capital-intensive and cost efficient enterprises run by managers and financed by absentee owners resident in Britain. Eventually, the sugar industries in the two colonies were taken over, almost entirely, by multinationals. This shift brought with it the demise of the British plantocracy in Guyana and Trinidad as English owners of small plantations were forced to sell. Most returned to Britain.

At the time the two countries gained their independence, then, the British presence in both colonies was confined primarily to the offices of the managerial and skilled staff in the British-owned agricultural, entrepreneurial, and commercial ventures, and to the group of British administrators and civil servants entrusted with running the two colonies. After

[14] The continued power, prestige, and wealth of the creole whites in Trinidadian society is indicated in the composition of the elite of the country at the time of its independence. Data collected by Charles Moskos in 1962 (Moskos 1967) strongly indicate a dominant role for whites in the business affairs of the country. Of 19 business leaders, nominated by a snowballing method of self-selection as the most powerful and influential in the country, 16 were white. By comparison, only 3 of the 7 economic leaders in Guyana were white (Moskos 1967: 109–11). In 1975 it was estimated that whites in Trinidad made up 53 percent of all the businessmen and that a further 24 percent were near-white (*Los Angeles Times*, 19 April 1975). Further, the business sector was perceived in Trinidad to play a much larger role in the leadership of the country. Of all the leaders nominated in Moskos' study 25 percent came from private business, because they were considered to be the most powerful and influential in the country. In Guyana, the comparable figure was 16 percent (Moskos 1967: 109–11).

independence, the majority of the government officials was repatriated to Britain. Even though most of the British staff in the private sector remained, they were over the years replaced by locals as a consequence of pressures exerted by both governments directed at ensuring the localization of managerial and technical staff in foreign-owned enterprises. The decline in the white populations in both countries between 1960 and 1970 can be almost entirely attributed to the repatriation of British functionaries after the granting of independence.

In colonial Guyana a group of white Portuguese occupied a position of status just below the British. Even though most were quite well off economically, with many engaged in successful business ventures, the members of this group were not quite accepted in to the social circle of the British. By and large, they did not participate directly in running the country – a role reserved exclusively for the British until well into the twentieth century.

Socio-economically, the Portuguese population in Guyana comes closest to the group of creole whites in Trinidad even though its members lacked the prestige, power, and wealth that came to characterize the latter. Furthermore, the wealth and political influence of the Portuguese population began to decline considerably following the Guyanese regime's shift to its socialist program in 1971. In the face of the subsequent weakening of the private sector, many chose to migrate overseas.

Blacks: While the Europeans (with the exception of the Portuguese) had come to Guyana and Trinidad as explorers and settlers from the last decade of the fifteenth century, blacks had been brought in as slaves from Africa to work sugar and cotton plantations from the seventeenth century until the early nineteenth century when the slave trade ended. Slavery was abolished in the two colonies in 1833.

Today, even though a small proportion of the black population continues to be engaged in the cultivation of small plots of land in the rural areas, blacks in both countries have become transformed into a proletarianized labor force. The bulk of the group is located within the lowest socio-economic categories in both societies. Black workers are concentrated in the urban areas and in the mining industries in both countries and many maintain ties with black villages, some of which continue to engage in subsistence farming; but the majority have been transformed into dormitory villages for urban and semi-urban workers.

The proletarianization of the black populations in Guyana and Trinidad followed in the wake of burgeoning opportunities for education. The process began during the latter half of the nineteenth century at a time when there was a growing need for a literate group of workers on the plantations and in the expanding urban and semi-urban areas of both countries. Even though rudimentary, a system of primary education was developed in both countries soon after the abolition of slavery and this provided for the black population the means of access into unskilled and semi-skilled occupations which, typically, required little more than an ability to read and write.

With a few notable individual exceptions, the education of the majority of blacks in both colonies remained confined almost exclusively to the primary level during the nineteenth century and the first half of the twentieth. During this time, the right to secondary education remained an exclusive privilege of whites. Nevertheless, the very expansion of primary education created in its wake a large demand for teachers which could not be met by the white population. To meet this need, teachers had to be recruited from the ranks of the blacks themselves. In time, post-primary teacher training served as a springboard for many blacks, giving them access to the more prestigious and high-paying civil service occupations. For those who remained in teaching, choosing to make a career out of it, upward mobility within the profession provided a certain degree of economic security while, at the same time, enhancing their status and prestige within the two societies.

A career in teaching, promotion within the teaching profession, and access to civil service occupations became the mainstays of black upward mobility in both countries during the twentieth century. As a result, the economic behavior of the black middle class became for the most part, crystallized within the narrow confines of salaried workers employed by the state. The educated black has, by and large, remained outside of the private sector which has been controlled and dominated by whites, who were later joined by East Indian businessmen and executives.

Over the years, however, blacks advanced from the most menial levels of the civil service to positions from which they now almost totally dominate and control it. This progression started first with an increase in opportunities for promotion as the service grew. It was enhanced with the localization of all but the top positions in the services that followed the democratization of politics in both countries during the 1950s. It culminated, finally, with the total replacement of the top-level colonial officials by locals when both countries were granted political independence from Britain during the 1960s.[15]

---

[15] See the International Commission of Jurists (1966) in a report which provides evidence and discusses the pattern of black domination of the government sector that had evolved in Guyana. The pattern was the same for Trinidad. See Braithwaite 1953.

Control of the post-colonial state 25

Most black workers remain in the proletarianized labor force in both countries. However, the black middle class of government officials and professionals – which has merged and developed a sense of common identity with a smaller group of coloreds (mulattoes) – has evolved into a most strategic and powerful constituency in the politics of both Guyana and Trinidad.

East Indians: East Indians, along with Portuguese and Chinese, were imported into the two colonies as indentured laborers to replace blacks on the sugar plantations after the abolition of slavery in 1833. Their importation was stopped in the second decade of the twentieth century.

Like the blacks, the bulk of the East Indian population is located within the poorest socio-economic categories in the two countries. Many continue to work as agricultural laborers in the sugar industries of Guyana and Trinidad.

During the nineteenth century, the planters and the colonial governments in both colonies began to offer the East Indians small plots of land in exchange for the price of their return trips to India. This was an effort to induce East Indians not to return to their homeland after the expiration of their contractual period of indentureship, and thereby to ensure the sugar industry of a continued supply of much-needed labor. So successful was the scheme that East Indians quickly emerged as the largest group of peasant farmers in both countries, cultivating rice in Guyana and sugar cane in Trinidad (see Williams 1962: 121; and McArthur 1912: 23).

The need for East Indian labor on the sugar estates set in motion a pattern of systematic discrimination against members of the group in most other sectors of the economy. Efforts were made to confine them to agricultural occupations. Moreover, they were exempted, by and large, from compulsory education laws that applied to all other racial groups, a practice that was fully remedied only during the third decade of the twentieth century. Without legally enforced access to education, East Indians became non-competitive in most non-agricultural areas of the economy.

Nevertheless, ownership of land set the stage for the upward mobility of many East Indians. During the twentieth century, many were able to use savings accumulated from their peasant undertakings to invest in small businesses. In some notable instances, such businesses have grown considerably.

The pattern of discrimination against East Indians in the public and private urban sectors impelled into the professions, particularly medicine and law, those who managed to acquire a secondary education, and who had the money to afford higher education at overseas universities. These occupations, by virtue of their relative independence, provided their practitioners with considerable insulation from the discriminatory practices of state and private sector employers.

Thus, through business activities and professional status, the East Indian began the climb into the middle and upper classes of Guyanese and Trinidadian twentieth-century societies. By the 1950s, East Indian businessmen had replaced most Portuguese among the group of the largest entrepreneurs in Guyana. While their rise in Trinidad was just as impressive, East Indian businessmen have not yet superseded the dominance of the creole white.

The cultural development of the East Indian populations in Guyana and Trinidad took on a character that was quite distinctive. Unlike the rest of the racial groups in both colonies, East Indians have remained firm in their commitment to Hinduism and to Islam (in the case of the smaller group of Muslims), and to the broader cultural trappings associated with these two religious systems. While there has been some conversion to Christianity among the group, the number of converts has been proportionally small.[16]

Notwithstanding the upward mobility of many East Indians, the vast majority in both countries continues to be plantation laborers and small-scale peasants. East Indian agriculturalists are numbered among the poorest of the socio-economic groups in the two countries.

The other racial groups: For most of the colonial histories of Guyana and Trinidad there was a group of mulattoes (coloreds) located in the status order just below the whites. During the twentieth century many worked as middle-level functionaries in government and in the private sector; they were also to be found among the local professionals. Over the years, coloreds have become less distinctive as a group, having developed, by and large, a common identity with the upwardly mobile black middle class. A few of the lighter-skinned upper-class coloreds have become identified with the creole whites in both countries.

Groups of Caribs and Arawacks (Amerindians) had inhabited both colonies before the arrival of the Europeans. All traces of these groups have disappeared in Trinidad, their members completely wiped out partly by European diseases and partly by the Spaniards in their attempts to recruit

---

[16] In 1970, three-quarters of the East Indian population in Trinidad was either Hindu (80 percent) or Muslim (20 percent). In Guyana, 83 percent of the East Indian population was non-Christian. Of these, 80 percent was Hindu and 20 percent was Muslim (*Census of the Commonwealth Caribbean 1970*).

them for plantation labor. In Guyana, the Amerindian population retreated into the interior of the country after European settlements were established on the coastlands and in the riverine areas. The group has since survived in almost total isolation from mainstream society and from the population of immigrants. Beginning in the 1950s, intense efforts were made to integrate Amerindians into the rest of Guyanese society, but the population remains almost completely socially, culturally, and geographically isolated.

Chinese indentures were brought into the two colonies as agricultural laborers after the abolition of slavery in 1833. This migration ended in 1866 when Britain bowed to protests from the Chinese mainland government against transportation and indentureship of its nationals. Some members of the originally small group chose to remain in the two colonies (see Fried 1956). Their descendants have become part of the urban middle class in both countries with occupations as small businessmen, civil servants, and professionals. New arrivals of Chinese migrants over the twentieth century have swelled the group's number. Most of the recent immigrants have established small- and medium-sized businesses. The Chinese have maintained some form of racial affinity which has been kept alive, in both countries, by the formation of Chinese associations. The cultural activities of the group have been revived in the wake of the twentieth-century arrivals.

Finally, in Trinidad there is a small but economically influential group of Syrians, Lebanese, and Jews (together numbering probably less than five thousand) who arrived later in the twentieth century. These groups are almost exclusively involved in business and their members are among the most wealthy in the country. Their business successes have increased the visibility of the light-skinned population and have contributed to its domination of the economy.

2. Mobilization for control of the state in Guyana and Trinidad

Nationalism and class mobilization: the initial phase

It was argued in Chapter 1 that when the structure of colonial organization is centered around the colonial bureaucracy, which functions as an instrument of power and domination socio-political change can come about only through mass mobilization. To be successful, such mobilization must be capable of disrupting colonial order and placing metropolitan interests in jeopardy. Mass mobilization is made necessary because of the rigid and impenetrable boundary separating the colonizer and the colonized and the closed nature of the political and social systems.

Mass mobilization is not invariably directed at the securing of sociopolitical reform; its objectives could remain confined to issues of economic and material welfare if the movement that inspires it does not become politicized. For politicization to occur, there must exist a group of leaders who are able to transform objective demands into political issues usually through the use of ideology. When the basis for initial discontent is economic and material, such an ideology must, of necessity, take on a class character. Ideology might also assume a nationalist character when the object of demands for change is a colonizing elite or a colonial power. Since colonialism implies class domination, nationalism can quite easily be appended to a class-based ideology.

Demands for change to a more representative government or for independence under a nationalist government also assume the existence of an elite with the wherewithal to take over administrative, legislative, and judicial functions from the colonial power. In other words, they assume, as a precondition, the existence of a domestic middle class from which the new set of leadership elite must come. There must be a generalized willingness, on the part of this middle class, to see itself in nationalist terms as leaders of the masses and a willingness to confront politically the colonial power.

Thus, politicization of the colonial masses can take on the character either of "bottom up" or "top down" mobilization. In the former, generalized discontent over material conditions leads to mass mobilization which is then harnessed by a middle-class leadership employing a class and/or nationalist ideology to confront the colonial authorities and demand change. In the latter case, a class or nationalist ideology is developed among the colonized middle classes and is employed as a mobilizing idiom among the lower classes by exploiting discontent over material conditions. Whatever its character, a fundamental condition of change to a more equitable and representative socio-political system is effective mass mobilization that is informed by a politicizing ideology rooted in class or nationalism, or both. The mass movement must be led and supported by a colonized middle class with the wherewithal to assume those legislative, administrative, and judicial functions normally performed by the colonizers. The strategy employed and the agenda for change can be determined by the willingness, on the part of the colonizers, to relinquish control, both political and economic, to a domestic elite. It was argued in Chapter 1 that such a willingness determines whether or not the nationalist movement will assume an incremental or an insurgent character.

In both Guyana and Trinidad, the nationalist movement assumed an incremental character. It began in the two countries with "bottom up" mobilization, born and nurtured in a twentieth-century tide of rising expectations that were constantly frustrated by the structural impediments to mobility presented by plantation society and a terminal economy. The nationalist era began with labor mobilization during the second decade of this century. Escalating labor unrest produced "heroic" charismatic leaders at the head of organized and unified labor movements demanding better wages, improved conditions of work, and the establishment of formal collective bargaining procedures (for Trinidad see Ryan 1972: 28–45; Oxaal 1968: 80–95; for Guyana see Chase 1964; Lutchman 1970).

Once labor became mobilized, middle-class leaders attempted to transform the movements into proto-nationalist groups by channeling their goals away from bread-and-butter issues of wages, salaries, and conditions of work towards demands for political reform. By the 1930s, these leaders had begun to call for more representative government, for a sharing of political power between colonial and local leaders, and for a shift of political control away from the Colonial Office and its representatives to local decision-making bodies (Ryan 1972: 28–45; Oxaal 1968: 80–95; Chase 1964: 72–82).

The early nationalists, while unable to organize fully fledged political movements, did enjoy some degree of political success. Labor mobilization was particularly widespread in the late 1930s and finally exploded, in 1937, into debilitating riots, first in Trinidad and then in other Anglophone

30   *Mobilization for control of the state*

Caribbean territories. The extension and severity of the unrest shocked the British Parliament into debate over the whole issue of existing colonial policy and practice (see R. T. Smith 1962: 163–5; Ryan 1972: 45–67; *Parliamentary Debates* 1937; West India Royal Commission 1939).

A Royal Commission was dispatched to investigate general social and economic conditions in the West Indian colonies. In its report the Commission made recommendations for far-reaching constitutional and social reforms that paved the way for an incrementalistic approach to the transfer of political control to locals and, eventually, to political independence (see West India Royal Commission 1939). Included was a recommendation for "representative government" in which local politicians, elected under universal adult suffrage, would fully participate in the political affairs of the two colonies.

The acquiescence of the British Parliament to demands for local political control reflected the success of local political leaders in tying the material concerns of the working classes to issues of political reform. There can be no doubt that working-class mobilization was the critical ingredient in the decision of the British Parliament to agree to the transfer of some aspects of state control to locals. Labor mobilization was clearly devastating as far as colonial economic and political interests were concerned.

Protection of economic interests and a consequent need to maintain social order were clearly preeminent in Britain's decision on political reform. During periods of political quiescence such changes were neither considered nor implemented – they were grudgingly made only when socio-economic order appeared to be threatened. Even after reforms were conceded, little effort was made to implement them, and none at all if socio-political order had been restored. This was particularly true for the recommendations of the West India Royal Commission. Soon after they were issued, there was an upsurge in economic activity in Guyana and Trinidad to cater to the needs of the Allied effort in the Second World War. This took the edge off working-class dissatisfaction. At the same time, with the promise of political reform and of an eventual transfer of some decision-making functions to locals, newly emergent leaders were reluctant to continue their mobilization campaigns against the colonial regime. As a result, the lower-class movement became demobilized, at least while hostilities raged in Europe (see Lewis 1968: 207–8 and 387–415; R.T. Smith 1962: 161–7; Dookhan 1975: 30–7).

After the war, the Colonial Government agreed to an increase in local political representation in the Legislative Councils of the two colonies. This new arrangement did little more than offer status and privilege to local politicians. While denying them any significant influence over colonial decision-making, it did signal Britain's willingness to consider reform. This willingness became the key ingredient in the incrementalist path taken by the nationalist movements in both countries.

Thus, in both Guyana and Trinidad there developed a generalized commitment to "gradualist" change. As early as 1946, Britain agreed to the introduction of universal adult suffrage in Trinidad as a prelude to more far-reaching constitutional changes. In Guyana, financial and property restrictions on the franchise were finally removed in 1953. Even though the Colonial Office and its local representative under the authority of the Governor continued to enjoy absolute political power, the introduction of universal adult suffrage was symbolically significant. It imbued local political actors with a sense of efficacy. It was also a statement of intent, on the part of Britain, that self-government and, eventually, independence was to be granted in the not too distant future. In effect, the introduction of universal adult suffrage took political pressure off the colonial regime with its promise of fundamental change in the future.

Britain's demonstrated willingness to concede to demands for more representative government and to promise eventual political independence was not entirely related to the success of mass mobilization efforts. There were also a number of factors, external to the two colonies, which made continued colonial autarchy highly improbable. In Britain itself, the stunning post-war electoral defeat for the pro-colonial Conservative Party by a powerful British Labour Party, and the democratic socialism of the latter, reflected a new ideological direction in the country. These, together, became the bases for a more responsive reception to appeals for self-determination in the colonies. Ideas of progressive socialism were becoming so rapidly diffused throughout the colonial territories that they had become responsible, to a large degree, for an increase in anti-colonial mobilization. Thus, the political sympathies of the British rank-and-file, imbued with these very ideas, were with the anti-colonial nationalist movements. In addition, the economic costs of colonial administration were becoming burdensome to the British taxpayer, who did not receive the direct benefits of economic exploitation. Finally, in the wake of the successful Gandhi campaign against colonialism in India, international opinion had swung in favor of self-determination as the undisputed right of any country.

While the above serves to explain Britain's receptiveness to demands for change, it was clearly the forging of nationalist movements out of lower-class discontent that acted as the catalyst for change. Ironically, it was the

32 Mobilization for control of the state

increasing strength of the British Labour Party and growing popularity of its Fabian socialism that provided the legitimacy and the ideological underpinnings for the anti-colonial struggles.

The first nationalist leaders in Trinidad emerged from the white creole middle class. This is not surprising given the group's economic power and the colonial practice of excluding its leaders from any form of political decision-making. Exposed to the Fabian socialism of the British Labour Party, these creole nationalists forged labor discontent in Trinidad into a unified labor movement between 1919 and 1934. They also laid the foundation for party politics in the country by forming a Trinidad Labour Party in 1934 patterned after the British Labour Party and based on the latter's ideological and organizational principles (see Oxaal 1968 and Ryan 1972). In other words, in Trinidad, Fabian socialism provided the ideological bridge between demands for material and economic betterment and political demands for national self-determination. It was the long-established white middle class which provided the leadership that successfully accomplished this transition.

Nationalist mobilization in Guyana

In Guyana, the emergence of a nationalist movement was delayed because of a weak and unsympathetic middle class. Even though the lower classes were as highly mobilized as those in Trinidad as early as the second decade of the twentieth century, attempts to politicize mass discontent and to create a nationalist movement were minimal up to the end of the Second World War. During the 1930s, there was a weak attempt to give the labor movement ideological direction. This came, not from the middle-class leadership, but from a lower class leader and founder of the British Guiana Labour Union (BGLU) which had emerged as a general purpose trade union in 1919. More characteristically, the middle-class leaders of the trade union movement were content to make moderate demands for incrementalistic political and economic change without challenging the colonial status quo. In other words, they persisted in defining the issues in material and welfare terms rather than in terms of political power and political representation.

Nonetheless, during the early 1940s, constitutional reforms were implemented in Guyana, although they were more the result of Britain's initiative than of any demands made by middle-class leaders. In implementing such reforms, the Colonial Office was responding to nationalist pressures occurring in the rest of the Anglophone Caribbean. While they provided expanded representation, their effects were minimal. Despite an increase in elective posts in the country's Legislative Council in 1943, based on a

Mobilization for control of the state

franchise qualified by property and income, and a guarantee of trade union representation in the Executive Council of the country, mass interests remained unrepresented. Local political leaders serving in the legislature quickly became co-opted clients of the colonial government and colonial economic interests. In this capacity, they began to direct their political efforts at the demobilization of the lower classes (Lutchman 1970: 22–7). They rejected bargaining and mobilization in favor of acquiescence and, in doing so, lost their legitimacy as leaders. The effect of their *volte face* became quite evident in Britain's decision to delay universal adult suffrage until 1953 while granting it to the sister colony of Trinidad in 1946.

Without middle-class leadership and lacking ideological direction, lower-class mobilization in Guyana suffered from an absence of unity and direction. During the 1940s, workers began to resort to wildcat strikes in making demands for socio-economic betterment. This remained the case until the emergence of a group of middle-class radicals, organized in a Political Affairs Committee (PAC), that managed to capture control of the trade union movement.

One of the PAC's leading members, an East Indian dentist named Cheddi Jagan, founded a new union, the Guiana Industrial Workers Union (GIWU), to present a radical alternative to conservative trade union leaders representing East Indian plantation workers. Thus, in the late 1940s, there was for the first time, a radical middle-class group of leaders, organized in the PAC, who were available to direct and channel the mobilizing efforts of the lower classes.

Membership of the PAC comprised largely overseas-trained professionals and intellectuals. Most were inspired by the radicalism of the British Labour Party and had converted that party's socialist ideology to suit the conditions of colonial British Guiana. This conversion translated into calls for representative government and eventual political independence. A few members of the PAC had become converted to the ideology and principles of Marxism-Leninism while overseas. This was true of the acknowledged leader of the group, Cheddi Jagan.

Thus, to middle-class leadership of lower class mobilization efforts, undertaken through trade union activity, was added a progressive and radical ideology. These conjoined to produce nationalist mobilization. Cheddi Jagan's radicalism and his willingness to confront the pillars of authority in support of the rights of workers made the GIWU an immediate success. He was quickly able to use the union as a basis for political mobilization in support of demands for radical change. Violent colonial retaliation against Jagan's mobilizing efforts served to dramatize to an already embittered labor force the very brutality and repressiveness of the colonial regime. It sanctified the appeal of the radicals for confrontational politics.

Cheddi Jagan's strategy among the East Indian workers was duplicated by Forbes Burnham, a young black lawyer with a berth in the powerful BGLU. Burnham was as popular among the black working class as was Jagan among his East Indian supporters. His radicalism was developed through direct exposure to the politics of the British Labour party while he was a student in England. Burnham immediately joined the PAC and later, with Jagan, formed the Peoples Progressive Party (PPP). As co-leaders of the PPP, the two were able to forge a powerful nationalist movement that was to pose a formidable threat to colonial hegemony. The movement was firmly rooted in lower-class mobilization.

Political scientist Ralph Premdas (1975) convincingly explains the party's success at lower class mobilization in its strategy of capturing control of the labor movement. Even before the PPP was formed, Jagan, through the GIWU, had gained control of the East Indian sugar workers. In 1950, two of the party's founder members (one of whom was Forbes Burnham) held leadership positions in the BGLU, the largest and most powerful of the black unions. Another of the party's core leaders had served as Secretary General to the Trades Union Council (TUC) which was the umbrella organization of the most important unions in the country. Indeed, as Premdas has argued, members of the PPP held leadership positions in most of the unions in the country during the early 1950s (1975). The workers were undoubtedly attracted to the militancy of the radical union leadership in pressing home demands for socio-economic betterment of their lot. It was the issues of bread-and-butter that concerned the lower-class electorate. The promise made by the PPP for a much more materially attractive future through the destruction of the overlordship of the white colonial class made sense to a working class whose demands for socio-economic change were being constantly rebuked by representatives of those very overlords.

General elections, held in 1953, were the first in the country to be conducted under universal adult suffrage. They were to usher in a new constitution of limited internal self-rule which placed legislative responsibility in the hands of a Legislative Council of 24 elected members and three colonial officials. The Executive Council was reconstituted to contain six ministers selected by the leader of the party winning a majority in the national elections, three colonial officials, a nominated Minister without portfolio, and the Governor. The new Executive Council was to be the "principal instrument of policy" (see Lutchman 1970: 27–9 and the *Colonial*

Annual Report on British Guiana 1953). A State Council was also added to the government. It comprised nine members nominated by the Governor (two on the advice of the party in power) and a nominated Minister without portfolio. Thus, the new constitutional arrangement represented a compromise by giving elected politicians virtual control of the legislature and of the Executive Council while guaranteeing in the State Council the participation of colonial business interests through the mechanism of nomination.

In both Guyana and Trinidad, therefore, it was radical middle-class leaders employing a socialist ideology, derived from the British Labour Party, who were able to unify and politicize lower-class mobilization efforts. They then used such mobilization to back nationalist demands. In both instances, Britain was forced to make the constitutional changes that ushered in representative governments and universal adult suffrage.

The fact that universal suffrage and the attendant constitutional changes were delayed until 1953 in Guyana may well have proved telling for the political direction of the country after the war. The pre-war radicalism of the Trinidadian nationalist movement was nipped in the bud. Political contentions shifted with the introduction of universal adult suffrage in 1946 to competition among local aspirants for eventual control of the postcolonial state. A radical and class-based ideology, so highly suited to an anticolonial nationalist struggle, became less important in this new phase of political organization. In Guyana, however, the anti-colonial struggle was then beginning. It came at a time of increasing legitimacy for nationalist and socialist movements in the wake of the success of the British Labour Party and of Ghandi's struggle in India. Moreover, the nationalist struggle was headed by leaders of a domestic middle-class intelligentsia that had become much more strategically placed in the Guyanese political economy after the war. The result in Guyana was that a radical group of political leaders was able to capture political office (even though their power was limited by the constitution) as soon as universal adult suffrage was introduced. In Trinidad, this was not the case. The leaders of the pre-war nationalist movement had come, primarily, from the creole white segment of the population and this group's identification with the private business sector served as a check on the radical direction of the movement.

The PPP scored an impressive victory in the 1953 elections winning in 18 of 24 constituencies and capturing 51 percent of the popular vote. All the party's successes came in predominantly lower-class constituencies (Premdas 1975: 16). It was helped, as Premdas (1975) again points out by "a sudden expansion of the electorate," many of whom were new wage earners interested in bread-and-butter issues. Party leaders, through their union activities, had demonstrated their preparedness to confront the colonial authorities in support of the interests of their mass supporters. The program of the PPP offered promises of a future even brighter than these wage earners had dared to imagine – if only the interests of the white ruling class could be expropriated. Thus, the ideology of the PPP made sense to the working class when translated into its practical consequences.

Political gradualism has its functions. It allows the colonial regime time to develop the mechanisms to guarantee the protection of metropolitan interests after independence. It does so by ensuring that the regime which inherits control of the state is sympathetic to these interests (see Chapter 3). Providing such assurances becomes quite difficult when a radical leadership captures political officer at the very beginning of the tutelary phase of representative government. For this reason, the experiment of representative government by Britain in Guyana backfired. It placed a group of radical leftists within a hair's breadth of controlling the legislative and administrative branches of the state. Calls made by the PPP for immediate independence were not lost upon the Colonial Office, and loomed ominously in view of the demonstrated capacity of the party to mobilize its ebullient supporters.

The PPP government posed a threat both to foreign capital with interests in the country and to the local propertied, professional and administrative middle class who stood to benefit from the very status quo that was under such vehement attack by the Party. Britain had no doubt hoped, and expected, that political power under a representative government would be inherited by this moderate middle class. This, as will be shown, was the case in Trinidad.

The rapidity with which the radical PPP burst onto the political scene allowed the Colonial Office no time to prepare for the possibility of its rise to power. The Governor had to lean heavily upon the repository of political control that he retained in the new constitutional arrangement to ensure the protection of the political and economic interests of metropolitan concerns. His actions forced Jagan and the new PPP government to complain constantly and bitterly that the party was merely "in office and not in power."

Notwithstanding the well-touted constitutional guarantees of representative government, the colonial powers showed themselves to be the ultimate political authority in the colony. Despite the supposed devolution of power to the locals, the new radical government was forced to mobilize its lower-class political supporters to back demands for political and economic reform. Britain demonstrated its authority by suspending the constitution

Mobilization for control of the state

after only 133 days of the PPP government. The country was reverted to an even more autarchic form of Crown Colony government with wholly nominated Legislative and Executive Councils, the functions of which became mainly advisory. The Governor and the Colonial Office once again assumed direct authority in running the colony's affairs. Thus, Britain used its coercive arsenal and the state apparatus of control to demobilize successfully the nationalist movement.

Incremental nationalism, communal politics and class interests

Bases for communal politics in Guyana and Trinidad

A commitment on the part of the colonial regime to transfer control of the state to a local political elite can act to defuse lower-class radical political mobilization. It creates a situation where the colonizers are no longer the object of demands for change and no longer serve as a rallying point for political action. When the issue of colonial control is settled or about to be settled, political leaders are forced to look for new organizing idioms better suited to internal political contentions (see Chapter 1). One of the arguments put forward in Chapter 1 is that to be guaranteed mass support, leaders must be able to exploit patterns of social organization which make sense within the existing context. The organization of colonial society in such a way as to make social and economic boundaries coterminous with those of race, culture, religion, language, and tribe can act to make an appeal to communalism most likely at the very time when the nationalist movement seems on the verge of success. The seeds of communal politics can be planted in the nationalist movement itself, particularly in the way it is organized. They can blossom in the process of organization of the party-political system after the introduction of universal adult suffrage.

In both Guyana and Trinidad, the communally exclusive nature of institutional and associational activities tended to reinforce racial identities. In the political arena, a constituency system and a trade union base for mobilization invariably led to racial exclusivity in political organization. For example, during the late 1930s in both countries, the mass-based, general purpose unions gave way to a proliferation of industry-specific and job-specific unions. Given the racially differentiated occupational system, the new unions that emerged became racially exclusive. In Trinidad, there were 17 unions formally organized by 1938 and almost all had memberships that came predominantly from one of the racial groups. This was especially true of two of the most powerful unions: the Oilfield Workers Trade Union

38   *Mobilization for control of the state*

(OWTU) which represented the predominantly black labor force in the petroleum sector, and the All Trinidad Sugar Estates and Factory Workers Trade Union, representing predominantly East Indian plantation workers. Similarly, in Guyana during the same period, over 20 unions representing specific categories of labor were registered, major among them being the British Guiana Labour Union (BGLU) representing black urban proletarian labor, and the Man Power Citizens Association (MPCA) which represented the predominantly East Indian sugar estate field workers. Near exclusivity in racial composition was the pervasive feature of almost all of the remaining unions organized in the country during this period.

There was also, in both countries, a high degree of racial exclusivity in residential clusterings of the population in villages, communities, and in broader geographic areas. This was especially true of the East Indian and black populations which were concentrated, respectively, in rural villages in the sugar belt of the two countries, and in urban lower class neighborhoods and dormitory villages close to urban centers. The "light skinned" populations of whites, Chinese, and coloreds tended to be located in upper- and middle-class urban neighborhoods. In Guyana, the Amerindians lived in semi-isolated hinterland communities.

The constituency system, introduced in the transfer of the Westminster model of parliamentary democracy from Britain to the two colonies, served to reinforce racial patterns of political organization given communal exclusivity in patterns of residence. Constituencies shared, by and large, the same boundaries with these residential clusterings.

With the two major bases for political mobilization rooted in racially exclusive bodies – the constituency and the trade union – national political organizations came to resemble racial coalitions rather than monolithic and unified structures. Ideological appeals to class during the early phase of the nationalist movement served more as a cement holding these racially disparate groups together, rather than as a basis for the crystallization of a unified mass movement.

Given the factors noted above, a shift to communal politics appeared highly likely in both countries. The reasons are two-fold: first, communal politics can guarantee mass support for politicians competing against each other for control of the state; secondly, it delivers the support of powerful middle- and upper-class communal elites who might previously have opposed the nationalist movement. This is precisely what occurred in both countries. The democratization of electoral participation and the commitment by Britain to transfer control of the state apparatus to local political leaders led to intense internal political competition. The turning inward of the political campaign brought with it the need for a new mobilizing "idiom" as the issue shifted from colonial domination and self-determination to competition for state control. As a result, race became the preeminent ingredient in the organization of popular political participation.

Racial politics and class interests in Trinidad

The shift to racial politics became evident in Trinidad immediately upon the introduction of adult suffrage. With the democratization of the electoral system, majoritarianism came to be the basis of political power. The principle of majority rule favored political leaders who were capable of mobilizing the support of the largest voting blocs in the country, and in the absence of class mobilization, this meant the black and East Indian populations. Gradually, political leaders began to realign themselves along racial lines.

Local whites had been in the forefront of progressive politics prior to the Second World War, and indeed many had been radical leaders of the labor movement. But the injection of race into post-war political organization proved threatening to their own political aspirations. The combination of majority rule and racial mobilization brought with it the real possibility that whites would be excluded from the corridors of power. There was the chance that these leaders would be out of contention, purely on racial grounds, in the competition for control of the post-colonial state. In order to consolidate their own power, many chose to become increasingly conservative, identifying with and supporting colonial political and economic interests. They also became anti-nationalist. Their hope was that their new identity with colonial interests would catapult them to power if the process of democratization could be checked, and in view of this they presented themselves as the logical choice in Britain's search for a domestic elite to inherit control of the state. Most began to rally around a new Political Progress Group (PPG). This new party, which was dominated by whites, represented most exclusively the interests of the small white population, and was strongly identified with the local business and professional elite. It resisted calls for immediate reform in favor of gradualism and moderation.

White politicians did not object to the transfer of political authority to locals, *per se*. What they rejected was majority rule as the basis of the transfer. Thus, they supported the retention of ultimate political authority by the colonial regime, and with it, the authority to select those local leaders to whom political decision-making would be entrusted. Their efforts in this regard met with initial success. In 1950, a new constitution was introduced which made five ministerial portfolios available to local politicians. Ministers were chosen by the Governor from among political leaders elected to the Legislative Council. By then, the relationship between creole whites and the colonizers had become so strong that all five posts were granted to persons sympathetic to the interests of local (hence white creole) and international capital. An erstwhile radical creole politician, now advocating moderate gradualism, was provided with the most powerful role of leadership in this executive group (Ryan 1972: 86–96). With the selection of these ministers, the economic and political interests of local whites were advanced while colonial interests were guaranteed continued protection. As an arrangement, however, the nomination of whites, under colonial tutelage, to positions of political leadership could only be short-lived given the agenda for eventual transfer of full political control and decision-making to locals.

There was undoubtedly, in 1950, a consensus of support for a gradualist path to moderate political reform within the group of creole whites. This was reflected in electoral victories for the PPG in two urban constituencies which contained a concentration of whites and the light skinned colored population. The crystallization of support around white politicians in the white community was accompanied by a dramatic decline in the popular mass appeal that these political leaders enjoyed when they were spearheading the political and labor movements during the 1930s

The racial mobilization of blacks and East Indians convinced members of the tiny white population to become mobilized around the PPG. Without mass support, however, the only hope for the white political leadership of this party was alignment with powerful colonial interests in an effort to postpone the inevitable transfer of power. The one-time radicals in the party were therefore compelled to adopt a conservative position.

Thus, the pace and nature of democratic political reform and the timing of the transfer of political power to nationals can become an issue in domestic political contentions. Local segments of the population that have enjoyed privileged status (economic, political, social, or otherwise) in the colonial system are likely to resist any change unless it involves transfer of power to representatives of their own interests. In Trinidad, the exclusion by the British of the wealthy and prestigious creole white community from the corridors of power catapulted white politicians into the nationalist struggle. Then, the very success of that struggle began to place in jeopardy any chances for creole whites to succeed the British in positions of power. More and more, white politicians began to depend upon the support of the white population and to shift away from mass mobilization and from demands for political democratization. Given the class interests of the white population and particularly of the white business elite, there was a natural ideological shift to conservative politics among white political leaders.

The political mobilization of the white population was triggered by the shift to racial politics among the blacks and East Indians. One of the functions of communal politics is to effect a unity between the politically strategic middle class and the lower class, which becomes important for its sheer numbers. A communal appeal to the lower class can serve the same function as an ideologically rooted class appeal. Communal politics holds out to supporters the chance that representatives of their own interests will replace the colonial elite in positions of political authority.

The issue of support is much more complex for the middle class. The interests of the latter's various segments are much more highly and differentially integrated with the colonial status quo. Moreover, middle-class socio-economic interests are quite variegated and highly prone to intra-class conflict. Thus, practical ideology, as defined in Chapter 1, becomes more important for political elites attempting to win the support of the various middle-class segments of the population. Political leaders employing a communal appeal must be sensitive to the interests of their middle-class followers. Contenders for communal political leadership who fashion their ideological appeal to suit the interests of their most strategic middle-class followers stand a considerably better chance of success. Thus, the major contenders to emerge in the competition for control of the state almost invariably become political representatives of the various segments of the middle and upper classes. A communal idiom is employed by these contenders merely as a strategy for mass mobilization.

Politicians representing middle-class functionaries in the state sector are best placed to secure control of the colonial state. It is this group which inherits control of the state bureaucratic machinery after the departure of the colonial elite. As such, it inherits the instrument of power upon which colonial domination and hegemony rests. In the post-independence era the bureaucracy becomes part of the political arsenal to be employed in competition for control of the ex-colonial state.

Members of the bureaucracies are much more inclined than other segments of the middle and upper classes to reject continued colonial domination. They stand to benefit (in terms of wealth, power, and prestige) much more so than any others from the expulsion of the colonial elite. Thus, they are much more prone to support a nationalist leader than any other segment of the middle and upper classes. They are also highly likely to be attracted to certain brands of socialist ideology. Socialism, especially of the

Fabian variety, is particularly consistent with the aspirations of the salaried middle class. Those who control and staff the public sector stand to gain enormously, socio-economically as well as in power and status, from the expansion of the state into private-sector activity (see Stone 1980: 111–21).

In general, members of the middle class whose income is not derived from business and property, particularly those excluded from private sector participation on racial or class grounds, are very inclined to support calls for an expanded role of the state in the economy. They are highly likely to endorse demands for income redistribution through taxation of business and wealth, and for an expanded state apparatus to provide welfare, services, facilities, and an infrastructure for human development to the general population. All these translate into bureaucratic expansion providing jobs, prestige and authority to the petit bourgeois.

It is not surprising, therefore, that nationalist politics go hand in hand with a progressive ideology. Both can appeal to petit bourgeois interests while mobilizing the lower classes. An appeal to communal sentiments can easily and successfully be appended to nationalist and progressive politics, given the convergence of communal and socio-economic boundaries in a colonial setting. When recruitment to the state sector is communally specific, political leaders representing the interests of state sector workers are easily able to forge a unity with one communal segment of the lower class. They do so by employing a communal appeal.

Thus, there may be a fundamental change in what might, on the surface, appear to be the continuation of the radical nationalist movement. This change is most likely to occur during the tutelary phase prior to independence. The initial phase of the nationalist movement is usually characterized by unified lower-class mobilization and a radical ideology geared to lower-class interests. Such an ideology is an initial prerequisite for politicization of lower-class movements. With the change to incremental nationalism, the lower class becomes important only for its numbers. Ideology becomes pitched to middle- and upper-class interests. This change can be ushered in after the embracing by the state sector salaried middle class of the principles of nationalism and democratic socialism. It is consistent with efforts by members of this segment to ensure that their own political representatives take control of the state and that the terms of transfer of power are such that their interests are significantly enhanced. In other words, the change might pertain to middle- and upper-class contentions for control of the state. Of course, the transition is not abrupt; elements of both types of nationalism can co-exist in the initial phases of the tutelary period. Usually, however, middle-class interests take over as the lower classes become divided along communal lines.

Such a change began in Trinidad soon after the Second World War, as soon as universal adult suffrage was introduced to the colony. In 1946, black and colored middle-class politicians formed the West Indian National Party (WINP) on a progressive platform which included calls for independence within the framework of a federation of Britain's West Indian colonial holdings. The party, and its successor, the Caribbean Socialist Party, made direct communal appeals to black lower-class voters in elections held in 1946 and 1950 (Ryan 1972: 87). Members of the lower class were slow to respond to a communal appeal since many were still organized in class-based political and labor groups. Middle-class progressive leaders had to compete with the powerful labor organization of the black-dominated Oilfield Workers Trade Union (OWTU) under the leadership of a charismatic black lower-class trade unionist-politician, Uriah Butler, who led his own party.

The Butler Party, as it was called, was a carry-over from the pre-Second World War era when nationalist mobilization was rooted in labor organization. As such, in its anti-colonial campaign, the primary emphasis was on lower-class mobilization rather than racial mobilization. Butler enjoyed enormous support from black oilfield workers and he was also successful in forging an association with powerful East Indian contenders for political office. This paid electoral dividends in 1950. The East Indian population voted, *en masse*, for East Indian candidates aligned with Butler (see Craig 1953: 166–8).

Racial issues soon destroyed any potential for lower class solidarity. There was a growing consensus among non-Indian politicians that federation with the rest of the British West Indies offered the best post-colonial political arrangement for the colony. The issue, however, inflamed the passions of the East Indian population and its political representatives who were already sensitive to the possibility of black political domination. East Indian leaders were strong in the belief that a federalist constitution would have the effect of relegating the East Indian population to an insignificant and permanent minority by encouraging and promoting mass migration of blacks into the colony from other less developed West Indian territories. East Indian leaders and their supporters alike felt that "Indians had worked to build the country, and that federation, if it came, would mean that Negroes would be able to get the better of Indians" (Gomes 1954: 690, cited in Ryan 1972: 100). The East Indian electorate was led by its leaders to believe that a West Indian federation would erase any possibility Indians had of true representation in a future independent government.

The issue proved to be the death knell for the Butler Party. After winning the largest number of seats for a single party in the 1950 elections (6 out of 18 electoral seats, 4 of them won by East Indian candidates in East Indian constituencies), Butler and his East Indian supporters became seriously divided over federation. The latter, in an act of apostasy, deserted him for a newly formed Peoples Democratic Party (PDP) headed by a wealthy right-of-center East Indian businessman and President General of the Maha Sabha – the organizing body of the Hindu religious community.

The appeal to race became the basis upon which East Indian support for the PDP rested. It allowed a conservative group of East Indian businessmen and professionals to catapult itself into positions of political leadership. By 1955 when a new constitution for self-government was to be written, these leaders appeared poised to assume control of the state. Britain, reacting to the party's declared position against the formation of a West Indian federation, to which it was committed, responded by postponing scheduled elections until 1956.

Prior to 1955, black political support was fragmented behind a number of black and colored leaders, each competing for positions of dominance in the colonial legislature. What was needed was a formula to bridge these political divisions; appeal only to race was clearly not enough. Race, while important as a mobilizing idiom among the black population, was still not effectively employed as a politically unifying principle. There was need for an ideological appeal which dovetailed with the material interests of the black middle-class population, concentrated in the salaried sectors of the economy.

Clearly cognizant of the threat posed by a unified East Indian party, the black intelligentsia banded together in an effort to form a unified political movement. Under the leadership of an internationally acclaimed former history professor, Dr Eric Williams, its members began to mobilize the black lower classes through "people's education" campaigns. In these campaigns, overt appeals to race were made, particularly to the black urban lower class. Their success quickly led, in 1956, to the formation of the Peoples National Movement (PNM).

The new party formalized the political tie between the black middle class and the black masses. It eliminated the need for a trade union base of mobilization by making direct racial appeals to the lower classes. As a result, political competition among black leaders employing different bases of trade union mobilization became irrelevant.

The program of the PNM catered to all segments of the black middle-class population. Reflecting the opinions of the black and colored petit bourgeois, the new party actively sought immediate self-rule for the colony and independence within the framework of a West Indian federation. The petit bourgeois was the very group that would inherit control of the state and federal bureaucracies once independence was granted. The party also called for a "welfare state" to ensure that the health, education, housing, and food needs of the population were guaranteed, an issue which appealed both to petit bourgeois and lower-class interests. The party platform also addressed bread-and-butter issues at the heart of the concerns of lower-class workers. It proposed the development of more viable trade union organizations with enhanced bargaining power and with facilities and resources provided by the state that guaranteed access to the information necessary for negotiating industrial contracts (see "The Peoples Charter" 1966).

At the same time, leaders of the PNM were most careful not to antagonize the powerful international and local business communities which saw their interests tied to continued colonial domination and protection. They made very explicit their disapprobation of socialism, stressing the importance of keeping and attracting foreign capital and emphasizing the need to develop local economic initiative (see Ryan 1972: 122). Thus, theirs was a populist ideology within the context of welfare capitalism, an approach which came closest to bridging the gap between the disparate elements of the middle and upper classes. A racial appeal ensured lower-class support.

The strategy quickly proved successful. It created the conditions for political unification of the black and colored population. In national elections held in 1956, the PNM captured 13 out of 24 elective seats primarily on the basis of its racial and ideological appeal. It was less successful, however, among rural blacks and oilfield workers. While the latter continued to support the now debilitated Butler Party, a large proportion of the former clung to the old progressive labor leaders. In the same elections, the East Indian PDP managed to win in only 5 of the electoral constituencies, relying almost totally on the support of the East Indian rural population concentrated in the sugar belt of the country. Thus, by 1956 the racial polarization of politics was firmly established.

National elections were again held in 1961 and the PNM; with the total and absolute support of the black, colored, and mixed population, was again victorious, winning in 20 of the 29 constituencies even though receiving only 48 percent of the popular vote (see the *Report on the General Elections 1961*). In 1962, with Eric Williams, the leader of the party, firmly in control of a cabinet government, the country was granted its political independence by Britain. Thus, through the PNM, political leaders representing the interests of the black and colored petit bourgeoisie had, by successfully appealing to racial sentiments, secured for themselves full control of the post-colonial state.

Racial politics and class interests in Guyana

Rather than creating the conditions for mass mobilization and insurgency, the suspension of the constitution of Guyana proved a catalyst for the racial fragmentation of the nationalist movement. The reason, of course, is that the suspension came at a time when Britain's commitment to eventual independence was firm.

The radical nationalist movement that came to power in 1953 under a PPP government posed as serious a threat to the domestic middle and upper classes as it did to metropolitan interests. To protect their interest, the political representatives of these local middle and upper classes launched the strongest lobby for the suspension of the constitution, making much of the "communist threat" and of a supposed communist conspiracy to take over the Guyanese government. It was these charges, made in an intense national campaign against the PPP, that were used by Britain to legitimize and justify political and military intervention. Thus, the strategy of the conservative representatives of middle- and upper-class interests was identical to their counterparts in Trinidad. To maintain control of the state they established a strong alliance with the colonial power. They were similarly rewarded. When the PPP was ousted, all the local leaders nominated by Britain's Colonial Office for legislative and executive posts came from among these political leaders. In other words, the suspension of the constitution can be explained partly in terms of domestic political contentions. It came about as a result of successful efforts by the local middle and upper classes, in an alliance with the colonial elite, to wrest control of the state away from those representing the interests of the lower classes.

It was proposed in Chapter 1 that, to be successful, the idiom of mobilization employed by political leaders has to make sense within the existing context of the situation. The nationalist movement was effective in Guyana in the face of generalized lower-class discontent and colonial intransigence. Because its platform, policies, and programs were geared to the general interests of the lower classes, the PPP provided the cement for otherwise racially exclusive mobilization of disparate constituencies and trade unions. With representative government, however, colonial intransigence was removed as a focus for lower-class mobilization. Constitutional reform came with the guarantee of eventual independence for the colony. As a result, the nationalist political movement soon succumbed to inter-class contentions for political power. These contentions had already resulted in the suspension of the constitution. They were also highly susceptible to racial political mobilization.

Mobilization for control of the state

The main strength of the PPP came from its rural East Indian supporters. In 1953, the East Indians (80 percent of whom were rural dwellers) were already 46 percent of the country's population. The black vote that Burnham brought with him, though critical to the PPP's electoral success, was certainly less important for continued electoral viability. In other words, the PPP was capable of winning elections just as much by appealing to the East Indian vote as by appealing to lower-class sentiment. At the same time, Burnham, as the black co-leader of the PPP, was alienated from the politically strategic black petit bourgeois and upper middle class because of the radical ideology of the party. The demonstrated opportunities for mobility available to the black middle class *within the existing status quo* made it impervious to any ideology which advocated radical transformation of the political economy.

From the beginning the PPP leaders had differed on the point of ideology. Burnham, as a product and representative of the black middle class, reflected that group's discomfort with calls for radical change. As a Fabian socialist, he was content to look to political solutions. He saw the immediate goal to be the gaining of political independence after which welfare policies would do the job of transferring economic surplus to the masses. By contrast, Jagan, a committed Marxist, saw economic exploitation as the fundamental problem. The solution to it was nothing less than state appropriation of private enterprise.

Burnham's future political success was hinged to an ideological position capable of fusing the interests of the strategic black middle class with those of the lower class. Both classes were likely to be attracted to a nationalist appeal for political independence and both were likely to favor the expansion of the economic and welfare functions of the state. This was not true for East Indian radical leaders. The limited political significance of the East Indian middle class and the electoral advantage offered by the mobilization of the East Indian lower class freed them from a dependence upon middle-class support. They were able to retain a radical class-based ideological position and still ensure electoral victory.

Changes in the economy were acting to intensify lower-class racial animosities. High birth rates and a declining death rate had caused the East Indian population to grow 46 percent, from 163,434 to 239,250 in the ten-year period between 1946 and 1956. Meanwhile, automated techniques that were being introduced with increased frequency on the plantations were leading to shrinkages in employment opportunities. Between 1956 and 1966 the labor force on the plantations declined from 19,523 to 14,322 (Thomas 1971: 31) while the East Indian population increased by another 100,000. In response, East Indians began to migrate in massive numbers into black urban preserves, making claims upon urban jobs. The economic interests of blacks were becoming seriously threatened by this migration. At the same time, the acculturating impact of education upon the East Indian youths led many to reject confinement to the agricultural sector. Between 1931 and 1946 the East Indian literacy rate moved from 26 percent to 56 percent and was continuing to rise. Even at the height of lower-class unity in the early 1950s East Indian demands for access to urban jobs were being opposed by the black urban population out of fear for its own economic interests.

The suspension of the constitution had the effect of polarizing the ideological cleavage within the PPP while intensifying pluralist pressures. Burnham was always careful to dissociate himself from the more radical rhetoric of his Marxist co-leaders in the party. In international politics he favored a neutralist "non-aligned" approach and was opposed to the recalcitrant anti-American position of the more radical members of the PPP. When the constitution was suspended, Burnham and some less radical leaders chose, against the directive of the party, to comply with orders curtailing their political activity and restricting their movement rather than face arrest and detention – the fate of the more radical party leaders.

At the same time, like Trinidad, the issue of federation with the predominantly black British West Indies was beginning to penetrate the politics of the country. Even more so than in Trinidad, the East Indian population in Guyana was vehemently opposed to any such political union on the grounds that it was a plot to deprive them of their electoral majority. Cheddi Jagan reflected this concern, and indeed, was the chief mouthpiece of East Indian opposition to Federation. By contrast, Burnham vociferously supported federation, a position that reflected black political opinion throughout the British West Indies, and no less so in Guyana.

The intensifying of these ideological and policy conflicts led, in 1955, to a split in the PPP. Initially, there were very few racial implications in the split: all the black radicals remained with Jagan while the moderate East Indians departed with Burnham. Soon, however, both political leaders changed their mobilization strategy from an appeal to lower-class sentiments to an appeal to race. In 1956, the use of racial rhetoric became so explicit in Jagan's faction of the party that all the leading black radicals resigned in protest. With their departure, the leadership became overwhelmingly East Indian.

The split of the nationalist movement along racial lines came just prior to the reintroduction of popular political participation and limited representative government. The suspension of the constitution could have been sustained only as a temporary measure. With international opinion in favor of political self-determination, there was a considerable amount of pressure

Mobilization for control of the state

to restore representative government to British Guiana. Given the popularization of democratic socialism by the British Labour Party (now out of power) in Britain, the threat of a radical government coming to power in its colony was no excuse for a continued denial of political freedom.

The Colonial Office was, therefore, under considerable pressure to work out a formula for excluding the radicals from office. Both the conservative government under Winston Churchill and the socialist opposition of the British Labour Party viewed the Marxism of the Guyanese radicals with considerable concern (see Spinner 1984: 53–5). Unlike the case in Trinidad, these radicals had demonstrated their ability to win at elections independently of middle-class alliances. The fragmentation of the nationalist movement was ideally suited to Britain's purpose. Racial politics ensured the political isolation of the Marxists while providing a much more ideologically acceptable group of leaders with a berth in lower class mobilization.

Bowing to pressure from within the British Parliament and from within the Commonwealth of Nations, Britain reintroduced a new constitution of limited self-rule in 1957 that was less representative that the suspended constitution of 1953 (*Colonial Annual Report*, 1957). Contesting the 1957 elections were the Burnham and Jagan factions of the PPP and two new parties representing the interests of the middle and upper classes.

Jagan's PPP provided a communal political identity for rural East Indian laborers and peasants and for frustrated East Indian youths with high school diplomas and no jobs. These segments turned out in full force behind the party, giving it 9 of 14 elective seats in the Legislative Council and 48 percent of the popular vote.

Despite the shift to racial appeal, black politics was still bifurcated by class factionalism. Lacking the support of the black middle class, Burnham managed to win in only 3 lower-class constituencies in Georgetown, the capital city. His share of the popular vote was 26 percent. As in Trinidad, racial politics, though necessary, proved insufficient for the political unification of the black population. There was need for an ideology which was compatible with the interests of the black middle class

With Jagan in power, the threat of an East Indian avalanche into the urban areas loomed large and fed fears of "Indianization." This was particularly true for government employees since they were the most vulnerable to overt attempt by Jagan's PPP to recruit East Indians into the public sector. Jagan's policies did nothing to allay these fears. He concentrated upon agricultural development schemes that were most beneficial to East Indians. He also instituted measures to free the educational system from the domination of the Christian churches. These churches had formerly refused to hire Hindu teachers (see Hope and David 1974). Jagan centralized the administration of education under the Ministry of Education and built a number of schools in the rural areas where there were large concentrations of East Indians. The responsibility for hiring and promoting teachers became solely that of the government. Aggressive recruitment of Indians had a dramatic effect upon the racial composition of the teaching staff: by 1964, 41 percent of the teachers in primary schools were of East Indian origin. The party made equally aggressive efforts to place East Indians throughout the public service and in most of the government institutions and agencies.

As politically charged racial animosities became heightened, ideological cleavages between black leaders who respectively represented lower- and middle-class interests began to lose their meaning. Anti-Indian sentiments were appended to the anti-communism of the middle class and this cemented the unification of black politics. In 1959, Burnham created the Peoples National Congress (PNC) in a merger with the United Democratic Party (UDP) which was headed by leading members of a black and colored middle class cultural organization. The UDP had received the overwhelming support of the black and colored middle class in the 1957 elections. The new party's sole commitment was to bring an end to East Indian and radical domination of the political system in the form of the PPP government.

Like the PNM in Trinidad, the formation of the PNC in Guyana institutionalized the political unification of the black middle and lower-classes. It also secured middle-class domination of black lower-class politics. With the party's formation, Burnham became converted from a representative of lower class interests to a defender and protector of the black and colored middle class. His political defeat in the elections of 1957 drove home to him the strategic imperative of middle-class support if his aspirations to power were to be satisfied. His importance for the middle class was his ability to capture lower-class votes. This ability remained uncompromised with the shift to a racial appeal. That shift paved the way for the adoption of an ideological position compatible with metropolitan and middle-class interests.

The political polarization of the two racial groups into a Marxist-led East Indian faction and a socialist-led black and colored faction left the more conservative Portuguese, Chinese, and near-white populations without ideological or racial representation. A group of businessmen and professionals, under the leadership of a Portuguese industrialist named Peter D'Aguiar, hastily formed the United Force (UF) – an extremely well-financed party supported by the Christian churches in the country, by the foreign multinationals, and by many Western governments.

This was the political situation when Britain agreed to a constitutional change that would introduce full internal self-government after elections slated for 1961. The decision only added to the racially charged political imbroglio. Full executive and legislative powers were to be turned over to the party winning a majority of the constituencies. In addition, Britain promised to begin discussing the terms of the country's independence soon after the elections. The apocalyptic specter of a Marxist East Indian government leading an independent Guyana loomed ominously on the political horizon and heightened racial tension.

After a racially charged election campaign, Jagan's PPP won a majority of the constituencies even though the party got only 44 percent of the popular vote. The superior numbers of the party's East Indian supporters, and East Indian majorities in the more numerous rural constituencies, assured victory under a simple first-past-the-post system. Thus, like the PNM in Trinidad, the PPP had managed to gain control of the state on the basis of sheer racial appeal.

To sum up, even though Britain had reverted to autarchic colonial rule rule in Guyana, the inexorable direction of political change was towards the transfer of political power to locals. Mobilization efforts, initially directed towards ensuring this transfer, shifted in the latter half of the 1950s to political contentions among elites competing to inherit political power. Racial mobilization became the strategy employed by these leaders in pursuit of their own class-related political interests. The East Indian PPP, by virtue of the superior numbers of its supporters, emerged victorious.

Metropolitan interests and the transfer of power

It was argued in Chapter 1 that, because of their enormous economic and strategic interests in a typical third world state, international actors are actively involved in the politics of these countries. Active intervention in politics ensures that their interests are not jeopardized by political outcomes. Under colonialism, the colonial regime serves the paramount function of protecting and catering to these interests. With the shift to representative government, there is the chance that these interests would be undermined by the leaders who eventually emerge in control of the post-colonial state. Ideology, as was discussed in Chapter 1, serves the function of signalling to these actors whether or not a particular local leader would continue to offer them the privileges enjoyed under the colonial regime.

The ideology of the PNM in Trinidad proved to be highly consistent with the interests of these international actors (see Chapter 3). As a result, the party faced little international opposition in its rise to power. This was not

52 *Mobilization for control of the state*

the case with the PPP in Guyana. As was quite dramatically demonstrated with the suspension of the constitution in 1953, the colonial regime had little hesitation in checking and even reversing progress towards the transfer of political power when external interests were threatened. It was clear that independence would not be granted if there was the slightest chance that these interests would be jeopardized.

The above facts figured heavily in Burnham's strategy for assuming control of the colonial state. It was clear that to do so, he must not antagonize metropolitan interests. So he opposed the use of mass mobilization and confrontation, favoring instead a bargained solution to the issue of colonial transfer of power. He refused to be associated with the blatant anti-Western rhetoric that characterized the radical wing of the PPP during the early 1950s and of Jagan's faction of the party after the split. He supported Britain's proposal for independence within the framework of a West Indian federation. The trade union which he controlled rejected affiliation with the World Federation of Trade Unions, the communist-controlled international trade union organization. Instead, it became a member of the US headquartered International Confederation of Trade Unions (ICFTU) formed in 1945 to combat communist influence in the international trade union movement (see Despres 1967: 196–201). There was, of course, his association with the country's progressive nationalist movement. As a welfare socialist, however, his ideological position was not radically different from mainstream politicians in the British Labour Party and in the major socialist parties of Western Europe.

By contrast, Jagan's Marxism proved dangerous to international political economic interests. Naturally, this all but eliminated his chances for assuming control of the post-colonial state. This was in spite of the prevailing constitution which provided his party with a clear electoral advantage. Regional events made it even less likely that he would be allowed to continue in power. The PPP's election to office in 1961 had come two years after Fidel Castro's revolutionary victory in Cuba and soon after the abortive Bay of Pigs fiasco. The United States was determined not to "lose" any other Caribbean country to the communist camp. It took a special interest in the outcome of the 1961 election and began to direct Britain's manipulation of Guyanese local politics. The United States government also intensified the efforts of the CIA to oust the Jagan Government (for an account of the US involvement see Sheehan 1967; Pearson 1964; and Lens 1965). Arthur Schlesinger, Jr., an advisor to the Kennedy Administration, actively supported a plan to bring about Jagan's demise. In his own words:

Mobilization for control of the state

An independent British Guiana under Burnham (if Burnham can commit himself to a multiracial policy) would cause us many fewer problems than an independent British Guiana under Jagan. And the way was open to bring it about because Jagan's parliamentary strength was larger than his popular strength. He had won 57% of the seats on the basis of 42.3% of the vote. An obvious solution was to establish a system of Proportional Representation. This, after prolonged discussion, the British finally did in October, 1963. (Schlesinger 1965: 779)

The path of constitutional change to proportional representation was cleared through intense racial mobilization. It was paved with violence and bloodshed. Proportional representation was backed by the predominantly urban middle- and upper-class supporters of D'Aguiar's UF and the black and colored population of all classes, politically organized in almost its entirety around Burnham's PNC. It was officially proposed to the colonial office by Burnham and D'Aguiar. Thus, the groups that the latter represented became aligned with Great Britain and the United States in the effort to oust Jagan's PPP.

A combination of race and anti-communism was employed by Burnham and D'Aguiar in an intense, urban-based campaign of anti-PPP mobilization (Premdas 1980). Among the major participants in this campaign were black and colored petit bourgeois supporters of the PNC who comprised, by far, the most numerous of the government employees, who held most of the senior positions not still in the hands of colonial bureaucrats, and who dominated the unions representing government employees (see the *Report of the British Guiana Commission of Inquiry, 1965* for ethnic representation in the Guyanese public service). With their mobilization, the administrative apparatus of the PPP government all but collapsed. Thus, as was the case in 1953, powerful sectors of the Guyanese population became mobilized to confront a legally elected government when a threat was posed to metropolitan interests.

In February, 1962, three unions representing most of the government employees declared a general strike against the Jagan government. Almost immediately, the strikers were joined by Burnham, D'Aguiar and their supporters in a march of over 60,000 persons through the streets of the capital city. There was rioting, arson, and the looting of several East Indian-owned businesses. The police and paramilitary units, sympathetic to Burnham's PNC, stood by idly. Lacking the support and loyalty of the armed and security branches of the state, Jagan was forced to rely upon the intervention of the British military to restore order.

There was a continued state of socio-political disorder over the next two years. Events reached a high point in 1963 when PNC and UF opposition to a proposed labor relations bill sponsored by the government sparked a debilitating general strike which lasted 60 days. The strike was covertly supported and financed by Western governments and multinational agencies. All in all, the entire period of anti-PPP mobilization cost the country nearly 300 lives in inter-racial warfare and left a legacy of racial hatred that has permanently scarred the national psyche of the Guyanese population.

The PPP's inability to govern the country with any semblance of order was the bargaining chip used to force Jagan to accept the constitutional change to proportional representation, and to agree to new elections before a decision on the country's independence was made. Elections were held under this new constitution in 1964 and the PNC with 40 percent of the vote joined the UF with 12 percent to form a coalition government. Thus, the alliance of the United States, Britain, and foreign business located in the country, with the Guyanese upper and middle classes, whose political leaders had succeeded in appealing to racial sentiments, was able to secure the ousting of the Marxist PPP.

In 1966, with Burnham as Prime Minister and with D'Aguiar, the conservative leader of the United Force, holding the powerful portfolio of Minister of Finance, Britain granted the country its political independence.

A combination of racial appeal and an intense anti-communist campaign assured Burnham and D'Aguiar control of the state after the departure of the colonial power. Burnham mobilized the black and colored population by the raw appeal to race. He was supported by a highly politicized black petit bourgeoisie that violently resisted Jagan's attempt at a radical transformation of the economy. The United Force spoke for the interests of the upper and middle classes in the private sector who felt most threatened by PPP radicalism. The coincidence of race and class in the country's stratification order became evident in the racial character of the UF. The party drew its supporters from the light-skinned Portuguese, Chinese, and colored populations concentrated in the higher class categories. Guyana thus provides a clear example of how the interests of the domestic middle and upper classes in LDCs coincide with those of metropolitan actors. This allows international intervention without the direct active participation of metropolitan actors.

The PNC/UF coalition that ran the government lasted until 1967. It was, in effect, more of a defensive coalition against the PPP, and, as such, it was incapable of resolving the real issue of who would control the post-colonial state.

Intra-Class Contentions and Control of the State

The conditions of power overwhelmingly favored the PNC. On the basis of racial appeal alone, the party was guaranteed the support of over 40 percent of the population as opposed to 12 percent or less for the UF. Moreover, the appeal of the party to the black petit bourgeois was reinforced by its welfare socialist ideological position. The majority of the salaried middle class stood to gain enormously from the introduction of a welfare state and from an expanded role for government in the economy.

Not surprisingly the PNC began efforts, soon after independence, to remove the UF from the sharing of power. Party leaders made an all-out effort to gain full and absolute control of the state. In this they had at their disposal (i) their control of the state bureaucratic machinery, (ii) the patronage resources available to them by virtue of that control, and (iii) the loyalty of the black and colored petit bourgeoisie who staffed and headed the state bureaucracy. The patronage resources of the state were employed to forge clientelistic alliances with powerful and influential leaders who would otherwise oppose the PNC on racial, class, or ideological grounds (Hintzen 1983). Elected representatives of opposition parties were co-opted and, in 1958, six months before scheduled elections, there were enough crossovers in the national legislature to give the PNC a parliamentary majority. PNC leaders were freed, for the first time, from the need for a coalition. They now enjoyed exclusive control of all branches of the state and sole access to an enormously expanded state coercive apparatus to be used against actual and potential political opponents.

With the constitutional requirement of periodic elections, however, there was no guarantee that the PNC could maintain its exclusive grip on the state. Its black and colored supporters did not constitute a large enough electoral bloc to provide the simple majority needed for an electoral victory. It could not rely on the leaders co-opted from the opposition to deliver the requisite votes. These leaders, by their decision to join the ruling party, had alienated their former supporters. The party thus found itself far short of the votes needed to win an election. To remain in power, the PNC had to circumvent the majoritarian requirement of the electoral constitution.

As soon as the UF was ousted, party leaders reconstituted the Electoral Commission which was responsible for the conduct and administration of elections. It staffed the body with its own supporters, thus giving party leaders full control of the electoral process. The first act of the reconstituted committee was to change the procedures of electoral administration. This opened the floodgates for massive electoral fraud which allowed the PNC to

56 *Mobilization for control of the state*

assure itself of a victory in 1968 elections. Evidence gathered by neutral observers incontrovertibly established that these elections were rigged, that they involved the use of tens of thousands of fictitious votes by the ruling party, and that they were conducted in the face of systematic disenfranchisement of supporters of the opposition (see *The Sunday Times* of London, 5 November 1968: 4; Mitchell 1968; Premdas 1977; Lernoux 1980; Jagan 1968). A state coercive machinery, in the form of a predominantly black army and police, ensured that political and social order was maintained and that political protests against the abnegation of the majoritarian principle did not spill over into mass disobedience, riots, demonstrations, and other forms of civil disorder.

Thus, after 1968, the PNC was able to assure itself of absolute domination of the state through racial mobilization, control of the machinery of elections, support from a loyal state bureaucracy, and control of a highly politicized army and police. Coercion, control, and racial mobilization became the three pillars of PNC power. The manner in which these were converted to serve the statist interests of the regime is the subject of the next chapter.

Summary

In summary, nationalist mobilization began, in both Guyana and Trinidad, with successful appeals to the lower classes who rallied in support of calls for the transfer of colonial power to local political leaders. When the commitment to such a transfer was made by Britain there was a shift in both countries to racial mobilization. An appeal to racial sentiments best serves the political interests of local elites who find themselves contending for power after the introduction of majoritarian politics.

Political leaders representing the interests of middle-class workers in the state bureaucratic sector stand the best chance of gaining control of the state. To do so, however, two preconditions must be satisfied. First, they must develop a formula to gain popular support; they can do this by appealing to subjective sentiments. Secondly, these leaders must guarantee the protection of the interests of strategic international actors; the advocacy and adoption of a moderate ideological position satisfies this condition.

These factors were all present in Guyana and Trinidad. Combined, they explain the emergence of leaders representing the interests of the black and colored petit bourgeoisie to take control of the post-colonial state.

3. Maintaining control of the state: strategies for regime survival in Guyana and Trinidad

In Chapter 1 it was proposed that the survival of a third world regime is directly related to its success in meeting three conditions: (i) the need to satisfy or neutralize powerful local and international actors; (ii) the need to demobilize or co-opt the organized opposition; and (iii) the need to retain mass support and to prevent outbidding. In its attempts at meeting these conditions, a regime usually employs a number of strategies. One is the use of "practical ideology." This entails the formulation of a socio-political program as a means of communicating to politically strategic actors that their interests will be furthered and protected in regime policy. Ideology can also be used in bids to counter the effects of powerful actors. In seeking to overcome socio-political threats, a regime might employ ideology to mobilize segments of the population or to obtain the support and assistance of actors with alternative resources.

A regime also has the resources of the state available for use as patronage. These resources can be employed to develop clientelistic ties with strategic elites, to generate and maintain mass support, and to generate and maintain the support of strategic groups. A regime also has the ability to strengthen and expand the machinery of the state. This provides it with the wherewithal to control political, social, cultural, and economic activity and to ensure the demobilization of those engaged in such activities who may prove politically threatening. By rendering potential opponents unable or unwilling to mount or support anti-regime challenges, it can preempt the use of resources controlled by these opponents for political and economic destabilization. Finally, a regime has at its disposal the entire coercive apparatus of the state to be employed against the political opposition.

The use of ideology, patronage, control, and coercion figured prominently in strategies employed by the Guyanese and Trinidadian regimes to retain control of the state. The success of such strategies is underscored by the longevity of both regimes. The Trinidadian regime came to power in 1956 and lasted until 1986 in an unbroken tenure of rule. The Guyanese regime was elected to office in 1964 and still held power at the time of writing (1986).

58 *Maintaining control of the state*

Both regimes managed to survive into the 1980s despite considerable sociopolitical crises and political challenges.

Ideology and regime survival in Guyana and Trinidad

Practical ideology and, more importantly, the announced program for its implementation, signals to the various organized sectors of society whether their particular interests would be protected, jeopardized, or undermined should a particular group of political elites assume control of the state. It is a most important determinant of support for or opposition to political leaders by segments of the upper and middle classes and by international actors. At the same time, ideology can prove unimportant for lower-class support. When a communal or nationalist appeal is employed, it becomes irrelevant for ensuring lower-class mobilization.

Practical ideology has to be consistent with the interests of the most strategic segments of society if a political leader is to succeed in the bid for power. Members of these segments, and others associated with them in one way or another, will mobilize or employ their resources to prevent leaders hostile to their interests from acquiring and holding on to control of the state.

In the pre-independence period when colonial control is still intact and when the terms for the transfer of power to local leaders are being set, the willingness to protect the interests of foreign economic and political actors becomes most critical in the efforts of local leaders to gain and retain control of the state. The point was made in Chapter 2 that political gradualism allows the colonial regime time to develop the mechanisms which would guarantee that the regime to assume power after independence is one which is committed to the protection of metropolitan interests. It follows, then, that the mechanisms developed will be fashioned to suit those whose ideology is in keeping with such interests.

PNM ideology and sectoral interests in Trinidad

The PNM's ideological position was ideally suited to the interests of major metropolitan actors and the most strategic sectors of the domestic middle and upper classes. As a result, Britain agreed to fashion a constitution that was guaranteed to ensure that the party inherited control of the state in the post-independence era. When this control was achieved, it went unchallenged by strategic and powerful domestic segments of the population. In fact, the primary challenge to the regime came from its own lower-class supporters.

Maintaining control of the state

When the PNM was formed in 1956, party leaders explicitly rejected a socialist direction for the country (see Richardson 1957; Ryan 1972: 120–7; "The Peoples Charter" 1966). Its moderate ideological position meant that Western governments and international investors had nothing to fear if the party managed to assume control of the post-colonial state. Britain became even more committed to a PNM government because of the party's vigorous support for a federal formula that its colonial office had advanced as a condition of independence for the English-speaking West Indies. Such a formula had considerable potential economic benefits for metropolitan entrepreneurial and manufacturing investors by providing opportunities for enormous expansion of markets in the region through the elimination of tariffs. Thus, the PNM's practical ideology was highly consistent with the interest of powerful segments of foreign business. Moreover, there was nothing in the PNM's position to threaten the interests of the domestic white population and the white-dominated domestic business sector.

For these reasons, the PNM had the best chances by far of succeeding the British at the head of a post-independence government. Britain backed the party's claim to power because of its support for federation. Its ideology was consistent with the interests of international business. And its proposed programs were consistent with the interests of the local business community even though the latter was represented by the political opposition.

Britain used its power to support the PNM in the political campaign to gain control of the post-colonial state. This became evident from the party's first foray into electoral politics in 1956. When the party came up two seats short of a parliamentary majority, the Governor, acting upon the advice of Britain's Secretary of State for the colonies, guaranteed its leaders a majority in the country's legislature. He did so by deferring to the PNM in the selection of five non-elective members of the Legislative Council. With the guarantee of a voting majority in Parliament, the party assumed executive authority under a constitution of self-government.

The powerful, white-dominated, local private sector, even though supporting the opposition, had little to be concerned about with a PNM government in power. The party's emphasis upon the development of local economic initiative and its plans for raising walls of protective tariffs around local economic activity sensitive to foreign competition catered directly to the interests of the group. While this did not immediately become translated into support, it prevented hostile rejection of the party. There was no anti-regime mobilization by members of the group, or by local business in general after the party came to power. Hence, by virtue of its ideological position, the PNM managed to satisfy the first of the conditions of power listed at the beginning of the chapter – the need to accommodate or neutralize powerful local and international interests.

Despite the success of the PNM, there was still the fundamental conflict between accommodating the interests of the powerful international and domestic private sector and satisfying the nationalist demands of its lower-class supporters. The conflict became manifest within the context of an ideological conflict among party leaders. Leftists within the ranks of the PNM, headed by a Trotskyite with international credentials, C. L. R. James, began to insist that the party adopt policies which were anti-colonial and anti-imperialist. This, of course, was in direct opposition to powerful moderates who had successfully chartered an ideological direction for the party in favor of accommodating western and private capitalist interests. Initially, there was a perceptible shift in party policy toward accommodating the leftists. This was undoubtedly rooted in a flawed reading of the political situation. It was evident that the PNM leadership believed that majority support guaranteed control of the state and that, with Britain's commitment to independence, there was nothing to stop the party from leading a post-independence government. The reality, however, was that majority support was rooted in racial appeal and not conditioned by ideology. A commitment to pursue policies that were demonstrably consistent with lower-class interests was not the critical factor in determining mass support. More important, with Britain reserving the absolute right to change the constitution until independence was formally granted, the determination of control of the post-colonial state rested with the colonial power independently of majoritarian considerations. It was more important, therefore, to pursue policies which Britain deemed desirable rather than those which catered overtly to mass interests if power was to be guaranteed. This was quite quickly demonstrated. Britain employed its constitutional authority to secure unequivocal accommodation to metropolitan political and economic interests and to obtain an absolute rejection of radical nationalism. In the process, it ensured that the radicals were purged from the ranks of the ruling party.

Britain's actions were sparked by the direction the new ruling party's policies seemed to be taking in the initial stages of PNM rule. Prodded by its left wing, the PNM had begun an attack on what it saw as the bastions of foreign domination (see Ryan 1972: 197–203). Because of its high visibility as a symbol of foreign domination, the party's left wing insisted that it take up the issue of an American military presence in the colony. As a result, an American military base in Trinidad became the focus of the party's mobilizing efforts. Party leaders began to demand the departure of all American military personnel and the return of the base to Trinidad (see *Nation*, 10 July, 22 July, and 8 August 1959).

In its anti-imperialist campaign, the party failed to recognize its almost absolute dependence upon Britain. The continuation of the PNM in power was tied to constitutional changes formulated, fashioned, and determined in the British Parliament and the Colonial Office. Most importantly, Britain had the exclusive power to make changes in the electoral boundaries that were demanded by the party. These changes were absolutely necessary if the party were to maintain its electoral majority. Under a first-past-the-post constituency system, patterned after the Westminster model, the drawing of constituencies was critical for electoral success and the party was extremely vulnerable on this score. During federal elections held in 1958, with a different configuration of electoral boundaries, the PNM suffered a stunning loss to the political opposition, winning only four of ten seats to the federal parliament. This put Britain in a position to determine any future electoral outcome merely by its power to configure electoral boundaries. In addition, Britain retained the full authority to determine the pace of political change. It could accelerate or check the pace of change to representative government and independence depending on its assessment of the party that enjoyed majority support.

Needing to consolidate its power by securing greater control of the state, the PNM leadership was anxious to assume the full constitutional powers of self-rule which gave its leaders jurisdiction in every area of state activity except defense and foreign affairs. Once again, the decision to transfer such constitutional authority to the PNM rested entirely with Britain.

It became clear, even though implicitly, that Britain was unwilling to reconstitute the electoral boundaries and to grant the constitutional powers of self-rule unless the PNM leadership was willing to repudiate radicalism, to drop its radical demands, and to return unequivocally to a moderate position. Realizing that the party's ability to retain political power and its chances to lead a post-independence government rested with Britain, Eric Williams, the party leader, acquiesced. Under considerable pressure from Britain, he agreed to a compromise on the issue of the American base and accepted a seven-year moratorium on the departure of the US military. This decision also set the stage for the satisfaction of the other conditions to guarantee continued PNM rule. In opposition to Williams' capitulation to Britain and the United States, James and his followers left the PNM, a decision which was the death knell for the left wing of the party. Britain rewarded the party leadership by acceding to its demands for changes in the constitution and the electorial boundaries (see James 1962; and Ryan 1972: 224–32).

Purged of its radical wing, with a constitution extremely favorable to its continued tenure, and with a black and colored population solidly behind it, the PNM fought and won the general elections held in 1961, the last before the country achieved independence from Britain. By then, the ideological position of Williams was unequivocally pro-West and pro-capitalist. Making reference to the former radical members of the PNM, he denounced communism as one of the five "dangers" facing his party (*Trinidad Guardian*, 1 October 1961).

In the process, the PNM was also able to capture strategic domestic support. Seeing no threat to its own interests in the policies of the party, the white-dominated business sector and the white population as a whole began a slow but steady drift to the PNM. More importantly, there was no white rejection of party legitimacy after its 1961 victory despite the prospect of independence, and thus no efforts to mobilize against it.

The political and strategic interests of the West, metropolitan economic interests, and local capitalist interests – all formerly protected and preserved by the colonial regime – were again guaranteed protection under a PNM post-independence government. This fact was clearly signalled by the ruling party's announced commitment to a moderate ideological position and to a pro-capitalist program of development for the country. There was very little reason for any of these interests to oppose the regime or to prevent party leaders from retaining control of the state once Britain had announced its intention to depart.

Without the rooting of mass support for the PNM in the black and mixed population, derived from an appeal to race, acquiescence to private-sector interests would hardly have been possible. Communal mobilization provides political leaders with considerable room for ideological flexibility which is not possible when class is employed as a mobilizing idiom. Racial mobilization was particularly important in Trinidad because it allowed the PNM to accommodate the powerful international and local private sectors before the decision was made on the transfer of colonial control to locals. At the same time, it guaranteed the party the majority support necessary to win at elections without catering to the interests of the lower classes.

After independence, the regime granted even more concessions to the private sector by giving the latter's representatives direct access to policy formulation. In 1963 it set up a National Economic Advisory Council in which a major role was reserved for the business community. The Council

Maintaining control of the state

was dissolved when labor, also a participant, objected to its pro-business direction. It was resuscitated in 1967 with private-sector participation considerably expanded and with trade union input vastly diminished. The new reformulated Council institutionalized and strengthened the already considerable influence enjoyed by the private sector over state policy. As a result, the regime became even more committed to a pro-capitalist developmental strategy for the country.

Party ideology also catered to petit bourgeois interest in its pursuit of a mixed economy approach to capitalist development. This translated into considerable state participation in the productive sector and expansion in the state welfare-delivery system. The beneficiaries of such a policy were the state bureaucrats whose jobs and promotion opportunities grew enormously, especially in the lucrative state corporate sector and in areas requiring professional qualification (see Chapter 5). Thus, by catering to the interests of foreign and local investors as well as the state bureaucrats, the PNM managed to assure itself of support from a majority of the middle and upper classes despite the retention of its racial appeal.

PNC ideology and sectoral interests in Guyana

Unlike the ideological consistency of the PNM in Trinidad, ideological flexibility in response to changing conditions of power became the critical ingredient in the PNC's continued political success in Guyana. An appeal to race makes such flexibility possible. Third world political movements which rely on subjective appeal have the freedom to respond to the most powerful domestic and international interests by changing their ideological positions without jeopardizing their mass support, even when the policies and programs implied by the new ideology act against the socio-economic interests of their followers. As conditions of power change, a third world regime that relies on subjective appeal is free to change its policies in keeping with the new realities with little fear of losing its mass support (see Hintzen and Premdas 1983).

Shifts in ideological position have been quite characteristic of the PNC's leadership in Guyana. Even though a Fabian socialist, Forbes Burnham, the leader of the PNC, began his political career by joining an alliance of radical Marxists when this seemed to offer, in 1950, the best chance of gaining control of the colonial state. By successfully appealing to lower-class interests, the Peoples Progressive Party (PPP) which he joined was catapulted to power in 1953. Burnham, as co-leader of the party, became a Minister in the government.

64 *Maintaining control of the state*

When the constitution was suspended after 133 days of PPP government, Burnham began an inexorable drift to a more moderate position. There was a clear recognition, on his part, that metropolitan political and economic interests and their local allies had to be accommodated if the transfer of colonial power was to be guaranteed (see Chapter 2, pp. 52–4). Given colonial control of the country and the domination of the economy by foreign capital, these interests had a virtual monopoly over decisions determining the future political direction of the country. In the case of Trinidad discussed earlier, it was the recognition of these very realities of power that led the PNM leadership to repudiate a radical nationalist position and to purge the part of its progressive membership.

Burnham's ideological shift led, eventually, to a split in the PPP. By 1955, he was labelling Jagan, his erstwhile co-partner, "a communist inspired stooge" (Glasgow 1970: 110; *Guyana Times* VI, 2nd quarter 1955: 1) while, at the same time, making direct appeals to the country's middle classes (see Burnham 1955: 4). In 1959, he agreed to a merger with the moderate United Democratic Party (UDP) support for which was anchored in the black and colored middle class and which vociferously opposed the leftist politics of the PPP. The merger was made possible by Burnham's shift from a class appeal to a racial appeal. Racial politics mitigated the importance of ideology and created the conditions for mobilization of the moderate black and colored middle classes in support of a leader who was ideologically to their left. It also assured Burnham of the continued support of the black lower classes despite his ideological shift.

Britain began to take particular pains to prevent a PPP government from inheriting control of the state before its promise of independence was granted. Its efforts in this regard were actively supported by the middle classes, by foreign and local capitalist investors, and by Western governments, primarily the United States. The concern of all of these actors for the political future of the country deepened dramatically after a PPP electoral victory in 1961. With the active involvement, encouragement, and support of these actors, a massive and extended mobilization campaign was mounted against the Jagan government. The success of the campaign derived from its ability to fuse ideological and racial opposition to the PPP to produce a multi-racial and multi-class alliance. These events, which I have already discussed (see Sheehan 1967; Lens 1965; and *Report of a Commission of Inquiry into Disturbances in British Guiana 1965*), forced the PPP's leadership to accept new terms for the granting of independence that were designed to ensure a transfer of power to the opposition parties. There terms, which included a change to proportional representation in the electoral system and

Maintaining control of the state   65

an agreement to elections before the transfer of power, all but guaranteed a political victory to a PNC/UF coalition.

Elections were held in 1964 and the coalition assumed power. The moderate socialism of Burnham was tempered by the conservative United Force. The latter party represented the interests of the local and foreign private sector and was committed to the protection of Western political and strategic interests. Under Burnham's leadership, and with UF leader Peter D'Aguiar as Minister of Finance, the government of Guyana began to cater directly to the interests of local investors while offering protection and economic guarantees to foreign industry.

All efforts were made by the Western governments to ensure that the coalition succeeded. They began to provide massive amounts of economic assistance, especially for the development of infrastructure and to finance a return to levels of production enjoyed before the crisis (see Address to PNC Congress 1968). Foreign assistance was also provided for the expansion and strengthening of the coercive arm of the state. When the country was granted its independence in 1966, an army, funded largely by Britain, was added to the country's coercive arsenal. Finally, there was an enormous influx of foreign private capital and increased levels of local private-sector investment leading to unprecedented economic growth (see Bank of Guyana *Bulletin* no. 8, October 1974: Table 8).

The shift by the leaders of the PNC to a seemingly pro-business, pro-Western ideological position must be viewed in politically strategic terms. It was the only possible way to ensure that the party would head a post-independence government. Party leaders had to accommodate the private sector and provide guarantees that Western political interests would be protected by entering into a coalition with the conservative, pro-business, pro-Western United Force. Though junior partners in the coalition, the leaders of the latter were put in a position to dictate the content of political and economic policy.

Once independence was granted, however, conditions for assuming and maintaining control of the state were no longer tied to terms dictated by Britain. The interests formerly protected by the colonial government became subject to new conditions of power. The extent to which they would be accommodated by the new regime came to depend on how strategic a role they played in the new power equation.

The state bureaucratic sector emerged the most powerful element in the political equation after the departure of Britain. Those who staffed it inherited control of a highly centralized civil service administration as well as an enlarged and more powerful coercive apparatus. They also controlled the small but growing state corporate sector. The trade union movement also emerged from the political crisis of the 1960s as a formidable political force. It was the success of labor mobilization that resulted in the PPP's capitulation to Britain when the terms of independence were being discussed. Thus, the key to power in post-independence Guyana rested with the powerful state bureaucracy and the massive trade union movement. The PNC was firmly tied to those two highly politicized bodies. The party's political successes derived directly from the unequivocal support it received from them. Thus, to remain in power, its ideological position had to cater to the interests of the members of these two groups. The fact that its lower-class support base was locked in through racial politics freed party leaders to concentrate, almost exclusively, on policies and programs directed toward these middle-class groups.

The members of the powerful state bureaucracy were predominantly and disproportionately black and colored, as were the leaders of the trade union movement representing urban workers and workers in the mining industry. Both bodies had become politically mobilized behind the PNC as a result of the combination of the party's racial appeal and its ideological opposition to the PPP. The total and absolute support of these two most politically strategic sectors of society was directly responsible for the party's assumption of power as part of the coalition government. It was this support which eventually provided its leaders with the wherewithal to oust the UF from the coalition and to assume full control of the state.

The party's ideological position became one of the major pillars upon which sustained support from the state bureaucracy and the trade union movement rested. An ideology advocating expanded state control was consistent with the interests of both groups. Socialist programs, it has been argued, are particularly attractive to a state-controlling bureaucratic elite. State penetration of the private sector offers to state employees almost unlimited opportunities for improving their socio-economic position because they are called upon to fill the high-paying and prestigious posts vacated by private-sector workers. The introduction of new welfare programs, the enlargement of old ones, and the expansion of state services and facilities also require an expanded state administrative bureaucracy which, in turn, generates considerable growth in the job-providing capabilities of the state sector. Increased revenues which come with expanded state participation in the economy and increased taxation of the private sector can be, and usually are, utilized in ways that are most beneficial to members of the civil, corporate, and armed service branches of the state bureaucracy (see Hintzen and Premdas 1983). Trade unions are also attracted to socialist programs because of their advocacy of the paramountcy and power of the worker and their commitment to welfare and social services. In the case of the PNC, the unions from which its support was derived represented the country's civil servants, teachers, urban employees and mine workers in semi-urbanized areas. With the exception of the latter, these were all to be direct beneficiaries of any program of state expansion undertaken under the aegis of socialist reform.

Thus, the advocacy and implementation of socialist policies were highly consistent with the power interests of the PNC once independence was achieved. This reality was quickly evident. When, in 1968, the efforts of the PNC to oust the United Force from the coalition finally succeeded, party leaders almost immediately began an ideological shift toward socialism. Social services and programs were increased, albeit to the benefit of the urban areas. There was a concomitant enlargement of state bureaucracies. Between 1971 and 1976 the regime nationalized all major foreign firms in the country. These included American and Canadian bauxite companies, a substantial part of the distributive network through which exports and imports were organized, and sugar plantations and factories owned by British interests. Foreign banks were "miniaturized" into an insignificant domestic role. The growth of the public sector was dramatic, incorporating about 80 percent of the productive sector by the latter half of the 1970s. Government ministries increased from 12 in 1968 to 21 in 1977. The number of state corporations also increased dramatically from 3 in 1968 to over 25 in 1977 in addition to 5 government banks (Sackey 1979; Mandle 1976).

Hence, between 1967 and 1977 the leaders of the PNC consolidated and strengthened their position of power by responding to internal factors. An expanded state bureaucracy and penetration of the private sector assured and guaranteed the resources necessary to cater to the demands of the regime's most strategic supporters: the black middle class who controlled and staffed the state sector. Since the ideological legitimation for state expansion was socialism, the party's policies appealed to the interests of those of its working class supporters organized in highly politicized unions. The latter, of course, constituted another strategic segment of its support base. The support tripod was completed by the black lower classes who predominated in the urban areas and in the mining towns and who were locked in by the powerful racial bond existing between their members and the party. Thus, mass support for the party was guaranteed and sustained through racial mobilization.

The adoption of a socialist ideology invariably brings a third world regime into conflict with powerful international economic and political interests. If regime survival is to be guaranteed, these interests have to be accommodated or neutralized or the regime has to adopt measures to insulate itself from the destabilizing consequences of their retaliatory actions. In pursuit of its new socialist program, the PNC had nationalized the lucrative assets of foreign investors against intense resistance from multinationals and Western governments. This produced a major campaign of Western retaliation, spearheaded by the United States and involving the exertion of political and economic pressure, in an attempt to destabilize the Burnham regime (Burnham 1974; Omag 1976). In view of this response, the regime faced the choice of acquiescence and accommodation or of developing alternative international alliances to protect itself from the Western onslaught. It chose the latter and this became reflected in its ideological position.

The PNC began to turn increasingly to Eastern Europe, Cuba and China for assistance and for some degree of protection. This turn was accompanied by a decidedly Marxist–Leninist orientation to the regime's ideological position. The government's foreign policy became markedly and radically anti-Western and Burnham's international image skyrocketed as he became ranked among the most "progressive" of third world leaders.

It seemed that the intention of party leaders was to develop political, economic and strategic relations with the Eastern bloc in order to neutralize the impact of Western retaliation and to protect the regime from the consequences of western actions. By signalling its ideological commitment to the Eastern bloc and by supporting these countries at international fora, the regime no doubt anticipated that economic, political, and strategic support necessary to offset the effects of Western action would be forthcoming. Soon, however, the state-controlling elite came up against the structural impediments to a shift of this nature in international economic and trading relations (to be discussed in Chapter 5). It soon became clear that the regime's efforts to substitute the Eastern bloc for the Western would meet with very limited success.

A combination of a US directed campaign of economic destabilization with the post-1973 recession in market economies began to produce a deepening economic crisis in Guyana. To maintain economic stability the regime was forced to adopt measures that were bound to prove unpopular among the members of its support tripod. It had to make drastic cutbacks in recurrent and capital expenditure and this resulted in massive retrenchments of state employees and in the removal of subsidies on food and consumer essentials. It was also forced to raise revenue from new taxes on income and from increases in custom duties, purchase taxes, and the like. Balance of payments deficits forced cutbacks on imports, leading to severe shortages of essentials

Maintaining control of the state

and affecting the capacity of the state to deliver basic services, particularly in the urban areas (see Hintzen 1981: 225–8; and *Guardian* (USA), 15 October 1980). The impact of the new policies was most severe among the regime's most strategic supporters: the black and colored middle class. Given the conditions of power, the regime would be hard-pressed to survive a mobilization campaign from this sector.

There was a desperate need to secure international resources to be used for meliorating the economic crisis as it affected the PNC's middle-class supporters. What became clear was that the regime's ideological direction was quickly becoming inconsistent with the terms of survival. Its embrace of Marxism–Leninism did not produce the resources necessary to avert an economic crisis. Nor did ties with the Eastern bloc act as a buffer against Western retaliation. This realization quickly led to repudiation by middle-class party supporters of the progressive ideological turn of its politics. A moderate alliance of professionals, leading executives in the state and private sector, trade unionists, and priests organized themselves into a Compass Group which began to join in a chorus of calls for a change of regime policy, if not of the regime itself. Leaders of the group demanded an immediate shift to a more moderate and pro-Western political and economic program. Such a shift, it was argued, was more consistent with international conditions for economic stability. Its advocates had come to the firm belief that any hope of economic recovery now depended, in no small measure, upon increases in western bilateral and multilateral assistance. In the face of mounting internal resistance and increased Western pressure, it became clear that the regime's continued commitment to a radical political and economic program would act to its detriment. It was forced to face the reality of a structure of dependence upon the international capitalist economic system. Clearly, the path of least resistance open to it was a swing to the right (these events have been fully discussed in Hintzen 1981: 343–55). In light of the above, the regime made the decision to return to the path of ideological moderation. Its advisors began, once more, to talk favorably of attracting the participation of foreign private enterprise to the Guyanese economy (*Guyana Chronicle*, 16 June 1977). In 1979, a New Investment Code was unfolded which invited foreign capital to participate in the development of the country and which took special pains to give guarantees against nationalization (*Financial Times* (London), 5 May 1978). At the international level, the regime's radical anti-West rhetoric cooled noticeably.

The United States took notice of the change and responded favorably. A sympathetic Carter administration intervened to ensure the transfer of bilateral and multilateral assistance to alleviate the effects of the economic

70 *Maintaining control of the state*

crisis (see Lernoux 1980; *Caribbean Contact* December 1980; Monroe 1980). The end result was that the regime, previously on the brink of collapse, was provided with enough resources to bide time while implementing a machinery of coercion and control that became the new basis of its own survival (this is discussed in more detail in Chapter 5.).

To summarize, the PNC's ability to capture power and to retain exclusive control of the state apparatus depended upon its willingness to fashion and implement policies and to adopt or accommodate ideological positions consistent with the interests of the most powerful and strategic international and domestic actors. Changes in the regime's ideological position served to signal its willingness to acquiesce to these interests. Ideology was employed by the PNC regime to obtain the support, assistance and intervention of strategic domestic and international actors during critical periods when its attempts to capture control of the state and its efforts to maintain a hold on political power seemed to be in jeopardy.

Clientelism and control of the state

Clientelism is rooted in the use of state resources by the regime to provide financial rewards, status and prestige benefits, services and facilities, and/or protection to individuals in exchange for support and loyalty or for a commitment not to oppose the political leadership (see Scott 1972: 92; Stone 1980: 91–110). In Chapter 4 I will discuss the important role played by clientelism in the decisions of powerful elites to support the PNC regime. Here, I will examine the relationship between clientelistic support and continued regime control of the state.

Clientelism and regime support in Guyana

In Guyana, PNC control of patronage resources played a major role in its assumption of absolute control of the state and in its subsequent ability to survive. In 1968, the distribution of patronage and the development of clientelistic ties created the conditions for the ousting of the United Force from the coalition. Party leaders offered elected representatives of the opposition, whom it convinced to "cross the floor," powerful and lucrative positions in the state sector and in government (see Hintzen 1975: 110; Premdas 1972: 31). This provided the party with the parliamentary majority that allowed its leaders to sever their relations with the UF and to gain absolute control of the executive branch of government.

In a similar manner, the party was able to attract top leaders from the most powerful East Indian organizations in the country.[1] Co-optation of these leaders played a critical role in the political demobilization of the East Indian population. The transfer of their support to the ruling party served effectively to deny the PPP use of their organizations for anti-regime mobilization.

In 1968, the President and top executives of the Maha Saba, "the most important cultural and religious organization for Hindus in Guyana" (Premdas 1972: 31) and formerly a strong pillar of support for the PPP, switched their allegiances to the PNC. Later, the Gandhi Youth Organization – the youth arm of the Maha Saba – and the United Sad'r Islamic Anjuman, one of the most important Muslim organizations in the country, also declared support for the ruling party. In exchange, many leaders of these organizations were given ministerial positions in the government while others were provided with senior government or political positions.

Patronage was also employed directly against the PPP itself to weaken its political effectiveness by attracting away many of its most capable, popular, and powerful leaders who controlled political resources on their own account. These resources were made available to the PNC, or at least were denied the PPP in its mobilization efforts.

Thus, clientelism served the interests of the PNC regime by acting effectively to demobilize the political opposition and to co-opt the leaders of strategic mass-based organizations. With the co-optation of these leaders, their organizations were no longer available to be used for mounting challenges to regime power.

Clientelism also ensured the continued loyalty and support of strategic elites in control of the civil, security, and corporate branches of the state. It is well recognized that "the distribution of patronage is highly centralized in the Prime Minister", who has to approve personally every senior-level appointment in the state sector (Milne 1981: 148). Loyalty to the Prime Minister (later the Executive President) and to the ruling party became an absolute necessity for appointment to these senior-level positions (see Milne 1981: 117; Enloe 1973; *Guyana Graphic*, 6 January 1972; *Caribbean Contact*, October 1978; *Guyana Chronicle*, 19 May 1978).

Patronage was less important in the regime's efforts at maintaining mass appeal in Guyana. This is because of the declining significance of majoritarian support for regime survival. Much more important was the support of powerful middle-class groups associated with the state sector and of elites

---

[1] Smooha (1980: 273) considers this strategy of co-optation important if regime power is to be maintained in the face of communal opposition. These co-opted elites become "mediators for the dispensation of benefits." It is also a means of gaining regime control over the institutions which they head.

who controlled politically strategic resources. Whatever mass support that was needed was secured through racial appeal. Otherwise, absolute control of the electoral machinery and a resort to electoral fraud ensured the party's continuation in power.

The patronage resources available to the PNC came directly through its control of the state. They included the distribution of state jobs and the enormous perquisites of senior bureaucratic office with its high salaries, access to foreign exchange, opportunities for foreign travel, lavish housing and car allowances, duty free goods, guaranteed supplies of consumer commodities that are in short supply, access to guaranteed low interest mortgages and loans, and cheap housing. Such perquisites are differentially distributed according to seniority. They are also differentially available across the various agencies of the state.

The most important factor in the patronage system, as it applied to state-sector employment, came to be not merely, or at all, the reward of a government job, but rather promotion to senior-level positions and transfers to more desirable branches and locations. Indirect patronage benefits also emerged in the form of access to opportunities for corruption. The availability and extent of such opportunities also came to depend upon one's position, one's geographic location, and the agency of the state in which one was employed.

To the extent that it was directed at securing support from members of the powerful state bureaucracies, patronage involving the distribution of state jobs became highly generalized. By contrast, clientelistic ties to powerful elites was much more personalized. They involved the distribution of patronage to senior-level state bureaucratic officials, leaders of voluntary and mass organizations, leaders who controlled strategic economic resources, and persons who fashioned public opinion. The resources involved in the more personalistic patronage network varied according to the specific needs of the clients. Powerful state bureaucrats might be provided with additional perquisites and access to corruption over and above that normally associated with their position; non-state elites might be provided with highly lucrative contracts, with guarantees that the state would not interfere in their affairs, with positions of power, prestige and status, with protection from arrest and prosecution for illegal activity, and with the opportunities to engage in graft and corruption and access to the proceeds from such activities (see Chapter 4).

To conclude, patronage requires that enough resources be available for transfer to clients. As such, it is quite tenuous, depending upon the economic fortunes of the state. The most serious challenges to the Guyanese regime

Maintaining control of the state 73

have therefore come during periods when it was experiencing a diminished capacity for patronage. The principle of reciprocity which is central to clientelistic relations implies a withdrawal of the support and loyalty of the client whenever the patron fails to deliver on his/her end of the bargain. It can be expected, therefore, that as a regime's capacity for patronage becomes restricted it will experience increased challenges to its authority.

Clientelism and regime support in Trinidad

The institutionalization of majoritarian politics in Trinidad rendered generalized patronage much more important in the political equation. Patronage resources have to be distributed in such a way as to generate and secure the retention of mass support. This demands a different pattern of patronage distribution than that needed to secure the support of *strategic* members of the elite and middle classes. Since all segments of the middle classes, together with the lower classes, must be included in considerations of mass support, generalized patronage requires enormous amounts of state resources. The bountiful revenues from the oil producing sector provided the PNM with the necessary prerequisites for supporting this pattern of patronage. At the same time, the PNM's ability to distribute patronage came to be directly related to the fortunes of the petroleum sector.

Three distinct types of patronage were employed by state political leaders in Trinidad during the PNM's tenure: (i) direct generalized patronage; (ii) indirect patronage; and (iii) elite patronage.

Direct patronage: The typical manner in which direct patronage was distributed was through direct allocations of jobs, services, facilities, loans and housing to individuals on a massive scale. Under the PNM government, the beneficiaries of these allocations were primarily the black urban-based lower classes who constituted the majority of its supporters. There were also some attempts to employ direct patronage to gain inroads into the rural East Indian electoral base of the major opposition.

In the area of jobs, the patronage mechanism was formalized in 1970 after black lower class political opposition almost toppled the regime. A 5 percent Unemployment Levy was legislated on incomes to finance a Special Works Program aimed at providing jobs for the unemployed in community works, housing, and urban rehabilitation. The program was transferred in 1980 to a newly created Development and Environmental Works Division (DEWD). Some indication of the enormity of this patronage package is provided when one considers that DEWD employed between 50,000 to 124,000 workers out of a total work force of 383,000 in 1982 (*Caribbean Contact*, September 1980: 5; *Sunday Guardian*, 12 December 1983: 6; Central Statistical Office 1983: 12).

Typically, DEWD workers were contracted on ten-day stints to work on community and housing projects. In actuality, these jobs were distributed through the ruling party. The vast majority were located in make-work projects where most recipients showed up for less than two hours per day. Moreover, paysheets were typically padded with nonexistent names (see *Trinidad Express*, 26 March 1983; *Trinidad Guardian*, 6 February 1983 and 20 February 1983). There were also reports of payments made to suppliers in respect of materials never supplied to DEWD projects (*Trinidad Express*, 11 October 1981: 1). In 1982, the state's total expenditure on DEWD amounted to TT$565·1 million which represented a deficit of TT$410 million on total receipts of TT$155·1 million coming primarily from the Unemployment Levy.

Another mechanism for patronage allocations was a Carnival Development Committee which had, as one of its responsibilities, the granting of highly lucrative franchises in the country's internationally famous and extremely profitable preLenten Carnival celebrations. In the rural areas, patronage was distributed through a "Best Village Program" which allocated state funds for cultural activity and village improvement projects.

The lion's share of direct generalized patronage was used to guarantee and ensure continued lower-class black support for the PNM. Nonetheless, some efforts were made to use such patronage to woo East Indian voters away from their racial party. For example, PNM electoral victories in East Indian constituencies in 1981 were linked to the use of state funds slated for Agricultural Development to provide patronage to residents in these predominantly agricultural communities. The claim was made that most of the funds allocated in this way were not used for agricultural purposes but to enhance the income of the recipients (from an interview with a leading member of the political opposition in August 1983).

Indirect patronage: The regime also exploited the position of the state as a major employer to provide jobs to its supporters. After the political unrest of 1970, direct job creation by the state became central in the policy agenda of the PNM government. State employment increased by 33 percent between 1973 and 1978, from 37,000 to over 49,000 workers. In 1982, this figure stood at over 60,000 and direct employment by the state amounted to 22 percent of the total employment figures for the country (*Trinidad and Tobago Review*, vol. 6, no. 6 1982: 3). With the increased numbers also came substantial increases in the wages of state employees. Between 1976 and 1980 wage levels in central and local government increased by close to 100 percent (*Trinidad and Tobago Review*, vol. 6, no. 6 1982: 3).

The regime also capitalized on its direct role in mediating industrial disputes, through the terms of an Industrial Stabilization Act, to provide exaggerated wage and salary increases and benefits to pro-PNM unions and to unions representing black workers in the country. Predominantly black unions representing oilfield, waterfront, transport, and industrial workers were continually guaranteed wage increases in excess of 100 percent over three-year periods in rulings by the regime-controlled Industrial Court. These wage settlements came with considerably expanded benefits to the workers. This was most particularly the case for unions that were directly linked to the ruling party. One typical example was the Seamen and Waterfront Workers Trade Union (SWWTU) which, as a result of agreements worked out in negotiations with the Ministry of Labour and the Port Authority (the latter also a government agency), managed to guarantee its workers an average income of TT$100,000 per annum for work as labor dockers (*Trinidad Guardian*, 30 June 1983: 1 and 26 June 1983: 7).

The link between union contract and state patronage was well recognized. One writer in the country's leading newspaper expressed views that were typical of those critical of the practice:

These are illegal violations of other people's constitutional rights and it sometimes appears to me that the trade unions have accepted the surrender of the politicians for no matter what the voters say at elections, it appears the unions win, and the present Government is so concerned with future votes and politics that it not only gives in to outrageous union demands, but in most cases seems actually to encourage these demands. (*Trinidad Express*, 21 November 1977: 5)

Elite patronage: This was the most visible, though the least important, component of the patronage network of the state during the PNM's tenure. Generally indirect, it was based on the use of state authority and jurisdiction to provide individuals with access to business contracts, or to opportunities for graft, corruption, and illicit financial gains, all involving enormous sums of money.

State political leaders used a program of massive state investment as the basis for providing patronage rewards to its most powerful elite supporters. Between 1978 and 1982, TT$7·5 billion in state contracts were awarded to foreign companies. To guarantee the award of such contracts, the paying of bribes to persons of influence with close connections to the political leadership of the country became almost commonplace. Included among the foreign companies that paid such bribes to influential Trinidadians are Tesoro Oil, McDonnell-Douglas, Lockheed, and a US construction company, Sam P. Wallace (see *Caribbean Contact*, April 1983: 9-10).

Local subcontractors made enormous profits from these projects, which typically involved substantial cost overruns and delays of a year and more on completion times (*Trinidad Express*, 1 August 1983: 6). Access to subcontracting thus constituted an enormous patronage resource for the regime. Final costs for the majority of projects were typically more than double the initial estimated costs (*Sunday Express*, 13 June 1982: 6). Cost and time overruns acted to inflate an already bloated patronage largess for local contractors and businessmen associated with the various projects.

Elite patronage was also distributed through the award of high-paying jobs in the state corporate sector. Somewhat typical was the national airline, British West Indian Airways, which in 42 years of operation never recorded a profit and the losses of which between 1979 and 1983 averaged TT$100 million annually (*Trinidad and Tobago Review*, vol. 6, no. 10, 1983). Not only did the airline provide high-paying jobs for regime supporters, their families and friends, but it was also pivotal in the distribution of the perquisite of free or cut-rate international travel for its employees and for state officials and their families.

Businessmen favored by state leaders were exempted from the country's laws and regulations in areas where their profitability and competitiveness would be enhanced. This was particularly true for foreign exchange currency regulations, for the payment of customs duties, and in the granting of protection from competition from overseas products (see *Sunday Guardian*, 26 June 1983: 10).

Patronage and regime legitimacy

State leaders used regime legitimacy to institutionalize, justify and protect the system of patronage. This was helped by 23 years of unbroken PNM rule which produced among members of the population a tendency to identify the party with the state. Such a tendency was nurtured to a large degree by the words and actions of party officials themselves. In general elections held in 1981, party leaders, including the Prime Minister, made it quite plain to those enjoying the benefits of state programs that they had an obligation to vote for the PNM (*Trinidad Express*, 23 June 1983: 20). This was intended partly as a warning to local government districts voting for the opposition that they would be denied the state funding from which all their revenue was derived.

Maintaining control of the state

The PNM protected itself from legal challenges to the system of patronage by putting strong pressure on the country's judiciary. As an example, in 1983, a judge was publicly censured in the Cabinet for "his wholly unwarranted attack on the Executive." The precipitant to the censure was the judge's observation, in making a ruling against the state, that there was increasing party interference in the administrative arm of the government "in the form of political patronage" (*Trinidad Express*, 13 June 1983: 1 and 23 June 1983: 6).

Thus, the identification of the party with the state in popular opinion protected the practice of using state resources for party patronage. Such a practice was popularly viewed as being legitimate. Otherwise, party control of the judiciary protected the regime against charges of illegality.

The enormous size of the regime's patronage package, when combined with its racial and ideological appeal, was enough to guarantee electoral victories and to ensure political order in the country until 1986. This is not to deny that there were conflicting pulls upon the loyalty of party supporters. However, such conflicts were normally resolved in favor of the party. This was particularly true for radicalized segments of the black working class. It is significant that while oilfield, transport, and industrial workers, represented by predominantly black unions, rallied strongly behind their union leaders in contract disputes with both the state and private sectors, they consistently failed to support these very leaders in their electoral bids to defeat the PNM. The strategy employed by the ruling party of giving in to industrial demands in exchange for political loyalty and support during elections paid enormous dividends. With the conflicting pulls of race and patronage on the one hand, and loyalty to their radical union leadership on the other, many black workers usually made the decision to stay away from the polls rather than to take political sides. In other words, race and patronage acted to neutralize ideological opposition to the regime even though they were not enough to cement and sustain direct overt support. Nonetheless, low polls in elections, typically way below 50 percent for the 1970s and 1980s, proved highly beneficial to the ruling party since those from among the black working class who stayed away were the ones most likely to be enticed by the appeals of the radical opposition.

Coercion and control in regime power

In Chapter 1 it was pointed out that a regime has at its disposal the entire coercive apparatus of the state. This apparatus is available to be employed against the political opposition, dissident groups, elite contenders for power, disenchanted segments of the population and anyone who chooses to engage in behavior with adverse political implications. For coercion to be effectively employed, the regime has to have absolute and exclusive control over military and paramilitary organizations, the police, and agencies of surveillance. Without such control, a regime becomes vulnerable to counter-mobilization from within these coercive segments of the state.

It was also pointed out in Chapter 1 that regime survival is considerably enhanced when the state strengthens and expands its control over the activities of individuals, groups, and organizations in the country. Such control effectively limits the availability of the resources associated with these individuals, groups, and organizations for use by political opponents.

Both coercion and control are particularly important for securing the demobilization of actual or potential challengers to regime authority. If a regime is to retain power, it must seek to neutralize its actual and potential opponents. Continued challenges mounted by opposition groups render their demobilization an imperative condition of political order. A regime must also seek to prevent outbidding among its own supporters. A ruling party becomes highly vulnerable to outbidding when its popular support is rooted in a communal or class appeal. Groups politically mobilized in communal or class organizations are highly likely to undermine regime autonomy by making demands for exclusive favor.

Trinidad

In Trinidad, mobilization of the black population, ideologically rooted multi-racial middle- and upper-class support, and an extensive system of patronage acted together until 1986 to ensure the PNM of electoral majorities. Until then, East Indian political opposition posed little threat to regime power. This had to do, partly, with the alienation of powerful East Indian leaders from their mass political organization. Their consequent support for the ruling regime effectively weakened the East Indian communal opposition.

Nonetheless, challenges to the regime in Trinidad did come in the form of outbidding, especially during periods of economic crisis. During economic downturns, state political leaders became quite vulnerable to the outbidding efforts of counter-elites who made appeals both to the racial and class interests of the black lower-class population. To assure itself of continued control of the state, the regime had to resort, periodically, to its repository of violent and non-violent coercion.

Effective working-class mobilization placed the trade union movement in the forefront of organized radical challenges to the regime. Left-wing leaders, the majority of whom are black, managed to gain control of the country's most powerful trade unions and developed alliances with the country's radical intelligentsia in attempts to oust the regime from office. The first such challenge to the post-independence government occurred in 1965. The country was in the throes of an economic crisis after a decline in its rate of annual growth from 10 percent to 3·5 percent in just one year. East Indian sugar workers called a strike which escalated into widespread violence resulting in the total shutdown of the industry. Encouraged and supported by radical unionists, industrial unrest spread to every other sector of the economy threatening the fragile political order.

The regime responded by falling back on its repository of coercion to contain the crisis. It quickly imposed a State of Emergency to deal with the immediate challenges to its power. It also took immediate measures to control the trade union movement. The government hastily legislated an Industrial Stabilization Act (ISA) which gave the Minister of Labour jurisdiction in questions of union recognition. An Industrial Court was instituted as the final arbiter for resolving industrial disputes, for registering industrial agreements, and for setting the prices of specified goods and commodities used to calculate the costs of living in the negotiation of wage settlements. Most important, punitive and financial penalties were imposed upon persons participating in strikes (see Industrial Stabilization Act 1965).

Though the language of the ISA suggested parity in government's dealings with workers and employers, it was clearly a bill aimed at preventing growing worker dissatisfaction from escalating into mass political confrontation. In the short run, it was highly successful. Between March 1965 and December 1969, the number of work stoppages in the entire country totalled a mere 27, causing a loss of only 40,000 man-days over the five-year period, as compared with an average of about 50 work stoppages per year between 1960 and 1964 resulting in the loss of close to 200,000 man-days per annum.

Regime strategy in response to the 1965 crisis was, therefore, two-fold. It deployed the state's coercive arsenal, under a declared State of Emergency, to contain the crisis. This allowed the regime to bide time until the politically explosive situation was defused. It also legislated measures which gave the administration direct control over critical areas of trade union activity. These included the right of representation, the right to strike and the bases for negotiating wage settlements. Its authority was enforced by punitive sanction.

As long as trade unions remained the primary agencies for anti-regime mobilization, regime control proved to be an effective demobilizer. When discontent spread to other sectors of society, however, these measures proved ineffectual. This was the case in 1970. In the face of continued working-class dissatisfaction, members of the radical intelligentsia began to develop ties with leaders of the most powerful trade unions in the country. The association began in April 1969 when radical university students demonstrated in support of a strike by the Transport and Industrial Workers Union (TIWU), one of the leftist unions in the country. Later that year, radical students and long-standing radical intellectuals in the community organized the country's youth and unemployed in the National Joint Action Committee (NJAC). The radical leadership of NJAC attracted enormous popular support among black lower-class residents in economically depressed areas. These areas were hit especially hard by an economic crisis which began in 1969. In that year, the country's GDP had registered zero growth and petroleum production, the major industry in the country, had experienced a decline in real growth of 11·5 percent over its 1968 figure (Inter-American Economic And Social Council 1974). Deteriorating economic conditions led to escalating unemployment and underemployment. As a result, political dissatisfaction with the regime was running high.

The radical leaders of NJAC capitalized on growing political and economic frustrations to organize the predominantly black urban lower classes. They also made racial overtures to the group by employing "Black Power" as their mobilizing idiom, a term that was borrowed from the civil rights struggles then enjoying currency in the United States. In February 1970, NJAC mobilized 10,000 marchers, mostly urban lower-class blacks, in a massive demonstration against the government. The protest was precipitated by the regime's attempt at coercive retaliation by arresting five student leaders of the group. Several more demonstrations were organized between March and April 1970.

Once again, the regime employed an immediate coercive retaliatory response to the crisis. Armed police, who on occasion shot at crowds of demonstrators, were deployed in a concerted effort to restore political order and to ensure effective demobilization. At least one demonstrator was killed. On 21 April, as its hold on political power slipped, the regime declared a State of Emergency, imposed a dust-to-dawn curfew, and abrogated the right of assembly amid skirmishes between demonstrators and police, and arson and looting in the capital city. Fifteen leaders of the movement, mostly university radicals and powerful trade union officials, were arrested (see Oxaal 1971 for a thorough account of the political upheaval of 1969–70).

Unlike 1965, however, the effectiveness of the regime's coercive response was limited. This had to do with the broader base of political mobilization.

To restore order, the regime had to call upon all branches of its coercive forces. However, regime control of many of its branches was quite tenuous and this was particularly true of the military.

There was, at the time, little strategic need for a standing army. It was formed only because the constitution under which the country was granted independence in 1962 stipulated the establishment of a military force. At the time, there already existed a well-established police force which was highly competent in matters of internal security. Hence, the resource outlay in developing the Trinidad and Tobago Regiment was minimal and its functions were mainly ceremonial. Compared, for example, to the 2,200-man army that was established in Guyana at the time of its independence, Trinidad, with a much larger population, opted for an army of only 750.

The army was more important as a patronage resource than for its function of maintaining national security. It was viewed by state leaders as part of their efforts at relieving unemployment. Senior army positions were distributed as political rewards to hastily trained loyal supporters of the PNM (Allum 1975). Many of the force's high-ranking officers were, therefore, incompetent. They were concerned mainly with preserving and expanding the enormous benefits that derived from their office. As a result, poor leadership and low self-esteem pervaded the army and contributed to endemic problems of indiscipline and low morale.

In contrast to their superiors, the junior officers in the Trinidad and Tobago Regiment were highly trained. Many had attended prestigious officer cadet schools in England and had received advanced training which qualified them for senior positions. They constituted a corps of highly professionalized soldiers, conditioned for leadership roles but frustrated by the absence of opportunities for promotion. Most remained Second Lieutenants while senior posts were distributed as plums in the patronage pie of the ruling party (see Allum 1975).

Naturally, deep-seated antagonisms pervaded the relationships between junior and senior officers in the Trinidad army. These soon assumed political proportions as the former became disenchanted with the regime, with its policies towards the military force, and with its practice of political patronage in making appointments to senior ranks. To this was added the low morale among members of the predominantly black rank and file. Both groups became quite sympathetic to the calls of the urban demonstrators for political change.

These were the sentiments and conflicts which pervaded the military when the political leadership decided upon massive coercive retaliation against the urban protesters. For the first time, the military was seen to be of strategic

82 Maintaining control of the state

importance for internal security. Under a State of Emergency, the Trinidad and Tobago Regiment was placed on alert in preparation for deployment against the demonstrators and for use in restoration of socio-political order. When the order for deployment was issued, it was disobeyed. Instead, two junior officers led a mutiny that was supported by most of the ranks. They took control of the only army base in the country, held their senior officers hostage, and began a march to Port-of-Spain, the capital city, in support of the demonstrators.

Without the control of the military and the loyalty of its junior officers and most of the enlisted soldiers, the ability of the regime to survive the crisis was placed in jeopardy. It was forced to rely completely on those branches of the state coercive apparatus over which it exercised absolute control. These branches, primarily the coast guard and the police, had the task of containing urban unrest in addition to checking the advance of the mutineers. Two coast guard vessels were hastily dispatched to the country's military base and began to shell the only road leading out of the compound. This timely action pinned down the anti-government forces averting what would have been the certain military overthrow of the PNM government.

The regime also called upon international allies to shore up its coercive power. In response, there was a veiled threat of US military intervention in support of the Williams government. On the very day of the mutiny, a United States naval task force appeared offshore amid reports of its declared willingness to come to the regime's assistance. This highlights the role of actual or potential international coercive intervention as a major factor in the conditions which determine whether a regime survives or not. International alliances can, therefore, come with the guarantee of protection in a crisis.

After a few days, a surrender was negotiated between the regime and the leaders of the mutiny. At the same time, the loyal police force managed to contain the urban demonstrators. The arrest of their leaders, the failure of the army mutiny, and the threat of US military intervention combined to dash any hopes that these demonstrators might have had for success. Soon after the surrender of the mutineers was negotiated, there was an abrupt end to anti-regime mobilization.

Despite the army mutiny, the regime was able to maintain the coercive capability of the state because of the strong loyalty of the police force and coast guard. Equipped with arms hastily flown in from the United States, these two branches were able to restore social and political order by ensuring that the terms of the State of Emergency were obeyed by the population. In all, 87 soldiers and 54 militants were arrested on charges of treason, sedition, and mutiny (for an account of events, see Ryan 1972: 462–70; Allum 1975;

Washington Post, 12 June 1970; *New York Times*, 9 March, 22, 23, 24, 25, 26 April and 1 May 1970). These events ushered in a brief period of regime reliance upon coercion to maintain its hold on the state. At the same time, the regime moved quickly to expand and strengthen its control over political activity and over the military and to increase its coercive capacity. To do so, the Prime Minister instituted a number of measures to bolster his government's weak hold on political power. The first was to purge the disloyal military of its dissident officers and to cut back on army strength. By 1972, it was estimated that the army had been reduced to two-thirds of its original 750 troops (*Tapia*, 26 November 1962). There was also a deliberate policy to make the army less attractive than before. The regime also strengthened the coercive capability of the state by upgrading and expanding the loyal police force and coast guard. Several new vessels were purchased for the latter while the former was equipped with new and modern weapons, including helicopters. Salaries in these two branches of the armed services were also lavishly upgraded relative to the army (see *Tapia*, 27 February 1972). Thus, when dependence upon the coercive arm of the state became critical for the political tenure of the regime, the coercive capabilities of loyal branches of the state security apparatus were increased while the strength of the disloyal military was weakened.

The second response of the regime to the political crisis was to keep the State of Emergency operative for several months after the 1970 disturbances and to strengthen its capacity to deal quickly and effectively with political dissent. One means at its disposal was legislation. On 7 August 1970, the regime made an abortive attempt to pass the Public Order Bill which: (i) gave to the Police Commissioner the power to prohibit public meetings, (ii) penalized the inciting of racial hatred and violence (a direct attempt to curb the Black Power movement), (iii) prohibited organization and training of quasi-military organizations, (iv) gave power of entry to police to any premises and the power to seize firearms, and (v) allowed the Minister of National Security to order the detention or to restrict the movement of anyone in the interest of "public order, public safety or defence" (National Security Act 1970). The sweeping powers granted to the police by such a law provoked resistance especially among middle- and upper-class regime supporters and forced withdrawal of the Act (see Ryan 1972: 467). Over the years, however, through several constitutional amendments, most of the clauses of the Public Order Act were passed into law.

The Prime Minister of the country assumed personal control of what was to be a much expanded police force and of the mutinous army, and created a National Security Council, headed by himself, to run the armed branches of government (see *Washington Post*, 19 June 1970). Direct control of the army, coast guard, and police ensured the strictest loyalty of the members of these agencies and guaranteed their availability and support for deployment against political dissidents.

Later, the regime developed a crack Flying Squad armed with sophisticated weapons and using modern equipment. Much of the activities of the unit were directed against political dissidents. An Assistant Commissioner (later promoted to Commissioner of Police) headed the squad and took personal charge of all of its major operations.

While the measures outlined above enabled the regime to contain mass mobilization, regime legitimacy, especially among the black lower classes, remained precariously low. The underlying causes of political discontent continued unabated. Poor performance in the oil sector between 1969 and 1972 affected most areas of the economy and by 1973 the economic picture was one of almost total disaster. Agriculture, services and facilities, public administration, and construction and trade all experienced negative growth in 1973. Manufacturing grew at a meager 1 percent as compared with 8 percent between 1968 and 1970.

This decline of regime legitimacy was visibly demonstrated during general elections in 1971 when 66 percent of the population heeded the calls of the radical opposition to stay away from the polls. The election was virtually uncontested except by the PNM and a few quickly assembled parties. While the regime was returned to power, it received only 28 percent of the vote of the total registered electorate. This attests to the effectiveness of the measures adopted by the regime to stay in power. An expanded coercive capacity and extremely effective measures of control over political behavior and over members of the coercive branches of the state kept the regime in power in spite of a loss of legitimacy.

Political participation and mass mobilization gave way to revolutionary insurgency. This was the response by young radical militants to the increased reliance of the PNM government upon coercion and upon strict control over political activity. The decision to go underground was, to a large extent, supported and justified by the loss of regime legitimacy. The National United Freedom Fighters (NUFF) began guerrilla activities from the forested hills of the country in 1972. Its young and well-educated leaders, who had the tacit support of much of the working-class population in the urban areas, led a series of attacks against police outposts and government installations, causing considerable damage to government and private property.

To meet the new threat, the regime escalated its coercive retaliation. The Flying Squad, the newly constituted army, and the police were employed in joint operations which resulted, in 1974, in a series of bloody confrontations with NUFF. Many of the group's leaders were killed and most of the survivors were arrested and imprisoned (see *Guardian Weekly*, 20 October 1983). Such operations continued against isolated and less threatening holdouts of this group and against weakly organized guerrilla groups that reemerged periodically throughout the 1970s and early 1980s. There was also an escalation of arbitrary search and seizure operations against known political opponents of the regime which became a permanent element of political control. Frequent targets of such operations were the houses of radical intellectuals, trade unionists, and even members of the elected political opposition and the premises of the organizations which they headed.

The defeat of the guerrilla movement came as much from the consequences of a post-1973 economic boom, fuelled by spectacular rises in oil prices, as from the effective coercive retaliation of the regime. Despite the implementation after the 1970 disturbances of a program of National Reconstruction to support job creation and patronage for the black lower class, the political crisis continued to simmer under the surface. Deteriorating economic conditions pointed towards political confrontation between the urban lower classes and the political leadership. In October 1973, the Prime Minister of the country announced his decision to resign, citing the escalating social, political, and economic problems faced by his government. All efforts to contain the situation had failed while demands for social and political reforms led by an increasingly effective and popular guerrilla movement, continued unabated.

Almost overnight, however, Trinidad experienced a dramatic economic recovery. The Middle East war of 1973 and the sharp increase in the price of crude oil brought immediate prosperity which bolstered the sagging legitimacy of the regime. The latter took immediate steps to exploit the boom and to use swelling revenues in a program of expanded job creation. By 1974, the insurgency challenge to the regime was all but eliminated.

With the reestablishment of regime legitimacy, the political opposition was forced to return to mass mobilization and electoral politics. The hope was that the radicalization of the population during the 1970-3 period of crisis had laid the framework for a new class orientation in the country's politics.

The events which followed the post-1973 economic boom serve to highlight a point made earlier in this chapter: that reliance upon coercion and control becomes increasingly critical for regime survival during periods of economic crisis. This is so for a number of reasons. As politically strategic sectors of society begin to be affected by the crisis, they withdraw their support for the regime and begin to capitalize on mass discontent to mobilize against the regime. Economic crisis also impinges upon the ability of the regime to honor its clientelistic commitments. When this occurs, many who were co-opted through patronage begin to withdraw their support. The regime also finds itself less able to reward its communal or class supporters from the coffers of the state. To survive, it is forced to rely increasingly on its machinery of control to preempt anti-regime mobilization. When such mobilization occurs, however, coercive retaliation might be the only recourse if order is to be maintained.

Despite a post-1973 economic boom, the result of spectacular rises in oil prices, economic hardships continued to be the experience of the bulk of the lower classes. Radical leaders continued to exploit economic dissatisfaction in efforts to topple the regime. They attempted to use their control of the country's major trade unions for class mobilization (see *Miami Herald*, 13 February 1974).

In February, 1975, trade unionists and radical intellectuals mounted a campaign of anti-regime mobilization to back calls for the outlaw of foreign firms. Together, they formed the United Labour Front (ULF) which later became a political party. The threat to the PNM government was all the more serious because of the group's multi-racial character. The new organization brought the most powerful of the black and East Indian working-class trade unions together in a united political effort (see *Miami Herald*, 20 February 1975). It was an unabashed attempt to redefine the terms of lower-class political mobilization from the politics of race to the politics of class.

In March, 1975, two of the unions, the OWTU and the All Trinidad Sugar Estates and Factory Workers Union, simultaneously called a strike. Ostensibly, the oil workers demanded a 147 percent pay increase and better conditions of work while the sugar workers called for a share of the profits of the state-owned sugar company. Underlying these demands, however, were calls for nationalization of foreign concerns in the country by the state (see *Christian Science Monitor*, 26 March 1975).

Industrial action by the two unions lasted over five weeks and caused an almost total immobilization of the country. Disruptions to the economy were severe. The supply of water and power was cut and there was an acute shortage of fuel, preventing the transportation of workers in other industries to and from their jobs. The estimated cost to the country was half a milion dollars a day (*Miami Herald*, 12 April 1975).

Again, the regime fell back upon its repository of coercion to restore social, political, and economic order. The leaders of the dissent were arrested early in the dispute and demonstrations by thousands of striking workers were broken up by police using tear gas, batons, and rifle butts (see *Los Angeles Times*, 22 March 1975). Armed police were deployed to protect all industrial and commercial properties in the country while security forces were used to distribute food, gasoline, and other petroleum products throughout the country. Faced with intense coercive retaliation by the state, the strikers returned to work without securing any concessions to their demands (see *Race Today*, April 1975). Thus, when the mechanisms of direct political control breaks down, a regime can easily fall back upon the coercive apparatus of the state to underwrite its own survival.

Party control over political behavior can also be indirect. Political leaders can define the terms of political behavior in ways that support their regime's own chances for survival. The encouragement and support for communal politics can be particularly important in this regard. Communal politics has the capacity to ensure that the regime retains mass support while neutralizing attempts by its opponents to employ ideological appeals to generate lower-class support. The PNM in Trinidad benefited enormously from such a strategy. Its continued encouragement of racial politics was important for maintaining control of the state. Efforts at lower-class moiblization by the opposition were constantly frustrated by communal conflict. During the crisis of 1970, anti-regime mobilization was confined to the black urban-based sector of the society, partly because of the black nationalism of the movement (which gave rise to some degree of anti-Indian hostility) and partly because of the suspicions harbored by the East Indian population against any black-led political movement. The radicals found themselves unable to recruit members of the East Indian lower class in significant numbers, even at the height of the crisis. Had the East Indian population been involved in anti-government confrontations, the regime would have been stretched beyond its limit, especially without the services of the mutinous army.

The post-1973 economic turnaround was extremely critical. It provided the resources necessary for the success of the PNM's renewed effort to reestablish racial mobilization. This was necessary for regaining the support of the black population. Between 1973 and 1980 the country was riding the crest of an economic boom which placed enormous amounts of resources at the disposal of the ruling party through its control on the state. A significant proportion of these resources was targeted at the black population and this mitigated black hostility to the party (see Hintzen 1981: 144–53). In 1976, one year after the ULF's attempt at class mobilization, the ruling party secured a massive electoral victory, winning 24 out of 36 parliamentary seats. In its shift from confrontational to electoral politics, the ULF was unable to translate its lower class mobilization efforts into victory at the polls. It was clear by the relatively low turnout of 56 percent that the PNM had not fully regained its legitimacy. However, those black voters who became alienated from the PNM during the political crisis of the early 1970s continued to refuse to participate in elections rather than support the political opposition. This testified to the effectiveness of the PNM in invoking the racial idiom. Blacks refused to vote for the ULF because of its racial identity with the East Indian lower classes and the domination of its Hindu leadership. This was despite the party's efforts at projecting a multi-racial image and notwithstanding the fact that many of its most powerful leaders were powerful and influential black radical unionists.

Economic prosperity, a capacity for lower class racial mobilization, an expanded system of generalized patronage, ideologically rooted middle- and upper-class support, control of political behavior, and coercive demobilization of the radical opposition all continued to serve the ruling party into the early 1980s. The party again won a resounding political victory in elections held in 1981, despite the sudden death of its founder and leader, Prime Minister Eric Williams, seven months earlier. The PNM's sixth term of office was secured with 26 seats in the 36-member Parliament despite renewed attempts by the opposition to forge a multi-racial movement to challenge it. Leading the efforts of the opposition was a former black Attorney General and, at one time, the second most powerful member of the PNM. He formed the Organization for National Reconstruction (ONR) which was aimed at mobilizing the middle and upper classes by adopting an ideological position somewhat to the right of the PNM. The new party emphasized its multi-racial character, choosing as its deputy leader a prominent East Indian intellectual.

There was a similar effort to move the idiom of political mobilization away from race by a coalition of moderate parties called the Alliance. The leading partner in the coalition was the ULF which, in 1977, had become purged of its radical wing. It was joined by two parties: one headed by a black moderate intellectual who enjoyed some appeal among the middle classes, and another which dominated the politics of the predominantly black population of Tobago which it represented in Parliament. The black founder of the latter was a one-time deputy Prime Minister in the PNM who resigned during the political disturbances of 1970. The only attempt at active mobilization of the lower classes was made by the National Joint Action

Committee (NJAC) whose radical class appeal was combined with black nationalism and directed at black and poor urban residents who continued to be dissatisfied with the economic program of the PNM (see *Caribbean Contact*, September 1981: 5).

The willingness of all these black leaders to challenge the PNM points to the susceptibility of a racially rooted party to outbidding (Milne 1981: 184–9). In order to preempt such efforts at outbidding, leaders attempt to demobilize party supporters during the periods between electoral campaigns. Demobilization, apart from denying potential challengers access to the organizational resources of the party, also serves to insulate elected officials from communally exclusive demands which compromise their autonomy (Cohen 1969: 4–5).

The structure of relations between the ruling party and government helped the regime's demobilization efforts. Members of the PNM had little motivation for sustained participation in its affairs because the party was almost totally isolated from the functions of governing the country (Hintzen 1981: 265–7). Party membership, even at the highest level, did not guarantee even indirect access to government decision-making, nor did it guarantee access to those who formulate policy. The political executive and elected members of Parliament were not closely identified with party activities, nor were they closely involved with its affairs.[2] The separation of those holding powerful positions in the state from party organizations served another function. Without roots in a mass following, elected and appointed officials became extremely vulnerable to the actions of party leaders and very dependent upon them. Thus, ministers in the government, many of whom were appointed as technocrats rather than recruited from among the ranks of elected parliamentarians, were constantly dismissed on the whim of the party leader without having recourse to popular mobilization. Even elected parliamentarians found themselves isolated from the party's mass following. When A. N. R. Robinson, the former Deputy Prime Minister who resigned during the political upheavals of 1970, left the PNM to form his own party, he became virtually isolated from the ruling party's support base, except within his small and politically insignificant constituency of Tobago. Similarly, a former Attorney General, Karl Hudson-Phillips, disappeared from the political scene after losing a bid to assume leadership of the party

---

[2] This has caused the relationship between party bureaucrats and the political executive to become strained. The former have been isolated from the corridors of power and a few have been dismissed for insisting upon a larger role for the party in national decision-making. See Hintzen 1981: 265–6 and *The Bomb*, 4 November 1977.

in 1973 when Williams announced his intention to resign. As a consequence, Hudson-Phillips became ostracized by the party leadership (see Hintzen 1981: 317). His reemergence at the head of the ONR had to await the death of Williams in 1981.

There were very few attempts by the regime to demobilize the East Indian opposition. The sustaining of the ruling party's racial appeal depended on the existence of an organized communal opposition. Such an opposition posed little or no threat to regime survival because it was strategically inconsequential (concentrated among the East Indian rural lower classes) and politically weak. For these reasons East Indian political organizations were allowed untrammeled participation in the political process. The concentration of the East Indian lower class in 10 to 12 constituencies served to blunt any potential electoral threat that its popular strength of close to 40 percent of the population might have posed to the regime. Moreover, East Indian political organizations were weakened by the loss of most of the population's powerful middle- and upper-class members to the PNM.

The regime's "hands off" policy ceased, however, when East Indian political leaders made attempts to cross racial boundaries in their mobilization efforts. Then, these leaders became the object of coercive retaliation. For example, when the ULF was formed out of a coalition of the Hindu Maha Saba party and radical black unionist-politicians, its leaders became subject to a considerable number of arrests and detentions. The party's premises, its personnel, and their homes were constant targets of police and security search and seizure operations. In other words, because racial mobilization was essential to the PNM's continued control of the state, there were no attempts to demobilize East Indian political organizations. However, when East Indian leaders engaged in political activity with the potential for cross-racial or class mobilization they became the immediate objects of the regime's coercive assault.

Guyana

The Guyanese regime effectively employed a racial appeal to secure absolute control of the military–bureaucratic state apparatus that was dominated by the country's black and colored middle class (see Hintzen 1983; Hintzen and Premdas 1981: 344–6). With this accomplished, it proceeded to decrease its dependence upon racial or class alliances. First, it rendered electoral politics meaningless by organizing an elaborate and effective system of electoral fraud. Secondly, through a policy of state expansion and appropriation, it skillfully converted the most strategic economic resources of the country into patronage while developing a structure of clientelistic alliances with powerful and influential leaders who would otherwise have opposed it on racial, class or ideological grounds (see Hintzen 1983). Finally, state expansion and appropriation allowed the development and organization of a powerful system of coercion and control which became the central pillar in its continued control of the state.

Political power in Guyana has come to rest, almost exclusively, upon an institutionalized system of political control rooted in regime domination of the apparatus of the state and in the use of state-directed coercion. This system of control is a logical outcome of the prerequisite conditions of political power in the country. These conditions, inherited from the colonial past, favor a black and colored political elite. Unable to win a majority in national elections, this elite has resorted to political control and coercion.

Today, the political directorate continues to rely upon racial mobilization. Unlike the PNM in Trinidad, however, it succeeded in restructuring racial support to serve its statist objectives. In other words it has been extremely successful in the regimentation of its racial supporters. The best example of this is the Guyanese military. When plans for the country's independence were being made in 1966, the need for a powerful military to maintain internal security was quite obvious. The country had just experienced a period of internal conflict, and political order was ensured only by the presence of the British military in the colony. The police force was ill-equipped to deal with large-scale political violence.

The need for a large military acted to the advantage of the black political leaders in the PNC/UF coalition government. It provided them with the opportunity to develop a larger and much more sophisticated coercive machinery whose loyalty to the PNC went unquestioned. The party's ability to do this rested upon an historically established pattern of black recruitment to the security forces in the country. This facilitated, justified, and legitimized discriminatory recruitment to the Guyana Defence Force (GDF) that was formed in November 1965 on the eve of the country's independence. Most of the new army's high-ranking officers were transferred from the British Guiana Volunteer Force which was a part-time unit organized in 1948 to supplement the police during periods of civil unrest (Enloe 1976: 28). This volunteer force had, by tradition, been predominantly black and was quite partisan in the racially changed politics of the country. It had, for example, come under strong criticism for its partisan support of the PNC during the civil disorders of the early 1960s. The younger junior officers of the GDF were recruited from the Cadet Corps of the prestigious secondary schools in Georgetown. Most of these cadets were black, as were almost all the recruits to the ranks.

There was little real demand on the part of the East Indian youths to enter the security forces. Most were rural dwellers (80 percent in 1965) who saw their future in the sugar and rice industries. Moreover, they were isolated from the centers of recruitment for the security services. The middle- and upper-class colored, Chinese, and white population showed little inclination toward a career in the armed services, or, for that matter, in the state sector. As a result, there was no expression of concern over black predominance in the 2,200-man Defence Force established at the time of the country's independence. (In 1970, the black and mixed racial groups made up 75 percent of the defense and police forces in the country. See Greene 1974: 75.)

During the 1970s the Burnham government relied more and more upon its control of the coercive apparatus of the state. The armed branches of government became pivotal for its continued political domination. The armed services also became crucial in the system of state-distributed patronage as the centerpieces of the regime's efforts to provide jobs for its racial followers.

In keeping with its expanded strategic, political, and patronage roles, there was a phenomenal growth of the armed services in the country, especially during the 1970s. In 1964, there were 2,135 personnel in the military and police forces. By 1977 this number had reached 21,751, representing one member of the armed services for every 37 citizens as opposed to one for every 284 in 1964 (Sackey 1979: 46). More recent estimates place the number of persons in the armed services of the country (exclusive of the police force) at between 23,000 and 31,000 (Thivolet 1979). Military and paramilitary expenditure rose from an estimated 8 percent of the national budget (G$22 million) in 1973 to 14·2 percent (G$113 million) in 1976 and went even higher during the years that immediately followed (Danns 1978). To the GDF was added a Guyana National Service in 1974. Apart from defense, the functions of the latter body came to include political education, hinterland development, and agricultural and industrial production (see Guyana Information Service 1977: 67). A Peoples Militia was formed in 1976 as a reserve supplement to the Defence Force.

The ruling regime increasingly institutionalized and formalized direct executive control of the military. The Prime Minister, and after 1980, the President, was the constitutionally designated Chairman of the Defence Board which administers the army. He had direct control of promotions and

Maintaining control of the state 93

appointments in all of the armed services (see Enloe 1976; 1980a; 1980b). Further, a group of committed party loyalists were appointed as his most senior army officers. Many were former members of a Social, Political and Economic Council (SPEC). Organized in 1970 as a branch of the party, SPEC's function was to bring together top military and police officers and leading PNC policy planners (see Enloe 1976).

Any hint of dissent among the officer corps of the army brought immediate and major reshuffles and the transfer of problem officers to civilian posts. Openly expressed dissatisfaction among the senior officers in 1979 was met by the removal of the Army Chief of Staff and the Brigadier General (the army's formal head) and their replacement by a former police officer highly loyal to the regime and with close personal ties to the Prime Minister. The total structure of command in the armed services was changed. The new Chief of Staff was given responsibilities for the police, the Militia, and the Guyana National Service in what constituted a consolidation of leadership and control of the entire armed services in the country (see *Caribbean Contact*, October 1979).

In 1973, for the first time, the army became directly involved in the electoral process of the country. The Guyana Defence Force was given the task by the Prime Minister of ensuring the orderly conduct of the elections and of transporting the ballot boxes to the capital city for counting. Members of all the opposition parties and most independent foreign commentators charged that the army's role of peace-keeping was a mere camouflage for its involvement in the blatant rigging of the elections. The army's involvement was a critical ingredient in giving the ruling PNC a two-thirds majority in Parliament, and with it, the numerical strength to change the constitution.

Charges were made, and substantiated, that army personnel were used to stuff ballot boxes with fictitious votes for the PNC during the course of transporting them to the city. During the campaign itself, the army intervened and broke up political meetings of the opposition parties, especially in rural areas with East Indian majorities. On the day of election, the army shot and killed three East Indians and used tear gas on numerous occasions in efforts to stop demonstrations which emerged to protest electoral rigging (see Jagan 1973; Mandle 1976; Premdas 1977; Lernoux 1980: 510).

As the country's economic problems deepened, the armed forces assumed a more critical role in ensuring political stability. The army was called out, even if only for a show of force, at the mere hint of civil disorder. Unannounced military exercises increased as political discontent became more openly expressed. Such exercises involved army occupation of government buildings, army blockades, deployment of troops to rural areas, and troops in full battle dress patrolling the streets.

The regime-directed coercive apparatus extended beyond the armed branches of the state. During the 1970s and early 1980s the most brutal acts of violence were carried out by members of a private, black religious cult calling itself the "House of Israel." It was headed by a convicted black American felon known as Rabbi Washington who had settled in Guyana in 1971 after skipping bail while facing charges of blackmail and grand theft in the United States. Over the years, the cult, with a membership of close to 8,000 black Guyanese (according to the estimates of its leader) developed especially close ties with the PNC regime. During the latter part of the 1970s it became an integral part of the regime's coercive retaliation against political opponents and against any form of anti-government dissent. The House of Israel was linked to violent attacks against anti-regime demonstrators and strikers, attacks against protesting high school students, and several political assassinations – including one of a priest who worked for a Roman Catholic tabloid that had become extremely critical of the directorate. Under considerable international pressure, the regime of President Desmond Hoyte, successor to Forbes Burnham, finally charged Washington with murder in May 1976. He was convicted with three of his "high priests" of manslaughter in October of the same year and sentenced to 15 years in prison.

At best, the effectiveness of coercion in maintaining political order is only temporary. For order to be maintained over any length of time, there needs to be developed an effective system of control over the behavior and activities of individuals, groups, and organizations which constitute actual and potential challenges to the dominance of the state-controlling elite.[3] This is particularly true for agencies of mass mobilization.

[3] What is said above is not to be misinterpreted to mean that third world socialist regimes must *invariably* employ political control to remain in power. The critical factor here is the existence of *politicized* communal segments which are available for mobilization by elites. Under conditions where communal fragmentation is not politicized or where it is politically unimportant (as for example, when one group comprises an overwhelming majority while the remaining groups have limited access to strategic resources of power), capitalist regimes may very well have to develop and have historically exhibited an exclusive reliance upon extreme forms of control (as in pre-socialist Viet Nam, Cambodia, Laos, and Cuba, and in most countries in Latin and Central America). There are other conditions where capitalist regimes depend upon extreme forms of control. One such is under conditions where the regime has exclusive communal ties to the midddle and upper classes and where the lower classes are communally distinct (as in Rhodesia [Zimbabwe] and South Africa). By contrast, when ideological commitment to socialism among the lower classes has become deeply entrenched, a socialist regime might need to rely less upon control and domination (as in the cases of China and Cuba, even though they do not fit into the definition of a third world socialist regime).

The Guyanese regime placed particular emphasis upon control of mass mobilization. The trade union movement received special attention. In Guyana, a pattern of industrial mobilization for political ends had become firmly established since the second decade of the twentieth century. All the major political changes in the century were brought about through the vehicle of trade union mobilization. To preempt the use of the movement by its opponents, the ruling party began to propose, support, and endorse party loyalists in elections for leadership positions in the country's top unions, and to blacklist office-seekers who were not party members and supporters (see Premdas 1972: 18). It also began to exercise strict control over the all-important Trades Union Council (TUC). Through the practice of direct party intervention, the state-controlling elite managed to gain effective control of most of the powerful trade unions in the country. This control was used, quite effectively, to prevent union-based mobilization against the regime. Nonetheless, party dominance of the trade union movement has been far from complete. It has had to face persistent political challenges from two affiliated unions of the PPP, a third union headed by radical anti-regime university intellectuals and a fourth which represents workers in the nationalized state corporations.

The regime also came to exercise strict control over the state bureaucratic machinery. The loyalty of the state bureaucrats, already strong by virtue of the party's racial appeal, came to be underwritten and strengthened by a system of patronage. The exchange of office and material gain for loyalty to the political directorate became critical in this apparatus of control. The Prime Minister and, after 1980, the Executive President was at the center of this system of patronage. He personally had to approve every senior-level appointment (Milne 1981: 148). Loyalty to him and to the regime became an absolute prerequisite for appointment to senior positions in the state sector (see also Milne 1981: 117; Enloe 1976; *Guyana Chronicle*, 19 May 1978). In return, this core of elites came to enjoy socio-economic status that was way above average for the population at large. They also enjoyed the numerous perquisites and privileges which came with their positions and considerable access to corruption in which they habitually engaged.[4] In 1978, the average annual income for the top leaders in the country, as reported in a survey which I conducted, was G$25,000 and the minimum listed salary for senior

---

[4] These include duty-free shopping and opportunities to purchase goods not available to the rest of the population (mainly confined to the military but with widespread access to them by non-military elites), duty-free cars and traveling allowances, opportunities for external travel with lavish travel allowances normally used as income supplements, easy access to loan privileges at government-owned banks, state-financed mortgages for low-priced homes constructed by a state housing corporation, and housing allowances. See Danns 1984.

government bureaucrats was G$12,000. This compared with an annual income of under G$3,000 for unskilled and semi-skilled full time workers in the state sector. At that time, 75 percent of the work force held lower-class occupations and the unemployment rate was over 30 percent (see Hintzen 1981: Chapters 2 and 5). Every effort was made to protect these state bureaucrats from economic downturns. When the Guyanese dollar was devalued in 1981, it was accompanied by a compensatory increase in salaries for the military and for senior government bureaucrats to offset the increases in the costs of living that devaluation entailed. All other employees of the state were denied similar increases.

The regime continued to maintain control of black mass organizations through communal mobilization directed by the party. Such mobilization, however, came to be channeled to the goals of statism and away from the particular interests of the black population. In other words, it took on the character of communal regimentation. Regime autonomy was therefore not compromised by racially exclusive demands. Racial mobilization also preempted the development of class politics among the lower classes.

The regime incorporated the party into the structure of the state. In 1974, it formalized this incorporation by declaring "unapologetically its (the party's) paramountcy over the government" (*Newsletter* no. 4: 1974). The Office of the General Secretary of the party was combined with a newly created Ministry of National Development headed by the Deputy Prime Minister. Significantly, the new Ministry was given the responsibility for overall co-ordination of the day-to-day running of the state and for overall development planning. It became one of the most strategic agencies of government.

The reorganization accomplished a number of things. First, state bureaucrats and the political executive came to have direct control of the party's resources and of its organization. With the state exercising control over the ruling party, the power and influence of party activists with local followings were all but eliminated as was their ability to make demands upon the regime. Secondly, by acting in the name of a paramount party, the political executive was able to free itself from the need to consult with the legislative branches of government and with other representative bodies in making and implementing policy. Finally, the reorganization created the machinery for the transfer of state resources to the ruling party to serve the functions of patronage, control, and mobilization in support of the political executive.

Control of the electoral machinery came to be another indispensable element in regime domination. Such control came to be important, not merely for winning at the polls, but for providing the regime with the exclusive authority to make constitutional changes which require a two-thirds majority in Parliament. Control of the electoral machinery was pivotal in efforts to centralize power around the Executive President. Before 1978, all constitutional changes required approval in a plebiscite as well as by a two-thirds majority in Parliament. The regime proposed a constitutional change that would abolish the need for the plebescite in future constitutional issues. A referendum was called to approve the proposal at a time when public discontent was running high. Because of the certainty of massive electoral fraud, all the opposition parties and anti-government groups called upon their supporters to stay away from the polls. Independent and verifiable evidence points to the success of the boycott movement with voter turnout assessed at just over 14 percent of the electorate, and some estimates as low as 12 percent. Nonetheless, with army intervention and massive electoral rigging, the regime was able to announce an official turnout of 71·45 percent with a 97·7 percent voter approval of the proposal (see *Covert Action*, August–September 1980; *Caribbean Contact*, July 1980: 13; Catholic Institute for International Relations 1980).

With the abolition of the plebiscite approved through electoral rigging, the PNC came to have the absolute authority to change the constitution without recourse to the elected opposition. For constitutional changes to be passed into law the regime now needed mere approval by two-thirds of the parliamentary legislators. Since 1973, electoral fraud had come to guarantee the ruling party the necessary parliamentary votes to secure such a majority.

With the plebiscite abolished, and enjoying a two-thirds majority in parliament, the regime passed a new constitution into law in October 1980 which installed Forbes Burnham as Executive President. The functions of the Prime Minister and President were combined to give the holder, in the words of Sam Silkin, a former Attorney General in Britain's Labour government, "virtually imperial powers" (*Nation*, 15 November 1980: 510). The new constitution gave the Executive President the authority to dissolve and suspend Parliament. He enjoyed the right of veto over legislation, and he had the constitutional authority to declare laws in the interest of "national security." In addition, the new president continued in his position as Head of State with supreme executive authority. Under the Executive Presidency, Burnham assumed the position of Commander in Chief of the armed forces with exclusive power to appoint and to dismiss the heads of all the branches of the security services (Monroe 1980).

Likewise, the judiciary also came under autocratic domination; *de facto* power to appoint the Chief Justice and the Chancellor of the Judiciary (head of the Court of Appeals), which formerly rested with the political executive, passed directly to the Executive President after the change of constitution. The appointment of judges and magistrates fell exclusively to the President who was to be advised by the Judicial Service Commission, comprising the Chancellor, the Chief Justice, and the Chairman of a Public Service Commission – all presidential appointees. In effect, every member of the Judicial Service Commission was dependent upon the Executive President for his or her job (see DeCaries 1979). In this manner, control of the judicial process was passed into the hands of the President through his power of appointment.

To consolidate its control of the judiciary, the regime passed the Guyana Administration of Justice Bill in 1978 against intense pressure from the Guyana Bar Association and from the Organization of Commonwealth Caribbean Bar Associations (OCCBA). This law abrogated the right of citizens to choose trial by jury where this was not mandatory. It gave the magistrates, whose appointment had to receive at least regime sanction and whose job was entirely at the mercy of the regime, the absolute power to determine guilt or innocence in most cases. More importantly, it preempted the use of the courts to mount legal and constitutional challenges to the actions of the regime and to its decisions. With regime control of the courts, the judiciary became incorporated into the coercive arsenal of the regime. The courts were now available to be employed against political opponents arrested and charged with various, and oftentimes trumped up, offenses.

Regime control of a dependent third world state cannot be sustained without access to international economic resources and without some form of external political support. The problem for the Guyanese regime during the latter half of the 1970s was that access to such resources was becoming increasingly difficult. Apart from the general political chaos that it caused, one of the most important consequences of the economic crisis of the 1970s was that it eroded the material basis of support for the lifestyles of the country's middle classes, and especially for the new group of bureaucratic elites. The crisis was also restricting the capacity of the state to sustain an effective coercive apparatus. Since the support of the bureaucratic elite and coercive strength were the two pillars upon which the political power of the regime rested, it became imperative that the economic crisis be meliorated, at least as it affected these two sectors. Important in this regard was the ability of the state to attract external financial and developmental support.

The hope for economic recovery was pinned to external assistance for financing planned developmental projects and to maintain current expenditures at existing levels.[5] In April 1978, the Prime Minister of the country set out on an economic mission to Eastern Europe and North Korea in search of such assistance. He returned with little more than friendship agreements and with few substantive commitments to provide financial and technical aid to the country (see *Guyana Chronicle*, 14, 19, and 23 April 1978; and *Trinidad Guardian*, 18 April 1978: 1).

Without commitments of aid in any significant quantities forthcoming from the communist countries, the Burnham regime was forced, if it wanted to stay in power, to seek increased assistance from the West. Burnham thus began to make appeals to the United States for assistance. Fortunately for the regime, they came at a time of revived efforts by the Carter administration to combat the growth of the radical left in the Caribbean. Undoubtedly fearing the possibility of a pro-Moscow PPP regaining power, the United States agreed to increase its aid package to the country. According to the then US Ambassador to Guyana, the country was, in 1979, "the recipient of the highest U.S. per capita aid of any country in the world" (*Guardian* (US), 15 October 1980: 16). In addition, the International Monetary Fund agreed to provide the country with four times its quota in aid while the World Bank suddenly agreed to help finance a massive hydroelectric project after years of steadfast refusals. The extreme generosity of these two agencies was, without a doubt, related to the emerging policy of support for the Burnham regime that had begun to typify the policy of the United States government particularly after 1978 (*Nation*, 15 October 1980: 510–12).

In exchange for the economic bailout, the regime cut back noticeably on its radical rhetoric both internally and at international fora. Its economic advisors began to talk favorably of attracting the participation of foreign private enterprise in the country (*Guyana Chronicle*, 26 June 1977). Thus, for regime power to be maintained, Western security and political interests had to be accommodated while promises had to be made that Western capitalist investors would, once again, be allowed to participate in the local economy.

In December 1980 the Burnham regime had managed to prop itself up with almost dictatorial powers, with absolute control over the country's formidable coercive arsenal, and with an economy that had begun to show signs of improvement. It was bolstered by a more favorable Western attitude and by US economic and political support. Combined, these led to the virtual

---

[5] Developmental plans included a program of industrialization centered around an enormous hydroelectric project to supply the country's energy needs and to allow industrial expansion for export. There were also plans to increase and diversify agricultural production and to develop small-scale industry.

disappearance of the protest movement against his government. Forbes Burnham used the opportunity to call general elections to confirm his presidency. Almost as soon as the elections were over, an international eleven-member observer team headed by a British Member of Parliament, Lord Avebury, Chairman of the United Kingdom Human Rights Group, reported massive evidence of widespread rigging and refuted the claim of the ruling party that it won 77 percent of the vote (see *Caribbean Contact*, January 1981: 1, 16). Unlike the referendum, however, the allegations of rigging generated very few public demonstrations, attesting to the success of Burnham's demobilization strategy. On 18 December 1980, Forbes Burnham was installed as the first elected Executive President of the country at a time when he was, once again, firmly in control of the country.

The Guyanese regime has depended upon coercion, control, and an appeal to racial sentiments to maintain its position of power. Internally, clientelistic co-optation produced support from state elites. The regime's willingness to succumb to powerful international interests guaranteed the supply of critical resources when they were badly needed. When combined, all these produced an effective system of domination that totally eliminated the need for a majoritarian base of power.

Conclusion

The factors responsible for the ability of the PNM regime in Trinidad to retain power for 26 years were its willingness to accommodate powerful interests, its capacity to mobilize mass support by appealing to racial sentiments, its extensive system of generalized patronage, and the development of an effective system of coercion. It managed to preempt efforts to use the party for political outbidding and to insulate itself from racial demands from its mass followers. With this, the political executive remained free, in its policy-making, to cater to the interests of the powerful private sector dominated by transnational investors and by local whites and East Indians. This did not come without costs. Periods of economic downturn spawned anti-regime mobilization among the lower classes and gave rise to the use of violent and non-violent state coercion. During periods of economic boom, large doses of patronage took the edge off abject poverty, enough to bring dissident supporters back to the fold. At the same time, attempts at lower-class mobilization were hindered by racial fragmentation. Lower-class political dissent failed to produce a unified multi-racial class movement even during serious political crises. The regime lost power only when a combined

Maintaining control of the state 101

opposition managed to put together a cross-racial political alliance during a period of economic crisis which severely restricted its ability to dispense patronage. The effect was a significant loss of middle- and upper-class support critical for maintaining control of the state, as well as a significant portion of the black lower-class vote through its diminished ability to dispense patronage.

The most important observation to be made is the intertwining of political order and economic performance. In 1980, there were the beginnings of a reversal in the once booming economy, sparked by declines in the output of crude and in refinery throughput. In addition, most non-oil sectors of the economy continued to exhibit negative growth and the country's energy-based industrialization program began to founder. Downturns in the price of crude, beginning in 1982, put further pressure on the Trinidadian economy amid signs of an impending crisis. The effects of all this began to produce an anti-regime backlash. In August 1982, for the first time, the regime suffered a stunning upset in local government elections, losing control of all but three urban municipalities and one county council to a combined opposition which managed to secure 51 percent of the popular vote to the PNM's 42 percent. This opposition was able to win 66 local government seats to the ruling party's 54. In December 1986 this same opposition won a landslide electoral victory by capturing 33 of the 36 parliamentary seats and 67 percent of the popular vote, thereby ending the 30-year rule of the PNM.

Thus, the middle and upper classes of the country appeared willing to continue their support for the ruling party only if its policies proved beneficial to their own economic interests. The party suffered severe losses in all upper- and upper-middle-class constituencies in 1986, winning in only black lower-class constituencies. At the same time, the regime's capacity to deliver political patronage, upon which a considerable proportion of its mass support rested, was severely affected by the economic downturn. This explains the willingness of many of its former supporters to vote for the opposition. Finally, the party's racial supporters had consistently shown a willingness to mobilize against it during periods of economic crisis. In the past, when faced with serious political challenges, state political leaders quickly resorted to coercion and political control. The depth of middle-class dissatisfaction with the regime acted to transform the state bureaucratic and security sectors into neutral agencies in the political conflict. Any attempt to use either to maintain regime power, as was the case in 1970, would most definitely have been rebuffed. Thus, loss of racial support, a significant drop in its patronage resources, and an erosion of dominance in the state

102 Maintaining control of the state

bureaucratic and security sector combined to produce an electoral defeat for the PNM regime. Lacking the resources for coercion and control, the party leadership had no option but to accede to the wishes of the majority.

Unlike the case of Trinidad, the Guyanese regime has survived by the institutionalization, over the years, of an increasingly elaborate system of oligarchic control and by an increasing reliance upon violent and non-violent coercion. At the same time, it has acquiesced to powerful international interests through a series of ideological shifts made possible because of the rooting of political support in racial mobilization.

The regime gained full control of the state through a combination of communal politics and political patronage. The former ensured the unified support of the black and colored middle class, the members of which had inherited control of the state bureaucratic institutions and who comprised the majority of state-sector employees. The latter assured loyalty, through co-optation, of strategic elites and of those who held strategic positions in the state and private sector. Racial support, patronage, and ideological acquiescence to powerful international interests became the pillars upon which the regime developed and institutionalized its system of coercion and control. In this manner, it freed itself from the majoritarian demands of popular democratic politics while developing the capability to demobilize any potential threat to its continued hold on the state.

4. Elite support and control of the state; race, ideology, and clientelism

One of the central arguments of the previous chapters is that regime survival is directly tied to its ability to accommodate, neutralize, or eliminate powerful and influential actors who control politically strategic resources. Such actors are able to employ their formidable resources to make the task of retaining power impossible for a political directorate. They have the wherewithal to mount or support mobilization efforts against a regime and to undertake efforts aimed at destabilizing the political economy and at disrupting social order.

Accommodation implies the commitment of a regime to formulate and implement policies and programs which protect and further the interests represented by powerful and influential leaders. Such policies and programs need not be consistent with the regime's ideological position. In the context of strategies for regime survival, ideology constitutes a means of gaining support from strategic actors through a declared commitment to further and protect their interests. The regime might find itself under no obligation to follow through on such commitments particularly when the conditions of power have changed.

In the *internal* power equation, the political directorate is by far the most dominant element because of the economic, political, and social resources under its control and because of its central role in conflict management and order maintenance, not to speak of its near monopolization of coercion.[1] To the extent that this directorate is unified and integrated, the regime, as its dominant element, has the wherewithal through its control of the state to preempt and overcome domestic elite opposition to its policies. Its ability to do so, however, is conditioned by the extent and nature of the opposition. A regime might not be able to withstand the brunt of opposition from a large

---

Parts of this chapter have appeared and much of the data have been reported in Hintzen 1983.

[1] This argument for the "overdeveloped" post-colonial state is made by Alavi 1972; Murray 1967, and discussed in Langdon 1977 and von Frehold 1977. It has been criticized by Leys (1976) on the grounds that it does not take into account the external (international) determinants of political power and external control of decision-making.

segment of the powerful and influential elite. At the head of a unified political directorate, however, it does have the capabilities to demobilize and neutralize elite opposition. It can do so in a number of ways. It might co-opt members of the elite and/or secure their support even when its policies and programs are detrimental to the interests of those whom such elites represent. The primary basis of such co-optation is patronage. This has been fully discussed in the previous chapters. Co-optation guarantees that the resources controlled by powerful elites would not be employed against a regime. As has already been discussed, coercion and control also ensure demobilization and neutralization. By expanding and strengthening regime control over the behavior of powerful elites and the groups, organizations, and institutions which they head or represent, a regime can secure their political neutralization. In this manner it can ensure that these groups, organizations and institutions are not employed for anti-regime mobilization. The regime might go even further and take direct control of such organizations away from powerful leaders. In addition to demobilization and/or regimentation, this also ensures that the basis of power and influence of opposing elites is undermined or eliminated altogether. Finally, a regime can employ coercion to eliminate elites altogether or to restrict their activities to non-political behavior.

There is another factor to be considered in a regime's relationship with powerful and influential elites. This has to do with its ability to appeal to communal sentiment. One might predict that communal support for the regime would be strong among elites who head communally rooted lower-class organizations. Based on what has been discussed before concerning the nature and character of middle- and upper-class support and its basis in accumulative and interest considerations, one might anticipate communal appeal to play less of a role among leaders representing middle- and upper-class segments of society.

The above formulations lead us to anticipate certain patterns in the composition of the group of powerful and influential leaders in countries like Guyana and Trinidad where regimes have managed to survive and endure. First, the group of powerful and influential should contain a predominance of leaders representing sectors of the middle and upper classes which have derived significant benefits from regime policies and programs. Otherwise, it would be difficult for the regime to survive given the inevitability of sustained and protracted opposition. The formulations also lead us to anticipate the pattern of relations between regimes and various segments of the elite. One might expect racial support to have very little predictive power in anticipating elite support, apart from among those leaders representing communal

Race, ideology, and clientelism 105

organizations. This is true because of the rooting of middle- and upper-class support in objective interests and of lower-class support in subjective identity. Clientelism might be expected to play a significant role in elite support particularly under conditions where regime policies and programs have had negative consequences for major segments of the population. This is because of the role played by patronage in co-opting the support of powerful and influential leaders.

To determine the extent to which the anticipated patterns outlined above proved true for Guyana and Trinidad, I conducted a survey of the powerful and influential leaders in both countries.

Methodology

In 1962, Charles Moskos did a study of leaders in six territories of the then British West Indies, including Guyana and Trinidad (see Moskos 1967). His findings provide valuable data for measuring any change that might have occurred over the years since Guyana and Trinidad were granted their political independence from Britain. In order to maximize the comparability of my findings with those of Moskos, I decided to use a similar methodology for selecting national leaders considered to be powerful and influential. I also decided to employ, where possible, questions comparable to those asked by him.

In selecting the group of powerful and influential leaders, Moskos used a two-stage, positional–reputational method (see Moskos 1967: 96–105). In the first stage he identified five sectors within which top leaders are most likely to be located, then he chose for interview one leader considered by convention to be the most powerful in each of the sectors identified. Thus, in the first stage, he ended up with five leaders: one each from the incumbent political group, the major political opposition, the private economic sector, the civil service, and the mass media. He "snowballed" the list of leaders by asking each of those selected for interview to identify other society-wide leaders considered to be most influential and powerful in national affairs. After the initial list was compiled, a leader was chosen for interview if he/she were nominated by at least one-third of those previously interviewed. This method ensured the selection of a near universe of top national leaders from every sector of society which, in addition, had been nominated by the group of leaders themselves.[2]

[2] This method has been successfully employed in studies of elites in the Anglophone Caribbean. In addition to Moskos 1967; see Bell 1964, 1967; Bell and Gibson 1978; Robinson and Bell 1978, among others.

The procedure used for selecting top leaders in Guyana and Trinidad in 1978 was identical to that used by Moskos in 1962 with the one exception that I made the decision to select for interview leaders nominated by one out of every five of the respondents. This provided me with a larger group of top leaders. It was done because my 1978 study was aimed at much more detail, in terms of elite composition and elite attitudes, rather than strict analytical comparison with Moskos' 1962 study. The new criterion of selection produced 48 leaders eligible for interview in Trinidad of whom 40 (84 percent) were actually interviewed. In Guyana, 31 out of 37 (83 percent) eligible leaders were interviewed. These percentages compare favorably with an 82 percent response rate for Moskos. Those eligible leaders not interviewed were either out of the country or could not be contacted for various reasons. A few refused to be interviewed.

Sectoral and institutional background of leaders

The context within which elite composition and elite support for the regimes in Guyana and Trinidad must be examined is (i) declared ideology and (ii) the choice of developmental strategy. Consistent with its own declared ideology, the Trinidadian regime implemented a program of capitalist development. Its policies and programs had enormous economic payoffs for most persons in middle and upper socio-economic brackets. Local entrepreneurs thrived upon the investment opportunities made available in the wake of business expansion and from direct and indirect state assistance. Managers and bureaucrats working in the private sector experienced enormous increases in income as foreign and local businesses expanded and became more profitable. Professionals were provided with greatly expanded opportunities for highly lucrative contracts and were able to avail themselves of investment opportunities that opened up with business expansion. Government bureaucrats benefited from state expansion that came with public participation in joint ventures, with infrastructural development for the private sector, with supportive services provided to local investors, with expansion of facilities to service the private sector, and with an active state role in financing local business. Government employees associated with these areas came to enjoy much higher salaries and more numerous perquisites of office supported by the increases in state revenue generated by a growing private sector.

One would therefore expect that the powerful and influential in Trinidad would be identified with the above-named sectors of the society while the

Race, ideology, and clientelism 107

PNM was in power. The reason, of course, is that as these sectors became strengthened by regime policy, one would expect considerable growth in the power and influence of their representative leaders. This expectation becomes even more justified in view of the regime's strategy (discussed in Chapter 3) of demobilizing mass organizations such as political parties and trade unions (the exception being the East Indian mass political movement which posed little or no threat to regime survival). Given the effectiveness of this strategy, one might therefore anticipate a lower representation of political and union leaders among the top elite in Trinidad during the PNM's political tenure.

The policies of the Guyanese regime have placed emphasis (i) upon state ownership and control of the economy through state appropriation of the productive assets of the private sector, (ii) upon strict monitoring and control of the professions with many of these functions being absorbed into the state sector, (iii) upon income redistribution from the upper to the middle classes, (iv) upon strict control of mass-based organizations, and (v) upon political regimentation. These have resulted in the significant increase in power and influence of leaders in the state sector. Given the strategy of co-optation, leaders of mass organizations can be expected to be highly represented among the powerful and influential since privilege, office, position, and perquisites come hand in hand with clientelistic co-optation. The strategy of regimentation rendered leaders of mass organizations more strategic for regime power. Hence, these leaders can be expected to be well represented among the influential and powerful. One might also expect heightened efforts by elite opponents to employ racial appeals to mobilize the lower classes against the regime. As a result, race can be expected to become a significant predictor of political support among the powerful and influential.

Finally, as opposed to Trinidad where wealth and power might be anticipated to go together, one might expect the income and assets of Guyanese leaders to reflect a middle-class salaried elite given the constriction and neutralization of the private sector and its representatives.

Table 4.1 shows that of the 88 leaders nominated in Trinidad, those from the private economic sector (27 percent) and from the political sector (24 pecent) had the largest representation among the groups of top reputational leaders. Leaders from the media, comprising 10 percent of the total group, were perceived to be next in importance with the rest spread among five other sectors. In Guyana, the politicians were clearly the most numerous (34 percent) followed by the professionals (22 percent). Leaders from the private sector made up only 12 percent of the nominated group. This reflects, in part, a historically limited influence of local business upon the political affairs of

Table 4.1. *Percentages of nominated reputational leaders by institutional sector of major occupation for Trinidad and Guyana, 1978*

Sector	Trinidad (%)	Guyana (%)
Political[a]	24	34
Union	7	8
Economic	27	12
Media	10	8
Professional	17	22
University	3	4
Clergy	3	2
Civil service	5	—
Armed services[b]	4	—
Public corporations	—	8
Not ascertained	—	2
Total	100	100
Number of cases	88	50

[a] Including professional/politicians
[b] Including police.

the country. It also reflects the effect of the regime's socialist policies in the miniaturization of the private sector and in the diminution of its political clout.

In Guyana, trade unions have been, singly, the most important instrument of mobilization for the mass-based parties (see Premdas 1975; Hintzen 1975: 46–81). Thus, political and trade union leaders amounted to 42 percent of the group of nominated leaders in the country. In Trinidad, the combined percentage of trade union and political leaders was only 31, a slim 4 percentage points above the economic leaders. Historically, private sector elites have played major roles in the country's politics. Their influence certainly increased in the wake of the PNM's capitalist policies (see Hintzen 1981: 109–13). At the same time, the lower representation of trade union and political leaders in Trinidad versus Guyana, (31 percent to 42 percent) emphasizes the effects of the former regime's efforts at demobilization.

There was a slightly higher proportion of professionals among the top reputational leaders in Guyana (22 percent) than in Trinidad (17 percent). This might also have to do with the higher degree of importance of mass-based organizations such as trade unions and political parties in Guyana.

Race, ideology, and clientelism 109

Such organizations are usually led by professionals. For example, 62 percent of political and trade union leaders interviewed in Guyana had prior occupations as professionals. In Trinidad the comparable percentage was 55 percent.

Distribution of wealth among leaders

The figures for the annual incomes of 30 of the 31 leaders interviewed in Guyana and of all 40 of the Trinidadian leaders were provided either by the respondents themselves or from reliable official sources – for example, the incomes of public officials in both countries are published.

Leaders who received one-fifth or more of the total nominations in Guyana had a mean income in 1978 of G$25,000. In Trinidad, the mean was TT$63,900 – a difference of TT$38,800 when compared with the Guyanese (the Guyanese and Trinidadian dollars were at the time almost identical in value). The median income of the top Guyanese reputational leaders was G$21,500 with a range of G$71,000 (the highest paid leader earned G$72,000). Thus, apart from the presence of a few extremely high-income earners, Guyanese leaders constituted a relatively homogeneous group of middle-income persons. In fact, only one Guyanese leader earned over G$50,000 per year. In Trinidad the median income was TT$49,833 with a range of TT$246,000 indicating a very heterogeneous group of income earners. Of the Trinidadian leaders, 23 percent (9) earned over TT$100,000 per year and 45 percent (18) earned over TT$50,000 in a country where 34 percent of the population lives below poverty level calculated on a sliding scale in 1978 ranging from TT$1,380 per annum for a single person to TT$3,960 per annum for a household of six or more persons (*Trinidad and Tobago Review*, June 1978) and where the average income for the lower middle class was TT$8,100 per annum that very year (*Trinidad Express*, 4 May 1978: 18). From an examination of the net worth of leaders in Table 4.2, it becomes very evident that wealth, power, and influence went together in Trinidad in a manner that far surpassed Guyana.

One-third of the group of top Trinidadian reputational leaders interviewed were millionaires and one-half had net worths of over TT$200,000. Only 20 percent had total net worths of less than TT$50,000. Among the Guyanese groups of leaders there were only two millionaires (7 percent) while the modal category of net worth was between G$50,000 and G$100,000. Sixty percent of the leaders were worth less than G$100,000. Thus, whilst monied interests were represented among the top leadership in Guyana, one cannot say – as one must conclude in the case of Trinidad –

110   Race, ideology, and clientelism

Table 4.2. *The net worth of the top reputational leaders in Guyana and Trinidad, 1978*

Net worth	Trinidad (%)	Guyana (%)
$1,000,000 and over	32·5	7
$750,000–$999,999	7·5	3
$500,000–$749,999	10	10
$200,000–$499,999	22·5	13
$100,000–$199,999	7·5	7
$50,000–$99,999	—	37
$10,000–$49,999	20	13
Under $9,999	—	10
Total	100	100
Number of cases	40	30

that these interests superseded all others. There was very little representation of capitalist interests among the Guyanese leaders even though they undoubtedly came from a property-owning group. In Trinidad, on the contrary, with 13 millionaires and with 42 percent of the leaders worth over TT$750,000, this was clearly not the case.

It becomes clear, therefore, that the composition of elites in the two countries reflected the success of government strategy in creating a cadre of elite representing sectors of society that were most dependent upon regime policies. The Trinidadian regime opted for policies which concentrated on the development of the local private sector and upon capital intensive industrialization through the encouragement of foreign private capital investment (see Hintzen 1981: 107–70). As a result, the political and economic influence of the local private sector increased tremendously and this was reflected in the higher representation of elites from this group among the nominated leaders when compared with Guyana.[3] Thus, the Trinidadian regime's commitment to a capitalist development strategy strengthened the

---

[3] In 1962 when Moskos did his study (see Moskos 1967) there were six private sector elites among 22 powerful and influential leaders that he interviewed, making them 27 percent of the top leaders. This percentage was increased slightly to 31 percent for this study. Moreover, the private sector gained direct and institutionalized access to national decision-making after the PNM regime set up a National Economic Advisory Council in 1963 in which the Executive, trade unions, and business met to formulate national economic policy. In 1967, the Council was reformulated with a larger role played by the business sector and the role of the trade unions minimized (Hintzen 1981: 112).

power and influence of those leaders most likely to support its policies and programs.

In implementing its economic policy, the Guyana regime nationalized all the foreign holdings in the country, with the exception of banks which were miniaturized. It also took over many of the large local enterprises (see Hintzen 1981: 72–228). In response, there was considerable capital flight from the country.[4] Many of the large locally owned firms closed and their owners migrated overseas. The miniaturization of the private sector is thus reflected in the small proportional representation of business elites among the nominated leaders as compared to Trinidad (12 percent versus 27 percent).[5] In other words, the effects of regime policy in Guyana was to minimize the destabilizing consequences of domestic capitalist opposition as businessmen lost their influence and power because of miniaturization of the private sector. In the process, there was a decline in the strategic importance of private-sector elites in the wake of state takeover of their assets, and thus their basis for power and influence.

Ideological consensus and party support among the leaders

In Chapter 3 I discussed ideology in strategic terms as a means of securing the support of strategic and powerful actors during critical periods in a political leadership's bid to gain and maintain control of the state. It was defined as a declaration of intent to protect and further the interests of these powerful actors in exchange for their support and assistance.

Ideological declaration need not be consistent with a regime's policy and program. The conditions for gaining power might not be the same as those for retaining control of the state. Likewise, the conditions for retaining power might change over time. This has implications for the degree of ideological congruence between a regime and the group of powerful and influential elites. When a regime's declared ideology is consistent with its policies and programs one might anticipate a high degree of congruence. The reason, of course, is that by following through on the policy implications of its ideology the regime is able to retain the support of those at whom the ideology was pitched. Secondly, the groups represented by elite supporters

---

[4] From an average annual rate of emigration between 1960 and 1970 of 3,000, the 1974 estimate rose to 7,000, about 1 percent of the country's total population (Milne 1981: 32–3). Many of these emigrants have come from the local business community and have moved to Barbados and Canada.

[5] When Moskos interviewed Guyanese leaders in 1962, 23 percent (3 out of 13 leaders) were from the business sector. In 1968, this figure dropped to 12 percent (Moskos 1967 and data provided in personal communication).

become the beneficiaries of its policies and programs and, as a result, are able to expand their power and influence.

By contrast, a regime might choose to retain its ideological position, as declared, while failing to follow through on the policy implications of such a position.[6] Under such conditions there would be less congruence between regime ideology and the declared ideological position of the group of powerful and influential leaders. The reason, of course, is that the actual beneficiaries, in power and influence, of regime policy are not those to whom the ideology was initially pitched. Moreover, leaders of these latter groups might lose their power and influence in the face of the regime's program of demobilization and neutralization. They may become the targets of such a program because of their actual or anticipated opposition to the sell-out of their interests. The effect of demobilization and neutralization can be to produce a further constriction in their numbers among the powerful.

For the purposes of the study, leaders were classified as either procapitalist or third world socialist. Given the wide degree of diversity within these two bipolar categories, and the possibility of overlap by those categorized as either capitalist or socialist in their support for specific policies,[7] some justification for the choice of a bipolar scale is warranted. First, the leaders themselves articulated the choices in capitalist versus socialist terms (see Hintzen 1981: 232–300). Secondly, such a dichotomized perception was also articulated by both the Guyanese and Trinidadian regimes and in the media (see Hintzen 1981: 107–228).

A second rationale for the choice of a dichotomous scale has to do with the particular focus of this chapter upon whether ideological congruence necessarily translates into support for or opposition to the ruling regime. The Guyanese regime consistently presented its ideological position as third world socialist while the political directorate in Trinidad presented its position as "mixed economy" capitalist. The ideological positions of the leaders have, therefore, to be assessed in these terms.

[6] This might occur for a number of reasons. Declared ideology might be used to ligitimize programs and policies which benefit groups other than those to whom the ideology was pitched. Socialism can be used to legitimize a program of state expansion for the benefit of the petit bourgeois middle class at the expense of the lower classes, in whose name the ideology was fashioned. Ideology might also be employed to retain the support of powerful actors despite the effects of regime policy. Regimes might continue to identify themselves as pro-Western and pro-capitalist to ensure international support and to prevent international sanction while, at the same time, adopting policies of state control and economic centralization and while expanding political and economic relations with communist and socialist countries.
[7] For example, some third world socialists saw a limited short-term role for the private sector. There were also some capitalists who favored state expansion into the economy and state control of economic activity, especially of the foreign multinationals. Most leaders supported some form of free education and state-provided pensions.

Respondents were considered pro-capitalist if they thought that private business and private capital had a positive role to play in the economy and if they did not advocate a socialist form of government or any radical structural reform in the politics of the country. Leaders were considered socialist if they advocated nationalization of the private sector and supported policies of national insurance, free education, and free national health, or if they openly advocated a socialist government.[8]

There is a high degree of congruence between the PNM's declared support for a capitalist ideology and its program of state-directed capitalist development within the framework of a mixed economy. Given the high level of representation of those whose interests were served by party policies and programs among the country's powerful and influential elite, one might predict a high degree of congruence between regime ideology and the ideological positions of the latter. At the same time, the regime's success in demobilization and neutralization can be expected to result in a low representation of those ideologically opposed to the regime's policies among the group of leaders. Given the highly beneficial effects of regime policies and programs upon middle- and upper-class interests and the negative consequences for the lower classes, ideological opponents can be expected to come from organizations representing lower-class interests.

Using the definitions previously stated, 36 of the 40 Trinidadian leaders interviewed (90 percent) were classified as pro-capitalist and only four (10 percent) as third world socialist. All of the socialists had lower-class family backgrounds, had institutionalized links with the working classes as politicians and trade union officials, and had a history of radical political agitation. They were all key figures in radically inspired political disturbances that almost toppled the regime in February 1970 (see Oxaal 1971). Among the pro-capitalists only one leader (a unionist/politician) was strictly identified with the lower classes in terms of representing lower-class interests (exempting the four members of the incumbent PNM who were all capitalists). Also included among the capitalists were a leader of a union representing middle-class workers, two members of the clergy, and six leaders from the media. Advocacy of a capitalist strategy by media elites can be anticipated since ownership and control of the media are either in the hands of local businessmen or of the state. In the latter case, local

---

[8] The reason for including the education, health, and welfare measure was that the distinction between socialism and capitalism was perceived in terms of the role of the state versus the private sector in income redistribution. Some pro-capitalists advocated state takeover as a basis of securing *local* control of the economy *vis à vis* foreign-owned enterprises. The Trinidadian government, itself, saw state ownership as a necessary temporary measure with plans for disbursement of state assets to the private sector at a later date (see *Budget Speech*, 1978).

businessmen and professionals are heavily represented on the various boards of directors (see Hintzen 1981: 267–71). One of the two religious leaders interviewed was Roman Catholic and the other was Anglican. The Roman Catholic church enjoys particularly strong ties with the country's white population which dominates local private commercial and industrial activity while the Anglican church is closely identified with the interests and concerns of the black middle class.

The conclusion to be made from the above is that, apart from those leaders who came to national prominence through institutionalized links with the working classes, the group of influential and powerful leaders in Trinidad and Tobago constituted an ideologically homogenous unit.[9]

Regime policy and program in Guyana have been consistent with the interests of the state-sector petit bourgeois. The party's declared ideology of socialism, while pitched to the interests of the lower classes, has not resulted in income redistribution to the lower strata of society nor in the significant expansion of the benefits of health, education, and welfare to the masses. In fact, the standard of living of the lower classes and, to a certain extent, the lower-middle classes, had suffered dramatic decline. During critical periods, lower-class support was sustained by a racial appeal. Socialism, however, was employed to justify and legitimize programs and policies that were directly beneficial to the middle classes. One might therefore expect middle-class leaders to have declared a commitment to the regime's program of socialist transformation.

At the time of the survey, most of the Guyanese population was politically mobilized around the ruling Peoples National Congress (PNC) and the opposition Peoples Progressive Party (PPP). Both parties were officially committed to a socialist transformation of the society. Moreover, of the several opposition groups and parties in the country, only two were capitalist. Despite this agreement by all major parties on the radical ideological direction for the country only 10 (32 percent) of the Guyanese leaders were socialist. Of the powerful and influential Guyanese leaders, 21 (68 percent) were pro-capitalist; in other words, they were in ideological disagreement with all the major political parties in the country.

The Trinidadian data indicate a higher likelihood that national leaders would be radical when their positions of power and influence depended upon institutionalized links with organizations associated with the lower classes. This is replicated in the Guyanese data. Of the Guyanese reputational leaders, 52 percent (16) came from trade unions and political parties, as did 9 of the 10 radicals interviewed. Hence, the higher portion of mass-based

[9] Details of these and all other responses are reported in Hintzen 1981: Chapter 5.

Table 4.3. *Percentages of top Guyanese reputational leaders having pro-capitalist or third world socialist ideologies by institutional sector, 1978*

Political ideology	Institutional sector			
	Political (%)	Union/ Bureaucratic (%)	Professional (%)	Entrepreneurial (%)
Pro-capitalist	25	91	100	100
Third world socialist	75	9	—	—
Total	100	100	100	100
Number of cases	12	12	3	4

leaders among the Guyanese elite might explain the higher incidence of socialists in Guyana (32 percent) as opposed to Trinidad (10 percent). Examination of the institutional origin of the leaders lends further support to this thesis. Of 12 political leaders interviewed, nine were radicals, seven of whom had formal links with trade unions. The three remaining politicians were conservative leaders in the right-wing parties in the country. Two were professionals and one was a powerful businessman in his own right. The four trade unionists who did not have formal links with political parties were all pro-capitalist. Of them, three represented middle-class workers and the remaining one had extensive business interests. There were no radicals among the leaders who earned their livelihood from the private professional, industrial, and commercial sectors of the society. Of the 12 leaders who came exclusively from trade unions or worked as bureaucrats, 11 were pro-capitalists. These findings are reported in Table 4.3.

As expected, therefore, congruence between the regime's declared ideological position and those of the powerful and influential leaders in Guyana was low and confined to those leaders representing mass interests or rooted in mass organizations. Almost all of the remaining leaders, who constituted a majority among the powerful and influential, were capitalists. The wide divergence can, no doubt, be partly explained by the events occurring at the time the interview was conducted. The country's middle classes had begun to blame the party's pursuit of socialist policies for the economic malaise and had begun to pressure for a return to more moderate policies. Their demands for change pertained more to the regime's foreign policy and its position on overseas investments than to state expansion *per se* since they were the major beneficiaries of the latter set of policies.

116   *Race, ideology, and clientelism*

Thus, both the Guyanese and Trinidadian regimes were able to create the conditions for the emergence and strengthening of a group of powerful and influential elites whose interests were, by and large, served by and dependent upon regime policy. The ideological congruence between these leaders and the PNM regime in Trinidad was not replicated in Guyana. The explanation has to do with the consistency between ideology and policy in the former and the absence of such consistency in the latter.

Racial, ideological, and clientelistic support among Trinidadian leaders

The question to be asked at this juncture is whether ideological commitment to capitalism became translated into support for the pro-capitalist PNM in Trinidad. The regime consistently followed a pro-capitalist approach in its policies and this had positive payoffs for middle- and upper-class occupational groups.

The expansion of the capitalist sector in Trinidad had spinoff benefits for the majority of middle- and upper-income earners. After 1973, the salaries of middle-class workers increased tremendously, not the least in the public sector where workers benefited from the bountiful revenues derived from the capitalist sector (see Central Statistical Office 1978). There was expansion of employment opportunities for the skilled and qualified; state expansion produced increasing opportunities for promotion for government workers; and professionals benefited from tremendous increases in business from clients who were able to afford to pay more as well as from opportunities to invest in the growing capitalist sector. The interests of the upper and middle classes therefore became closely identified with the policies of the ruling party which, in 1978 at the time the interviews were being conducted, held 24 of the 36 seats in Parliament.

To determine whether ideological agreement with the ruling party became translated into support, I decided to exclude from the analysis, elites who were nominated on the basis of leadership roles in any of the country's political parties of labor unions. Political leaders, by virtue of their membership in a specific party, enjoy no degree of freedom whatsoever in their choice of which party to support, irrespective of ideological compatibility. Trade union leaders were excluded because of the immense antagonism that existed between trade unions and the ruling party. Three of the four socialists interviewed were trade unionists and one was a leader of a radical party. The exclusion of these two sectors meant that all of the leaders considered were committed to a capitalist strategy.

Of the 40 Trinidadian leaders interviewed, 29 were nominated from

Race, ideology, and clientelism

institutional sectors other than trade unions and political parties. Fifteen of these 29 leaders (51 percent) claimed support for the ruling Peoples National Movement, while 10 (34 percent) professed no political affiliation. By comparison, only 4 (36 percent) of the 11 political and trade union leaders excluded from the above supported the ruling party. All supportes held leadership positions in the PNM.

Of the 15 PNM supporters from sectors other than political parties and trade unions, 14 were business and professional leaders while the one remaining leader was the sole representative of the country's university faculty among the lists of influential and powerful elites interviewed. His national influence derived from his position as a member of the boards of directors of numerous state and private corporations.

Clearly, in view of the high degree of ideological compatibility between the PNM and the leaders discussed above (the four socialist leaders were all in the political and trade union sectors that were excluded), support for the regime did not appear to be overwhelming. While most of the non-supporters were politically apathetic (10 out of the 14 who did not support the PNM), it still becomes important to examine the factors that would most likely militate against support for the PNM despite ideological agreement with its position. The racial factor becomes important in this regard. The PNM is identified and popularly perceived as the party representing the interests of blacks in the country. There is need, therefore, to examine the extent to which race enhanced or inhibited party support among the Trinidadian elites. All 40 leaders interviewed are considered in the following examination of racial patterns of party support.

Of a total of 9 white leaders, 6 (67 percent) supported the black-dominated PNM. Of 12 East Indian leaders, 8 (67 percent) did likewise. Of the 4 East Indian leaders not supporting the ruling party, 2 were members of the political opposition. What this means is that of 19 PNM elite supporters, only 5 were black while 14 were either East Indian or white. The latter supported the party despite strong objections, on their part, to the ruling party's continued commitment to its black identity (see Hintzen 1981: 248–55). It appears from the data, then, that the expressed ideology of the PNM and the way that was translated into policy was enough to overcome resistance to its continued emphasis on a black identity and to guarantee the party strong elite support across racial lines. This is consistent with the expectation that racial support would prove relatively unimportant among the middle and upper classes given policies and programs that favor these sectors of society.

The party was not nearly as successful in converting its racial appeal into elite support. In fact, an anomaly emerges in the pattern of black support for the PNM. There were 4 elites located in sectors other than political parties and trade unions who expressed support for one or the other of the opposition parties. Of these, 3 were black. Moreover, of 17 black leaders interviewed, only 4 (24 percent) supported the ruling party while 6 (36 percent) claimed to have no political preference at all. Among the 7 that remained, 4 supported 2 black moderate parties, 1 supported a black radical party, and 2, both socialists, supported the United Labour Front that was formed out of a merger between leaders of the East Indian mass communal party representing rural-based Hindus with radical black and Muslim trade unionists. While the United Labour Front lasted (it broke up soon after the interviews were conducted), it projected a radical ideological image even though the Hindu component of its leadership was ideologically moderate (see Hintzen 1981: 318–25; *Miami Herald*, 13 February 1974).

What the above suggests is that black leaders, irrespective of ideological orientation, have, by and large, refused to support the ruling regime. Apart from the university professor whose national influence derived from the numerous directorships that he held in the state corporate sector, all the black supporters of the PNM were office holders in the party. The reason for this seeming inconsistency was the high susceptibility of the PNM to racial "outbidding" defined by Milne (1981: 185) as the "act of making offers or promises to an ethnic group by an opposition party which is able to offer more than the government because, unlike the government, it is not under the obligation to reach compromise with other ethnic groups." Because of the domination of the private sector by whites and East Indians in Trinidad, the capitalist policies of the ruling party were interpreted by black opponents as a "sellout" of black interests. The party was especially vulnerable to these claims in view of exceedingly high unemployment among urban blacks and in view of the effects of high inflation upon the mainly salaried black middle class (see Oxaal 1971; Allum 1975; Ryan 1972: 462–70; *Miami Herald*, 13 February 1974; *Caribbean Contact*, August 1977: 1). Thus, members of the black middle class found themselves caught between conflicting pulls upon their political sentiments. On the one hand there were the obvious and demonstrable benefits of PNM policy upon their socio-economic status as privileged employees in the state sector – privileges that were protected by the PNM government. On the other hand, by far the major beneficiaries of PNM policy were the white, near-white, and East Indian upper and upper-middle classes. This was compounded by a tremendous influx of foreign experts, managerial and professional personnel, and skilled workers as a consequence of the regime's industrialization program. These foreign workers were also enjoying disproportionately larger benefits and were seen to have displaced members of the group. Finally, there was the effect of inflation upon their economic aspirations. All these combined to produce a certain ambivalence among the black and colored middle class. While many of its members continued to support the ruling party, however reluctantly, many more withdrew into political apathy.

Three black parties – two pro-capitalist (the Democratic Action Congress and Tapia) and the other radical (the National Joint Action Committee) – as well as one East-Indian dominated, multi-racial radical party (ULF) sought to exploit black discontent in attempts to oust the PNM from power. Both NJAC and the DAC attempted to highlight the seeming inconsistency of a black regime presiding over what appeared to be escalating black immiseration whilst members of the white and East Indian upper and middle classes were enjoying unprecedented prosperity.

In summary, the data strongly support the notion that the most important basis of elite support for the Trinidadian regime was ideological. The effect of outbidding and perceptions of the negative consequences of the party's capitalist policies upon the black lower and middle classes combined to erode racial support for the regime among the country's elites, irrespective of ideological inclinations.[10] Support based on clientelistic ties seemed to be nonexistent among the powerful and influential elites. One exception was the case where support for the ruling party coincided with appointments to the boards of state corporations. The importance of clientelism, therefore, was in securing and sustaining mass support for the regime and in transferring state resources to the private sector, thereby ensuring the commitment of domestic business to the regime. Patronage figured quite minimally in delivering the support of powerful and strategic elites to the ruling party. Finally, the fact that many of the powerful and influential elites not supporting the ruling party did not in the latter half of the 1970s become aligned with the political opposition was testament to the success of the regime's efforts at demobilization.

Bases of party political support among Guyanese leaders

The findings on Guyana confirm the existence of a deep ideological cleavage between the popular political leadership and elites coming from and representing middle- and upper-class segments of the population. This rift

---

[10] The party still managed, however, to maintain its black support base among the lower classes. This was especially true during elections when the party enjoys substantial communal mass support.

120   *Race, ideology, and clientelism*

was not only manifest between socialist politicians and leaders from the private economic sector but, even more importantly, between the former and elites in control of the state bureaucratic sector. This was the group upon which the regime depended for political and economic management and for administration.

Ideological congruence, however, emerged as not at all critical in predicting support for the ruling party. Of the 13 leaders supporting the PNC only three (two politicians and the head of a public corporation) were socialist. At the same time, race emerged as an extremely important, though not exclusive, determinant of party support. Of the 13 PNC supporters among the leaders interviewed, nine were black or colored.

Supporters of the political opposition among the group of powerful and influential leaders interviewed exhibited a high degree of ideological consistency. All three of the leaders who supported the two right-wing parties (United Force and Liberator Party) were conservative pro-capitalists: two were professionals and one was the owner and managing director of one of the country's largest firms. All three were active politicians. Of the eight supporters of the left-wing opposition parties (the Peoples Progressive Party and the Working Peoples Alliance), seven were ideologically socialist.

A combination of race and ideological appeal seems to explain the pattern of support for the opposition groups. As a party identified with the interests of the East Indian population, the PPP was unable to regain the support of non-Indian radicals despite its unquestionable commitment to Marxism–Leninism.[11] At the same time, a strong middle-class orientation within the PNC (as exhibited by the nature of elite support) served to alienate the more radical black leaders, in spite of the declared socialist ideology of the party. Most black radicals remained unconvinced of the sincerity of the PNC's commitment to a socialist solution for the country's problems.

Racial politics was a key ingredient in the support of the civil service and of the urban-based trade unions for the ruling regime. Members of the black middle class associated with these two sectors derived significant benefits from the regime's policies and programs and continued to support the ruling party despite their moderate ideological outlooks. Of the top reputational leaders interviewed, 12 were from the trade union and state bureaucratic

[11] The Peoples Progressive Party (PPP) began as a multi-racial party in 1950 and received strong support from both the black and East Indian populations of the country. Racial and ideological pressures soon led, however, to the splintering of the party into two racial segments, one the Peoples National Congress (PNC) led by Forbes Burnham, and the other, the present PPP led by Cheddi Jagan. See Premdas 1975; Despres 1967: Chapter 4; and Hintzen 1977.

sectors of the society and nine of them supported the PNC. The three remaining leaders claimed to have no political affiliation. Thus, none of the country's top leaders from these two extremely strategic sectors of Guyanese society claimed support for any of the opposition parties. The absolute success of the ruling party's strategy for control of these two strategic sectors is quite evident in this pattern of support. Party dependence upon racially based patronage for control of the civil service and the trade union movement was also quite evident in the racial composition of these 12 leaders, 10 of whom were black.

It is clear, therefore, that the continuing commitment of the black leaders to PNC rule was secured by continued emphasis upon race as the basis of distributing state-controlled resources. Ideology had little place in attracting members of this group to the party since they remained political moderates. As a result, there was only one socialist among the 12 state bureaucrats and trade unionists interviewed. The support of these leaders for the regime rested, instead, upon assessments of the effects of regime policies on the material welfare of those whom they represented.

The implications of an ideological cleavage between the regime, on the one hand, and strategic leaders of the black bureaucrats and black trade unions, on the other, are astounding. One can expect that support for the PNC from this group will only be forthcoming if the policies of the party were to continue to favor racial exclusivism and to continue to provide opportunities for the socio-economic mobility of its members. The regime had to face the very real possibility that leaders of the group would search for new black alternatives should the government fail to deliver on the above demands.[12]

Clientelistic ties rooted in patronage resources made available through control of the state were extremely critical in delivering elite support to the regime. In this regard, the regime's formal turn to socialism was extremely beneficial. First, it allowed resources of the private sector to be placed in the patronage arsenal of the ruling party. More importantly, the state takeover of the economy offered to state employees almost unlimited opportunities for improving their socio-economic position by filling the high-paying and prestigious posts vacated by private-sector workers. Socialism also justified

[12] This has been confirmed by events occurring between 1977 and 1980 when poor economic performance began to affect the economic well-being of black middle-class state-sector workers. In the height of the crisis, trade unions and government workers normally sympathetic to the ruling regime engaged in violent demonstrations and strikes against the government; see Hintzen 1981: 366–82. In Jamaica, the socialist PNP also suffered a loss of middle-class support when economic crisis affected its ability to distribute patronage; see Stone 1980.

expansion of the state administrative bureaucracy to staff a spiralling welfare program. This brought in its wake considerable expansion in the job-providing capabilities of the state sector.

Apart from employment and appointment to high ranks in the public service, patronage in Guyana also came to involve business allocation by virtue or of the enormous controls that the state came to exercise over the economy, its monopoly over imports and exports, and the gargantuan nature of state-generated business. Allocations of positions of status and prestige also became a significant part of the patronage largess of the state (see Milne 1981: 146–9). In exchange for its patronage, the ruling regime was able to co-opt the support of elites representing all racial groups in the country. This support helped to ensure the maintenance of order and political stability, to provide regime legitimacy, and to co-opt mass support from among the racial supporters that these leaders brought with them.[13]

The strength of patronage considerations in elite support for the PNC is quite evident. Of the 13 PNC supporters, four were East Indians (out of a total of 10 East Indian leaders). One was a very successful businessman who, like most businessmen in the country, depended heavily upon state-generated contracts to ensure his own economic survival. He also depended upon preferential exemption from the burden of state control to remain in business. His support for the regime was not atypical of the East Indian business community. In the words of one scholar "the more socialist the government became, the more it employed controls; consequently, although Indian businessmen liked its ideology less, they became increasingly dependent on it and were forced to give it greater electoral and financial support" (Milne 1981: 253). Another East Indian PNC supporter was a senior official in the public corporate sector, an office where the politics of the holder is as important, if not more so, as requisite qualifications. The remaining two East Indian PNC supporters, a professional and a trade unionist, had benefited substantially from long associations with the ruling party from which their positions of power, prestige, and status derived.

Thus, elite support for the PNC by leaders who were not black appeared to hinge upon the access to state and party-controlled resources that

[13] For Guyanese patron–client ties see Greene 1974: 140; Parliamentary Debates, 12 December 1973; *Sunday Graphic*, 8 July 1973; *The Mirror*, 18 November 1974. For discussions of patron–client relations that are generally revelant to the third world, see Scott 1972: 17. This is not to deny that clientelistic ties do allow the articulation of lower-class interests in the process of decision-making and in the determination of resource allocation. See for example, the case of Kenya discussed by Barkan 1979. Even though mass interests in Kenya were articulated and acted upon as a result of the clientelistic network of ties, Barkan also noted that dependence upon such a network goes hand in hand with increasing inequality (1979: 71); see also Holmquist 1979.

association with the party guaranteed. Without a doubt, the national prominence of all four East Indian PNC supporters was directly related to such association. It was well recognized that in Guyana "the distribution of patronage is highly centralized in the Prime Minister" (later the President) who must personally approve of every senior level appointment (Milne 1981: 148). Loyalty to the President and to the ruling party became an absolute necessity for appointment to senior positions in the state sector (see also Milne 1981: 117; Enloe 1973; *Guyana Graphic*, 6 January 1972; *Caribbean Contact*, October 1978; *Guyana Chronicle*, 19 May 1978).

Patronage also figured heavily in the support of black elites. Of the nine PNC supporters among trade union and bureaucratic leaders, seven were black. All seven owed their positions, clearly, to their association with the ruling party. The one black unionist who did not support the PNC held a leadership position in a multi-racial union that represented most of the remaining private-sector workers and many clerical, service, and sales workers in recently nationalized firms. Many of these lower-middle-class and middle-class urban workers were opposed to the regime. Thus, the position of power and influence of this particular leader depended upon his ability to shun ties with the ruling party and to be perceived as being critical of regime policies.

Of the 17 black leaders interviewed, only two were neither unionists, politicians, nor state-sector employees; one was a professional and another a freelance journalist and broadcaster. In other words, both were independent of party ties for their positions of national influence. Neither one supported the regime. Thus, all the black leaders who expressed support for the ruling party were involved, implicitly or explicitly, in the regime's network of patronage, if only through the requirement of party loyalty for holders of senior positions.

What can be concluded is, first, that the Guyanese regime's declared attempt to establish a socialist state did not have widespread support among the group of powerful and influential trade union and state bureaucratic leaders. Secondly, the important and influential left-wing leaders who would normally be expected to support the ruling party on ideological grounds, opposed the regime either because its policies were inconsistent with its declared socialist position or because these policies proved detrimental to lower class interests. Thus, the party became isolated from its "natural" ideological constituency while, at the same time, depending upon the support of those elites who were opposed to its declared ideological position.

Conclusion

The composition of the group of powerful and influential elites in Guyana and Trinidad in 1977–8 strongly enhanced the chances for regime survival. In Trinidad there was strong representation of elites from the country's capitalist sector, professionals, and middle classes among the group of powerful and influential. These groups were all beneficiaries of the policies and programs of the state and their members had developed a vested interest in regime survival. Since regime policies and programs followed directly from its declared ideological position, there was a high degree of congruence between the latter and the expressed ideology of members of the elite group.

At the same time, the negative effect of regime policies upon the lower classes produced conditions for the emergence of a few powerful and influential leaders rooted in mass organizations. Such leaders were opposed to the regime politically and ideologically. There was also some racial opposition to the regime, largely the result of outbidding, among black middle-class leaders. That such opposition did not affected regime survival until 1986 is testament to the regime's success in demobilizing mass-based organizations. While lower-class opposition was successfully contained, those among the middle and upper classes who opposed the regime found themselves isolated from the political resources necessary to challenge it. They thus remained uncommitted to any of the opposition parties until the local government elections of 1983 when they swung in favor of a combined multi-racial opposition. Thus, the Trinidadian regime was able to survive, maintain its legitimacy, and ensure order and stability until 1987 despite the disaffection of the lower classes and of black elites.

The policies and programs of the Guyanese regime were fashioned to service the interests of the black petit bourgeoisie. As a result, the regime alienated the upper classes and sectors of the middle classes, including professionals, not coming from its own constituency. It had to rely on the clientelistic co-optation of elites and upon control to demobilize the opposition. A combination of patronage, racial appeal, and favorable policies and programs ensured the regime of middle-class support. Racial mobilization became the basis of its lower-class support.

The Guyanese regime was highly successful in creating a group of elites whose interests were tied to its policies and continued tenure. This became manifest in the high representation of public-sector leaders and co-opted leaders in the mass organizations controlled by the regime among the powerful and influential. Its success in clientelistic co-optation is also manifested in its ability to gain the support of East Indian leaders and leaders in the business sector. The party was less successful in its efforts at demobilization. This allowed the emergence of powerful and influential opponents who represented upper-, middle-, and lower-class interests. As will be seen, the regime was forced to respond to these elites with a campaign of coercion, and to secure their neutralization with an expanded machinery of state control.

Both the Guyanese and the Trinidadian regimes survived by creating conditions for sustaining the power and influence of elites who represented segments of the population that had vested interests in the policies and programs of the government. In the Guyana case, clientelistic co-optation of powerful representatives of groups opposed to regime policies effectively secured the demobilization of such groups. At the same time, the employment of elite allies to control organizations of mass mobilizations ensured both mass support, regimentation, and demobilization. Coercion and control acted to neutralize and eliminate hitherto powerful elites.

In Trinidad, an extremely high degree of ideological congruence did not become translated into overwhelming support for the ruling regime from among the powerful and influential. Only a small majority of pro-capitalist elites supported the ruling party. However, the Trinidadian regime successfully employed a strategy of political control to separate political opponents from politically strategic sources. Where such a separation was not accomplished, a strategy of demobilization ensured the neutralization of powerful elite opponents.

5. Regime survival and state control of the economy

Control of the economy implies an ability and a capacity for authoritative decision-making in all areas of economic activity. Regime survival in postcolonial states such as Guyana and Trinidad is invariably hinged to an ability to secure the compliance to state decision-making of the powerful private sector, and particularly its international segment. It is also tied to the ability to neutralize politically powerful economic actors in the face of opposition to new nationalist definitions of state interests and to a new nationalist economic agenda. As was pointed out in Chapter 1, these normally produce a fracturing of the old relationships between the colonial state and the privileged private economic sector whose interests were typically protected and furthered by the former. It was demonstrated in the previous chapter how control of the economy through a program of nationalization can act to demobilize effectively the private sector and neutralize its political influence. As was also shown to be the case, state control of the economy can make available to the regime a significantly larger share of the country's economic resources to be employed in ways that enhance regime survival.

A regime is forced to weigh its decision to gain control over the economy against the potential consequences of its efforts to do so. Powerful actors might resist such efforts and might employ their resources to challenge the regime, to conduct or support a campaign of political and/or economic destabilization (which might involve the use of international resources), and even to secure the outright overthrow of the political leadership. Whatever policy emerges out of such deliberations, it must be informed by the availability to the state of the requisite skills and resources. The degree of control sought and how it is to be undertaken has to be determined, in the final analysis, by the ability of the state to ensure the continuation of economic activity and to guarantee compliance with its dictates. A policy of nationalization, for example, cannot be undertaken unless the state has access to the wherewithal to run the nationalized undertakings. If a state seeks to legislate increased revenues from the private sector it must have the ability to determine accurately business earnings and to prevent practices

State control of the economy

that deflate "book" profits. If it seeks to legislate domestic (whether state or non-state) participation in foreign enterprises this has to be undertaken under circumstances where these enterprises have no alternative but to remain in the country.

When powerful economic actors cannot be neutralized then the regime is forced to accommodate them. Economic policy has to be fashioned to protect and further their interests. This acts to limit state control of the economy since (i) these actors usually insist on preserving their prerogative to make decisions over their own activities, free from the encumbrance of state regulation, and (ii) these actors end up dictating state policy as it pertains to their own activities. Regime survival thus becomes tied to an expressed willingness not to extend state control to the activities of such powerful economic actors. At the same time, the state comes to be viewed as an instrument of political control by these actors.[1]

Despite the demands of powerful actors, there are particular and conflicting economic claims upon the state which have to be met if the regime is to guarantee its own survival. The ability to satisfy these claims implies some degree of state control over the allocation and distribution of economic resources. One set of claims has to do with the ability to perform state functions and to maintain socio-economic stability. Another set has to do with economic claims made upon the regime as a direct result of the conditions of survival discussed in the previous chapters. The state has to have the wherewithal to direct economic activity and the allocation of surplus in ways that satisfy these claims if the regime is to ensure its own survival.

The state functions to which authoritative allocations of economic resources must be made if the regime is to ensure its own survival are:

(i) Developmental functions: the state has to ensure itself of a capital budget for financing its developmental program and for securing the skills and technology necessitated by such a program. It also has to ensure that the economic behavior of all sectors of society conforms to that which is consistent with development prerequisites. The failure to meet developmental needs can lead to an endemic economic crisis which brings with it the likelihood of persistent anti-regime mobilization.

(ii) Civil administrations functions: the state has to have the resources

[1] It is for this reason that some radical political economists make a distinction between a state-controlling elite and a ruling elite (see Langdon 1977; Saul 1976; Murray 1967; Leys 1976; and Von Frehold 1977). Because powerful actors are able to dictate the terms of state decision-making their will can easily be imprinted upon state policy to the exclusion of the interests of others. Those directly involved in state decision-making become reduced to mere functionaries who control the state apparatus in the interest of the powerful.

necessary for undertaking its bureaucratic mandate, including civil administration and social welfare, and for supporting its legislative and executive activities. Without these the entire system or government would collapse.

(iii) Defense and law and order functions: The state needs the resources to maintain law and order internally, and to guarantee security against external aggression.

There are, however, competing economic claims upon the state which are much more impelling because they pertain, directly, to regime survival. Such claims include:

(i) Accumulative claims of strategic and powerful local and international actors: Powerful domestic and international actors in third world societies view the state as an instrument of economic accumulation. Because of its "overdeveloped" character, the state can set the terms of economic participation and income distribution. It also acts directly in the process of accumulation. One of the consequences of accommodation and acquiescence is that a regime is forced to employ state resources to cater to the economic demands made by these powerful actors.

(ii) Patronage claims (including racial claims): At the elite level, these claims are made by individuals in control of politically strategic resources. They must be met if the political loyalty of these individuals is to be guaranteed. At the level of the masses, patronage is used as an instrument of control by the regime. It acts to mediate the conflict between mass mobilization and demands for income redistribution. As such it serves to relieve the "distributive pressure" upon state resources (Scott 1972: 187–9) while assuring continued mass commitment to the regime (see Chapter 3). Patronage is, therefore, particularly important under the conditions of "marked inequalities in the control of wealth, status, and power" (Scott 1972: 181) which typify third world societies (see Hintzen 1984).

(iii) Coercion: A regime might have to finance and staff a coercive apparatus to be used for the political repression of dissidents if its survival is to be assured.

For the above claims to be met, the regime is forced to employ the state as an instrument of economic control to service the accumulative needs of the powerful. It must also employ the state as an instrument of accumulation to guarantee the revenue and financial resources necessary for meeting its patronage bill and supporting its coercive branches. It is in this manner that control of the economy becomes directly linked to regime survival.

Thus, there is a conflict between the need for autonomy in state economic decision-making to satisfy developmental functions and the need to employ state control of the economy to meet the patronage and accumulative claims of powerful and strategic actors. In its efforts to secure economic control, a regime has to navigate delicately between the two if it is to ensure its own survival. Ideally, the conflict is best managed when accumulative, patronage, and coercive claims can be justified in developmental terms.

Once again, the declared ideological position of the regime becomes critical. Ideology is employed to justify and legitimize patterns of economic control and resource allocations as being absolute prerequisites for development. In the process of implementing policies and programs derived from and legitimized by its ideological position the regime can and normally does seize the opportunity to meet accumulative, patronage, and coercive claims related to its own survival. This is as true of regimes adopting capitalist strategies of developmental as it is of those employing the third world variant of socialism.

When the ideology of capitalism informs a regime's developmental strategy, it can end up legitimizing a pattern of resource transfers and state decision-making which favors local and international private investors. It can also serve the accumulative interests of the local managerial, professional, and state bureaucratic elites. This is particularly true of the mixed economy approach which emphasizes joint ventures between the private and public sectors, outright state ownership of specific industries such as utilities, and some degree of control over the private sector with a view to increasing the latter's tax liabilities. Third world socialism justifies a policy of state appropriation of the productive assets of the private sector and strict control of the professions (when they are not totally incorporated into the state bureaucratic system). It is, therefore, ideally suited to situations where regime survival rests with its capacity to cater to interests of the "governing class" of administrative elites and to the group of "petit bourgeois" state employees. Thus, the ideologies of both capitalism and third world socialism can be employed to justify and legitimize the use of state control to service the accumulative claims of powerful actors. They are, however, consistent with the interests of different segments of the elite population.

Both capitalism and socialism can be employed to justify and legitimize the use of state resources for patronage. They could justify the undertaking of "developmental projects" by the state which offer opportunities for clientelistic recruitment of regime supporters, for the awarding of contracts

130 *State control of the economy*

to elite clients, and for providing opportunities for corruption to those loyal to the ruling party.

There is also an inherent conflict between the accumulative claims of powerful actors and the economic claims relating to patronage and coercion. The former places strict limitations upon state control over the economic activities of these powerful actors. The latter requires the authoritative reallocation of resources from the sectors under their control to the state apparatus. This conflict can be managed by justifying efforts at expanded state control in terms of meeting the costs of performing state functions. Thus, a regime can make claims upon economic resources based primarily upon the need for revenue to finance the functions of civil administration, security, and law and order. In doing so, the regime is provided with the opportunity to meet its patronage obligations. State employment can become transformed into a patronage largess and bureaucratic office can come with the opportunity for corruption. In this regard, the expansion of the civil and military bureaucracies have direct patronage implications.

A regime can also justify economic allocations for coercive purposes in terms of state functions of law and order. There is an obvious relationship between security and law and order functions on the one hand, and coercion on the other. The problem for the regime is the transformation of the former into the latter. Political scientist Cynthia Enloe (1984) suggests that this transformation is assured when functional distinctions between external defense, normally reserved for the military, and the law and order role of the police are eliminated. The functional integration of the military, paramilitary, and police creates the conditions for much more centralized and co-ordinated control of the state coercive machinery by the political executive.

The relationship between coercion and state control of the economy pertains to the need for enhanced state revenue engendered by expansion of the repressive machinery. The former can be secured only through the strengthening of the authoritative relationship between the state and the income earning sectors of society.

In summary, the areas of economic activities over which the regime exercises authoritative decision-making and the character of such decision-making determines the degree of control it has over the economy. At the least, the degree of control that it enjoys has to be such as to ensure that enough resources are available for the adequate performance of administrative, law and order, and security functions of the state. Ideally, regime control of the economy should also be such as to allow it to allocate the resources of the country and to determine how they are employed in ways that guarantee economic development. This implies autonomy in decision-making over a wide range of economic activities. Given the conflict which inheres between autonomy, on the one hand, and the allocative and patronage claims of powerful and strategic segments, on the other, a regime might have to settle for just enough control to prevent an endemic economic crisis of the sort of that threatens its own survival.

Economic control implies the capacity to determine how economic resources outside the state sector are allocated and utilized. It also implies a capacity to secure the transfer of such resources to the state sector. Both of these are affected by the degree to which the regime is forced to satisfy the accumulative and patronage claims of those powerful and strategic actors that it cannot neutralize. The degree of control which the regime exercises over state-sector resources is also affected by these claims and by the demands of the coercive apparatus. Powerful actors making accumulative claims upon the state do not merely demand autonomy in decision-making over their own economic activities, they also insist upon dictating to the regime how its economic policies and programs are to be formulated and implemented, particularly when these pertain to their own interests. These actors therefore come to exercise an inordinate control over the way resources are allocated by the state sector. Patronage and coercive allocations also restrict the regime's autonomy in the determination of how state-sector resources are to be utilized. Since both are directly related to regime survival there is little choice but to honor these commitments.

A regime might make efforts to increase its control over economic activities by citing demands of the administrative, law and order, and security branches of the state and by claiming increased economic control as being necessary to stave off economic crisis. A choice can be presented between administrative collapse, a breakdown of order, and economic crisis on the one hand, and the continued satisfaction of accumulative and patronage demands on the other. In this way, a regime may be able to increase its control over economic activities successfully both within and outside of the state sector.

The Trinidadian and Guyanese regimes have employed different strategies to resolve the conflict between the economic demands of state functions and economic obligations that come tied to the terms of regime survival. These differences are very evident in the attempts of the two regimes to strengthen and expand state control of the economy.

Economic policy and regime survival in Trinidad

Satisfying the accumulative claims of the oil producers

When they cannot be neutralized, transnational corporations can be the most powerful actors making accumulative claims upon a third world state. The reason for this is their control over and access to an enormous amount of international resources (including the resources of their home governments), their capital, skills and expertise, and their control of the markets for their products. Host governments are forced to acquiesce to their accumulative claims or face the possibility of economic collapse, political reprisal by their home governments, and even military intervention.

In Trinidad, oil producers constituted, by far, the most powerful of the international investors in the economy. The reason was the almost total dependence of the country upon its oil industry.

Figure 5.1 provides an overall picture of the country's economy. Two dominant characteristics are immediately evident: first, is the predominant role of the oil sector (30·7 percent), and, second, is the considerable importance of service-oriented economic activity (25·6 percent) which includes distribution (12·7 percent) and transport, storage and communication (12·9 percent). These services, together with finance, insurance, and real estate, rely heavily upon direct and indirect linkages with the petroleum sector. When one adds government (7·7 percent), which has an excessive dependence upon oil-derived revenue, one begins to appreciate more fully the preeminence of the petroleum industry in the economy of Trinidad and Tobago. As early as 1951 the oil industry was accounting for almost 77 percent of the country's exports and contributing one-third of the government's revenue.

From its inception, the PNM government recognized its obligation to meet the accumulative claims of the oil industry. A government-appointed Commission of Inquiry into the industry was convened in 1964, one year after the country became independent. It concluded that government had no alternative but to guarantee to the oil multinationals that they would be able to continue operating with the least possible risk to their investments while enjoying generous profit margins (see the *Report* of the Commission of Inquiry into the Oil Industry of Trinidad and Tobago, 1964). It advised Trinidadian policy-makers to take special pains to preserve the "legal, political, and institutional environments attractive" to the industry (see *Report* Commission of Inquiry: 11). The reasons for these recommendations had to do with the vulnerability of the regime to decisions made by the oil

State control of the economy 133

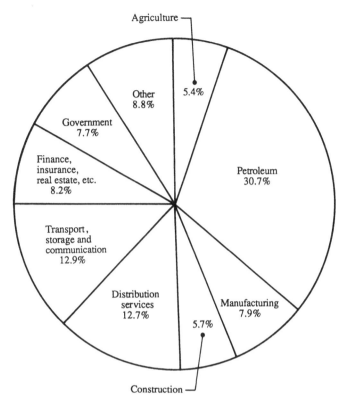

Figure 5.1. *Average annual percentage contribution of sectors to gross domestic product of Trinidad and Tobago at factor cost, 1966–76 (constant 1970 prices)*
Source: *G.D.P. of Trinidad and Tobago, 1966–76*: 7

multinationals. The regime could not afford to risk any negative reactions by the companies to unfavorable government action (see Trinidad and Tobago Budget Speech, 1964–5)

Regime vulnerability was directly linked to the centrality of the oil industry in the Trinidadian economy and its importance as a major contributor to state revenue. There was a direct link between oil production and refining, on the one hand, and economic stability on the other. At the same time, the operations of production and refining could not be carried out without the presence of foreign transnationals. This was so for a number of reasons. The state did not have available to it the requisite skills and resources necessary to run the operations of the oil producers. One

134   *State control of the economy*

consideration was the means to finance the industry. The newly independent government, with a total budget of TT$232 million (approximately US$100 million) would have found itself extremely hard-pressed to capitalize an industry where costs and expenses at the end of 1962 were declared at TT$246 million – more than the total budget of the state (Commission of Inquiry). There was also the problem of the unavailability of the requisite skills and technology domestically. Both sets of limitations were explicitly acknowledged by the regime, which took special pains to point out as late as 1971 that it lacked the wherewithal to provide initial finance, or to provide the management, know-how, training, skills, as well as the technology necessary to run the industry (see *Third Five Year Development Plan* 1971: 55).

The country's economic vulnerability to decisions made by the oil companies was compounded by the international organization of the industry and the way this impinged upon domestic operations. Given the presence of three massive local refineries, Trinidad had to import the major proportion of its crude throughput to secure the maximum benefits of economies of scale. Thus, the profitability of refining depended upon decisions made externally as to the price of imported crude and the volume to be supplied to the Trinidad refineries. Favorable terms and adequate volume are best guaranteed by intra-company transfers. Any attempt to secure control through some form of domestic ownership brings with it the possibility of retaliation through price hikes or reduced volumes of supplies. So important was imported crude for refining that, in 1963, 48 percent of the total imports of Trinidad was mineral fuel to be used as throughput. Economic vulnerability also pertained to access to markets for Trinidadian crude and refined products. Like all major oil producers, the three companies of Shell, Texaco and British Petroleum which had operations in Trinidad exercised an inordinate control over these markets.

Thus, the Trinidadian regime was forced to acquiesce to the accumulative claims of the oil transnationals because of the unavailability of domestic alternatives and because of the certainty that any negative actions on their part would create a severe economic crisis. Trinidad's oil industry was of minimal importance for the world market and could be dispensed with easily. The total share of the country's crude in world production, for example, was less than 0·5 percent. At the same time, the international political resources of the oil companies posed an even more direct threat to regime survival. There was the real possibility of economic retaliation by Western governments in response to efforts aimed at a significant expansion of domestic control of the industry. Important in this regard was the

State control of the economy 135

vulnerability of the industry to decisions made in the United States, which was the major market for Trinidadian crude and refined products. Access to this market on competitive terms depended upon preferential marketing arrangements which allocated special quotas to the country's crude and refined products. The "vital importance" of these quotas was given particular prominence in the report of the Commission of Inquiry (*Report*: 26). Any effort aimed at expanding domestic control faced the possibility of the companies involved using their influence to secure the cancellation of these special arrangements. There was also the possibility of direct political and military action against the regime. This was specifically recognized by the Prime Minister of Trinidad who, in referring to the immediate post-independence period in a speech in 1974 pointed out that any thought of domestic control and nationalization had to be absolutely ruled out: "The decade of the sixties," he said, "was not an easy time for small countries; just think of Viet Nam and the Dominican Republic. A campaign would have been mounted against us on the grounds that we were nationalizing a foreign enterprise." (Williams 1974: 28).

Thus, at the time of its independence, national policy was forced to accommodate the interests of the oil producers in Trinidad; to have done otherwise would have meant certain economic crisis resulting from the flight of foreign investors in the oil industry and the possibility of international political retaliation and even military intervention by the home governments.

Accumulative claims of the oil companies versus domestic prerequisites for regime survival

The problem for the Trinidadian government was to satisfy the accumulative claims of the oil multinationals while, at the same time, securing enough control over the economy to meet the domestic conditions for regime survival. It was pointed out in Chapter 3 that the major domestic threat was class mobilization and outbidding which seemed to invariably follow upon the heels of economic crisis. In every instance these crises were linked to performance in the oil sector. The first problem was, therefore, to ensure that enough resources were made available so that the economic conditions of the black lower classes did not deteriorate to levels which made members candidates for anti-regime mobilization. The second problem was finding ways to insulate the general economic condition from the performance of the oil industry. Given the centrality of petroleum production and refining, the resolution to both problems demanded some form of increased control over the activities of the oil companies.

136 *State control of the economy*

The major need among the lower classes was for employment generation. In 1963, one year after the country became independent, close to 15 percent of the Trinidadian labor force had no jobs and entertained little prospect for finding any. An additional 16 percent of the workforce was underemployed. This had a direct link to oil production.

Oil and oil-related activity accounted in the early 1960s for almost 25 percent of the country's GDP but yet employed less than 5 percent of the country's work force (OWTU, 1968). Thus, regime acquiescence to the oil industry had to be tempered by the political expedient of employment and income generation. This demanded the use of the state to secure the transfer of a larger share of the surpluses of the industry to the country's lower classes.

Insulating the economy from the performance of the oil sector could only be achieved through a policy of economic diversification. While this might have been accomplished partly by securing some form of external developmental funding, the major thrust of the effort was bound to come through the reallocation of surpluses generated domestically. This meant employing the authority of the state to secure a larger share of oil industry surpluses for reallocation in the non-petroleum sectors of the economy.

Thus, both economic diversification and employment and income generation had to rest upon the ability of the state to secure a larger share of the surpluses generated by the industry. In its efforts to do so, the regime chose to employ the least offensive of the alternatives available to it. This appeared to be the best strategy to manage the conflict between the accumulative claims of the oil producers and the need to prevent an endemic economic crisis that threatens its own survival. In its efforts to control the oil producers, a more aggressive policy of limited participation was postponed for the future and nationalization of the industry was ruled out absolutely. Instead, government sought to monitor the operations of the oil companies to prevent intra-company pricing practices that artificially deflated "book" profits for taxation purposes (see *Third Five Year Development Plan* 1971; and Hintzen 1981: 118–25).

There were some tentative efforts to secure a greater degree of state participation in the industry, even though great pains were taken to exclude the existing operations of the oil multinationals. Singled out were activities concerned with future operations. Legislation was passed (i) to revise the terms of lease of oil-bearing land and marine areas, (ii) to expand the functions of a strengthened Ministry of Petroleum and Mines, and (iii) to establish a National Petroleum Company. The role of the new company was to formulate policy on the activities of multinationals on concessions and leases and to act as a holding company for the purposes of establishing "wholly owned or joint venture subsidiaries for producing crude oil products, natural gas, petrochemicals and other related products" (*Third Five-Year Development Plan* 1971: 171). Soon after its formation, the company entered into a joint venture with Tesoro Petroleum Company of Texas to work concessions left idle by British Petroleum Company after the latter unilaterally pulled out of Trinidad when profits began to decline.

The policy of the Trinidadian regime toward the oil companies underscores the dilemma of a third world government faced with an economy that is dominated by foreign multinationals the local subsidiaries of which, for a combination of reasons, cannot be immediately localized or nationalized. While efforts at economic self-determination demand some degree of state control of the operations of these multinationals, the ruling elite is forced into the least offensive – and least effective – strategy through a fear that stronger measures might provoke negative reactions from the companies concerned. The result is that the state remains just as impotent in dealing with the foreign firms after its efforts at control as it was before them.

It was the hope that these limited attempts at extending state control over the oil industry, minimal though they were, would be enough to provide the additional revenues needed to embark on a program of economic development outlined in three five-year development plans spanning the period from 1955 to 1973. The first such plan concentrated primarily on infra-structural development; the second emphasized import substitution; and the last concentrated on developing export-oriented production. The overall thrust of the regime's efforts was upon programs aimed at generating growth in the labor-intensive sectors of the economy – particularly agriculture and small-scale producer and commercial co-operative ventures (see Williams 1970: 20–7). A program of agricultural development, as outlined in the Third Five-Year Plan, aimed at a growth rate of 5 percent per annum to be achieved through diversification and the application of modern techniques to cultivation. There were hopes for an anticipated increase in agricultural employment to well above the then existing level of 22 percent, and significant increases in agricultural incomes such that they approached parity with the rest of the economy. In addition, regime plans called for the development of a "peoples sector" consisting of small-scale industry, handicrafts, small service activities such as distribution and transport, small hotels and guest houses, credit unions, cottage industries, and trade union enterprises. The co-operative was to be promoted as a basis for organizing these activities.

138 *State control of the economy*

Economic control and satisfying the accumulative claims of the private sector

The strategic importance of political support from the domestic private sector for regime survival in Trinidad has already been discussed in the previous chapters. This support is underwritten by the willingness of the regime to meet the accumulative claims of local businessmen through the use of the resources of the state. It has been pointed out that ideology can serve to justify and legitimize the use of state resources to meet such accumulative claims. This is so because it allows the employment of state resources in such a manner to be justified in terms of developmental prerequisites.

The embrace of an ideology of capitalism by the PNM regime in Trinidad justified and legitimized a pattern of resource use to meet the accumulative claims of the domestic private sector. Basing its policies upon the claim that the development of the local capitalist sector and local industry was "the pivot of efforts at economic transformation" the regime poured resources into these two sectors (see *Third Five-Year Development Plan* 1971: 224). As a result of its efforts, local manufacturing grew between 1963 and 1968 at a rate of 7 percent per annum. Government legislation provided protection to local industry in the form of prohibitive tariffs and, in some cases, outright restriction against competitive imports. State loans were made available for financing local industry and for training in relevant industrial skills.

To push the development of local production, the regime set up an Industrial Development Corporation (IDC) in 1969 which offered manufacturers technical assistance and a centralized channel of access to government. Part of the function of the IDC was to conduct industrial research and to assist in identifying viable manufacturing undertakings. In 1970 a Small Business Unit was set up to provide similar services to smaller enterprises. A Management Development Centre, set up in 1965, was expanded. Finally, medium- and long-term financing for local industry was made available through a Development Finance Corporation set up in 1970.

Even though satisfying the accumulative claims of the private sector, the policies of the regime had the potential for the considerable expansion and deepening of regime control of the economy while, at the same time, contributing to its efforts at economic diversification. In the process of implementing these policies, the private sector became highly dependent upon the state for financing, for infrastructural support, and for favorable legislation. As a result the regime was able to dictate the terms of transfer of resources to the private sector and, thereby, impose its own program for

State control of the economy

economic development. It was also able to increase significantly its capacity for authoritative decision-making over the activities of the private sector.

Domestic demands versus the reality of oil dependence

The Trinidadian regime attempted to manage the conflict between the accumulative claims of the foreign private sector on the one hand, and domestic accumulative claims and developmental demands on the other without seeking to expand its direct control over the activities of the oil corporations. Instead, it used its authority to legislate measures that would secure an increased volume of surplus transfers from the oil producers to the state. This could have succeeded only if the levels of performance in the oil sector remained high. This performance is affected by conditions in the industry and by production decisions made by the managers. The efforts of the regime were doomed to failure on both counts. There was a recession in the industry between 1968 and 1972 reflected in a precipitous decline in its contribution to the GDP from 25 percent to 14 percent over that period. Moreover, decisions to cutback on refining produced a significant decline in throughput between 1971 and 1973 of around 6 percent per annum (see Inter-American Economic and Social Council 1974). The recession in the industry brought with it a serious budgetary deficit forcing severe cutbacks in state spending on both capital and current accounts. With this cutback went any chance for realization of the targets set out in the three developmental plans (see Inter-American Economic and Social Council 1974: 115). The effect of the failure upon the chances for regime survival became immediately evident. The anti-regime rebellion and army mutiny that occurred in February 1970 was a direct result of the continued high unemployment and poverty among the regime's lower-class supporters. Even though the regime survived the political onslaught, during the three years following 1970 it was plagued by a loss of generalized legitimacy and by intense radical opposition, especially among the black population (see Chapter 3). In other words, the degree of control the regime exercised over economic activities and its ability to allocate economic resources were so limited that it found itself unable to stave off an endemic economic crisis that threatened its own survival.

The dilemma for the Trinidadian regime was that it had to secure the economic means for preventing an endemic crisis while severely constrained in its efforts to reallocate surpluses from the major sector of the economy. It was clear that the oil producers were not prepared to tolerate any conditions, including those legislated by the state, that impinged upon their profitability.

140 *State control of the economy*

This was forcefully brought home in 1968 when British Petroleum Company made a unilateral decision to pull out of Trinidad, leaving its assets idle, when profits began to decline. It became equally evident in 1971 when oil refiners decided to use alternative facilities in other countries as a consequence of the uncertainties in the wake of the military and civilian uprisings of the previous years. The result was a decline in local refinery throughput.

In terms of regime survival, the most pressing domestic claims upon state resources came from the urban and semi-urban black lower classes. The chances of assuring political stability were enhanced if their demands could be met, and it became imperative that the regime find a source of financing, independent of the oil companies, to meet these demands. It was within this context that the decision to shift to generalized patronage was made (see Chapter 3). The program of "national reconstruction" constituted an attempt by the regime to use its legislative authority to transfer income from the domestic sectors of the economy into the hands of its black lower-class supporters. Unable to increase the tax liabilities of the oil corporations, the regime decided to finance the program by revenue from an Unemployment Levy placed on all incomes and by supplemental loans raised locally and overseas. This capacity for authoritative decision-making in the domestic sectors of the economy was undoubtedly enhanced by the growing dependence of the domestic private sector on the state. It also had to do with the perception of the regime as the defender of the interests of the middle and upper classes against a radical onslaught which led to the 1970 uprisings. In this instance, the regime was able to justify the levy in terms of the necessity of staving off economic crisis which brought with it the potential for a radical takeover of the government.

The breakdown of socio-political order stemming from the economic crisis could not be long forestalled unless the regime could find a successful way for the state to secure more of the oil-generated surpluses. This meant seeking much more direct control of the industry. The problem was how to do so without risking a negative reaction by the oil companies. The regime strategy was to institute measures aimed at securing for the state a share of future discoveries of oil and gas as a condition for the granting of new concessions. Companies planning to work such concessions were required to sign an agreement to surrender 50 percent of their acreage, upon request, to the National Petroleum Company after a period of six years. These plans were incorporated into the regime's program of National Reconstruction, and therefore, were justified and legitimized in terms of the necessity to stave off economic crisis. In other words, the regime was using the argument of the preservation of state function, and particularly law and order, to increase its direct control over the oil industry. This was to be done by expanding the assets of the National Petroleum Company through a process of reallocation from the oil-producing transnationals. At the same time, however, it left untouched the *existing* arrangements between the state and the companies already established in the local industry regarding their already developed productive assets. This strategy was formulated with the knowledge that intense exploration and development efforts had produced considerable results which had already begun to pay dividends. New and extensive deposits of oil and gas were discovered by the transnationals offshore and had begun to come onstream as early as 1971. It was by gaining some form of shared ownership in the production of these new discoveries that the regime hoped to resolve its dilemma.

The problem for the regime was that the economic crisis facing the country's lower classes demanded immediate and significant increases in state revenue. The Unemployment Levy and supplemental loans were vastly inadequate even for the task of raising the requisite revenue to support a system of generalized patronage on the scale demanded to forestall a political crisis. Thus, in 1973, more than two years after the introduction of the program for National Reconstruction, conditions remained basically unchanged. In October of that year, facing escalating social, political, and economic crisis, the Prime Minister of the country announced his decision to resign. The regime appeared to be quickly losing its ability to survive as a result of its incapacity to manage the conflict between the accumulative claims of the country's transnationals and the prerequisites of economic control necessary to stave off economic crisis.

As "price takers" the fortunes of economies such as Trinidad's are firmly tied to conditions and events occurring outside the country's borders to the degree that they affect the prices and terms of sale of exports and imports. The problem for the Trinidadian regime was that the state did not enjoy the necessary control over domestic allocations of economic resources to stave off an economic crisis. Given the nature of the Trinidadian economy, the only way to secure such control was to increase significantly state revenue. In this manner, the state could act directly in the process of reallocating domestic resources particularly to its lower-class supporters. The problem was dramatically and suddenly resolved in the wake of the consequences of the Middle East War of 1973 for international oil prices. It ushered in a period of dramatic economic recovery and a veritable explosion of state revenue.

From close to US$3 per barrel at the beginning of 1973, the world market price of Trinidadian-type crude rose by January 1974 to over US$14 per

142 *State control of the economy*

barrel. The industry's direct contribution to total tax revenues, excluding the Unemployment Levy, shot up to 70 percent as compared with a previous high of 35 percent in 1968. Increased petroleum taxes led to an increase of 160 percent in government revenues between 1973 and 1974, in a budget which jumped to TT$1,229·4 million from TT$450·5 million the previous year. The oil companies alone contributed TT$881·5 million to the budget compared with TT$120 million in 1973 – an increase of TT$769 million.

Government policy after the Middle East War

Political leaders in countries like Trinidad are at the mercy of external decision-making and of international circumstances over which they have no control and which they can neither foresee nor predict. Policy-making, under such circumstances, becomes reduced to reactive responses to fortuitous or damaging events occurring in other parts of the world.

Given the dramatic increase in oil prices, the profits to be made from the production of crude in Trinidad, in absolute terms, shot up phenomenally. Under existing arrangements this meant phenomenal increases in revenue for the state. For a number of reasons, it also meant an increased willingness on the part of the oil transnationals to tolerate an expansion of state control over their activities. Given the radical challenges to the regime, it was in the interest of the oil companies to ensure that the PNM remain in power. This implied giving in to demands by the country's leaders for greater control when the issues of economic stability and the maintenance of socio-political order were raised. Secondly, with increased revenues the state became a potential source of capitalization for the industry through some type of joint venture arrangements.

Taking advantage of the new situation, Parliament passed the Petroleum Taxes Act in June 1974 that introduced several changes in the tax structure which had direct implications for regime control over pricing policies and organization of accounting in the oil multinationals. In the Act, (i) tax liabilities for crude production were to be calculated from a tax reference price per barrel decided by government, rather than on actual price received, as was prior practice; (ii) separation of production, refining, and marketing was made mandatory for the computation of company tax, and each new oil concession was to be considered as a separate tax entity; (iii) oil operations were divided into land and marine tax zones and exploration and drilling costs had to be treated apart from operating costs; and (iv) direct taxation on refinery operations was legislated for the first time. The prior practice of

State control of the economy 143

including refinery earnings within the total corporate income was changed to a tax on throughput per barrel. The unit price of a barrel of refined oil was to be set by the Minister of Finance. All of these measures were aimed directly at the practice by the oil companies of deflating book-profits for tax purposes by offsetting high returns on investment in one area with high costs in another and at the practice of transfer pricing. The regime also increased the tax liability of the industry; the government raised corporate profit tax on oil companies from 45 percent to 47·5 percent.

State leaders also adopted indirect measures aimed at control of refinery operations through fiscal incentives. Lower priced fuels which contributed little to the economy were taxed excessively to discourage production. At the same time generous tax concessions were granted to encourage the refining of higher priced fuels where value added was considerably larger and which, in consequence, contributed more to the local economy. In this way the regime hoped to influence a shift in refining practices to ones which produced larger contributions to state revenue and to the domestic economy.

The measures adopted to increase the amount of oil-generated revenue were accompanied by efforts to secure increases in the direct share of profits by the state. The regime announced plans to obtain equity participation in all the operations of local subsidiaries of foreign oil companies. It also insisted that oil companies agree to a production-sharing arrangement which would provide the state with between 60 percent to 80 percent of future output of crude as a condition for the granting of new oil concessions. Finally, it nationalized the properties of Shell Oil, including its small refinery, and all the local marketing and distributing facilities of the oil producers.

The entirely fortuitous circumstances of the post-1973 oil boom enabled the regime, through authoritative decision-making, to employ the state as an instrument for reallocating the phenomenally expanded oil income into politically strategic sectors of the domestic economy. It was able to do so without affecting the accumulative claims of the oil-producing transnationals given dramatic increases in profitability. With the tremendously increased revenue, the regime was able to sustain and expand the system of patronage directed at the black lower-class population (see Chapter 3). It was also to meet the accumulative claims of the country's middle and upper classes, while at the same time increasing its control over the non-oil sectors of the economy. One way in which this was accomplished was through an expansion of direct participation of the state in the economy. At the end of 1977, government investments totalled TT$921·7 million in 21 wholly owned government companies, 13 majority owned companies, and 12 companies in which the state held minority interests. Through an Industrial Development Corporation, another 12 industries and hotels were either fully owned by government or financed by state funds.

The regime justified the tremendously expanded participation of the state in the economy in terms of the latter's economic development functions and of its role in transferring resources from the transnational to the domestic private sector. In this manner it was able to legitimize its own expanded control of the economy. The Prime Minister explained that the program of state participation was undertaken on behalf of local investors in need of protection from the "traditional encroachment of conglomerates." It was necessary to prevent the "heavy concentration of shares in the hands of a few large investors" (*Budget Speech* 1978). The state would continue its high degree of participation until "appropriate institutions have been developed to facilitate planned and equitable divestment" of its shareholdings to the private sector (*Budget Speech* 1978). Returns on state investments were to be used for the "long term restructuring and diversification of the national economy, to develop the foundation for long term economic viability and to increase national participation in resource based industries" (*Info*, December 1977: 7).

Regime survival has to do with an ability to ensure that politically strategic actors are unwilling or unable to behave in ways which disrupt social, political, and economic order. The measures adopted by the Trinidadian regime to expand its participation in the economy did just this. With tremendous expansion in state revenues and state-sector jobs the regime was able to satisfy its patronage obligations and considerably enhance the income earning opportunities for the salaried middle classes and the lower classes. As a major investor and a major source of finance capital it was able to satisfy the accumulative needs of the domestic private sector while increasing the latter's dependence upon the state, and hence its own control over the activities of local business. Similarly, with the expanded role of the state in economic activity, income generation, and as a source of financing, the regime became paramount in satisfying the accumulative claims of professionals in the country. The latter came to be highly dependent upon the state and upon a continuation of regime policies.

The regime was able to manage the conflict between domestic demands and the accumulative claims of the transnationals by acting as a major source of capitalization for the oil industry. It did so through its policy of establishing joint ventures where state surpluses were employed to enter into partnership with foreign investors. From the point of view of the transnationals, state participation meant giving up a proportionate share of the profits without relinquishing control of productive operations. The reason, of course, was that they still retained autonomous decision-making by virtue of the skills, expertise, resources, and access to markets under their exclusive control. Again, given enhanced profitability, absolute levels of profits were hardly affected. The exception, of course, was in domestic distribution where the state obtained full ownership and control.

The role of the state in the capitalization of foreign ventures meant that a lot of its efforts would be invariably concentrated in high-risk, highly capital-intensive ventures. This emphasis became very evident in ventures justified by the regime in terms of "industrial diversification." Foreign investors were attracted to the Trinidadian economy, not merely because of capital availability through state equity participation, but also because of the presence and easy availability of cheap energy, particularly natural gas reserves discovered in the early 1970s and estimated to total around 17 trillion cubic feet. The state had also undertaken the task of financing the infrastructure, service, and facility prerequisites for investments in energy-intensive industry both directly on its own account and indirectly by making capital available to the private sector. Thus, joint projects were entered into between the state and foreign transnationals for the production of liquified natural gas for export, for the construction of an iron and steel plant, an aluminum smelter, and several petrochemical and fertilizer plants. The transnationals involved included Amoco, W. R. Grace, Tesoro Petroleum, and Texaco, all American companies, Hoechst and Kaiser Aluminum of Germany, and Mitsui Chemicals of Japan.

All the above products were to be included in a Point Lisas Industrial Estate located in the oil belt of the country to be developed at an estimated capital cost of US$5 billion. Additional state expenditure was necessitated because of related new and massive infrastructural undertakings to expand and develop electricity generation, roads and ports, transportation, water, and housing facilities. In other words, the needs of foreign transnationals for capitalization, risk sharing, and infrastructure to allow further exploitation of the country's energy resources were perfectly satisfied in the strategy chosen by the regime to gain enhanced control of the economy. While such a strategy meant a larger transfer of the earnings of these transnationals to the state in the form of revenue and shared profits, it hardly affected absolute profit levels while providing considerably increased opportunities for profitable business undertakings. In this manner, the regime was able to resolve the conflict between autonomy and the accumulative claims of the transnational sector of the economy. It resolved it in favor of the latter while adopting measures to secure the transfer of a massive amount of financial resources from the transnational to the state sector. Such transfer allowed the regime to meet its patronage obligations, to finance its coercive apparatus, and to satisfy the accumulative claims of the domestic private sector, whilst at the same time increasing its control over the domestic economy and over political behavior (see Chapter 3).

The accumulative claims of the domestic private sector were also served by the regime's program of industrial diversification involving joint ventures with foreign transnationals. Local businessmen, financed directly or indirectly through state funding, began to exploit highly lucrative opportunities provided in support services related to the energy-based industrialization program and through contracts and subcontracts in the program of infrastructural development. These opportunities emerged particularly in construction, manufacturing, and insurance, which became the high-growth sectors of the local economy (see Hintzen 1981: 152–8).

Finally, the massive transfer of oil earnings to the state sector financed a tremendous expansion of the state administrative system as well as an expansion of state participation in the economy. The result was enormous increases in wages and salaries in the public sector. There was also a tremendous expansion of incomes from direct and indirect patronage allocations and from growth in the domestic and transnational business sectors. The effects of these increases were twofold: first, they created the conditions for the satisfaction of the accumulative claims of the salaried middle classes, whose members were the major beneficiaries of this growth in income; secondly, they generated an expanded demand for the products and services of the domestic private sector.

By employing the revenue derived from the transfer of oil earnings to the state sector, the regime was therefore able to resolve the inherent conflict between state expansion and the accumulative claims of two sets of powerful domestic actors: local business and the domestic middle classes. In the process, both became highly dependent upon resources of the state and upon state expansion in which their interests became vested. They also became dependent upon state policies and programs that were specifically targeted to their needs. Given the regime's role in protecting and furthering the interests of these two powerful domestic sectors, relations between the latter and the state came to take on a character similar to that under colonialism. That is to say that these domestic actors became almost exclusively dependent upon the state for furthering and protecting their economic interests. The state also came to serve as an agency of reconciliation in the face of inter-sectoral conflict and competition. As a result it managed to enhance its legitimacy and

State control of the economy

control since its decisions were considered binding by powerful interest groups (see Chapter 1).

Through patronage the regime was able to secure the loyalty of its lower-class supporters while it was able to enhance its capacity for coercion and political control by employing the revenue largess of the country's oil earnings (see Chapter 3). It was therefore able to satisfy all the conditions for regime survival.

The regime justified the transfer of state revenue into the international and domestic private sector in developmental terms. Such a strategy, as earlier stated, is a means of managing the conflict between the accumulative claims of powerful economic actors and the need for autonomy in economic decision-making to satisfy developmental functions. In this manner, it can justify in developmental terms its own abrogation of autonomy in favor of meeting the accumulative claims of the powerful. The Trinidadian regime did this by formulating a program for disbursement of the enormously increased state revenue through the establishment of several "special funds" in 1974. These funds, according to the regime, were aimed at "the long term restructuring and diversification of the national economy, to develop the foundation for long term economic viability and to increase national participation in resource based industries" (*Info*, December 1977: 7). Under the program, monies collected from revenue were earmarked for future capital projects and invested in fixed deposits in state and commercial banks and trust companies, in bonds and securities, and in loans. In this way these funds became available as capital financing to the private sector while accruing interest for the state. Among the projects allocated funds were petroleum development, infrastructural development, industrial development, community development, and state facilities and services. By the end of 1977, 29 special funds had been established with a target allocation of TT$5·7 billion (see Table 5·1). Simultaneously, between 1973 and 1976 over TT$698 million in state funds had become available to local companies in the form of equity, loans, advances, and other grants. In making the attempt to implement the above strategy, decisions on the investment of the bulk of state-controlled capital came to be based on the attractiveness of projects and programs to foreign investors.

This followed naturally from the regime's decision to channel much of its capital resources into joint ventures with foreign firms. Apart from the direct implications for foreign control, such a decision also caused most local businessmen to tie their investments to these joint ventures. In addition, the new capital-rich conditions combined with state policy to channel local

Table 5.1. *Long-term projects fund (special funds)*

Date fund created		Withdrawals of 31 Dec. 1976	Balance 31 Dec. 1976	1977 income (TT$million) Appropriation	Interest
		TT$000	TT$000		
1974 (1)	Food development	6,760	30,873	5·3	1·5
1974 (2)	Fisheries development	18,461	25,701	32·0	2·4
1974 (3)	Omnibus renewals	38,544	12,520	50·0	2·7
1974 (4)	Petroleum development	292,432	529,430	31·3	23·8
1974	Institute of Banking[a]	nil	3,223	—	—
1974	Petroleum Institute[a]	nil	3,223	—	—
1974 (5)	Scholarships	nil	2,294	nil	0·1
1974 (6)	Reserve for primary school improvement	2,000	1,396	nil	nil
1974 (7)	Reserve for building projects	2,533	5,699	9·7	0·6
1975 (8)	Infrastructure development	48,076	201,589	49·6	10·5
1975 (9)	Central Marketing Agency	nil	5,277	0·4	0·2
1975 (10)	Caribbean integration	2,856	2,614	nil	0·1
1976 (11)	Education	66,820	55,917	55·1	5·1
1976 (12)	Port development	22,222	4,471	52·6	2·5
1976 (13)	Water resources	17,674	3,679	102·2	4·3
1976 (14)	Roads	14,918	9,675	108·3	5·0
1976 (15)	Housing	1,144	1,409	50·0	2·0
1976 (16)	Sports	1,238	1,350	98·5	4·0
1976 (17)	Drainage	1,463	2,838	3·3	0·1
1976 (18)	Telecommunications	4,718	410	26·9	1·1
1976 (19)	Electricity	19,020	4,766	26·4	1·4
1976 (20)	Health	nil	nil	6·5	0·3
1976 (21)	National Training[a]	965	501	0·2	0·2

1976 (22)	Recruitment and settlement of nationals	nil	nil	1·5	nil
1976 (23)	Air transport	12,701	7,440	102·0	4·1
1976 (24)	Airport security	nil	nil	2·0	nil
1977 (25)	Culture	nil	nil	20·0	0·8
1977 (26)	Pre-investment	nil	nil	20·0	0·8
1977 (27)	Social and community development	nil	nil	7·1	0·3
1977 (28)	National parks	nil	nil	15·0	0·6
1977 (29)	Co-operative societies development	nil	nil	13·0	0·5
		574,545	916,295	888·9	75·0

(a) The Institute of Banking Fund and the Petroleum Institute Fund are incorporated in the National Training Fund.
Source: Info, April 1977: 11.

productive investments into areas involving a high degree of capital intensity and into the production of goods with a high import content, usually high priced consumer items. Massive injections of income into the economy by the state assured guaranteed markets for such products.

Massive transfers of oil earnings into the state sector provided the Trinidadian regime with the wherewithal to underwrite its own survival after the post-1973 economic boom. The availability to the state of massive amounts of revenue allowed the regime to meet the allocative claims of the domestic and international private sector as well as those of the middle classes and the black lower classes. Dependence of these sectors upon the state for capitalization, job creation, patronage, and income generation served to enhance state control over the allocation and distribution of economic resources. The regime chose, however, to accommodate the needs of the international energy-based sector for capitalization in exchange for a share of profits without seeking control over decision-making. It justified this strategy by making the claim that state participation in the lucrative energy-based sector of the economy, with future plans for divestment, was the best way to ensure local investors of future ownership and control. With respect to the domestic private sector, high levels of profits came to be guaranteed by a state legislated program of protection and support. Domestic business undertakings were made possible and even more lucrative by the availability of massive amounts of state capital at low interest rates. Finally, a program of state infrastructural development, state expansion, and patronage acted to satisfy the accumulative claims of the middle classes and the black lower classes. It also served to create a high demand for the goods and services of local industry and commerce. Middle-class accumulative claims were also satisfied by an expansion of high-paying job opportunities that became available with state and private sector expansion. With the legitimacy of the Trinidadian regime enhanced, with the state playing a critical role in the management of conflict among the powerful and politically strategic actors, and with state capacity for coercion and political control considerably enhanced, the PNM government became firmly entrenched. The problem, however, was that with such a strategy, regime survival came to be linked even more to economic performance in the oil and energy-based industries. The implications of this are discussed in Chapter 6.

State control of the economy 151

Economic policy and regime survival in Guyana

Regime strategy for state control of the economy

The implicit but pervasive argument in the discussion of the efforts of the Trinidadian regime to expand its control over the national economy is that whatever strategy emerges has to be linked:

(1) to the prevailing economic conditions as they relate to the viability of the country's major productive sector; and
(2) to political conditions as they pertain to the strategic claims on state resources made by those actors whose support and loyalty are critical to regime survival.

Guyana's strategy for economic control followed along the lines of the third world variant of market socialism. As such, the regime embarked on a program of state ownership of all major economic enterprises. This was accomplished through full-scale nationalization, especially but not exclusively, of foreign-owned firms. All remaining private economic activity became subject to strict state regulation and control.

Economic factors and state control of the economy

The most arresting feature of Guyanese political decision-making when compared with Trinidad's has been its high degree of independence from the foreign-owned economic sector. In other words, regime survival was not as inextricably linked to a willingness to satisfy the accumulative claims of the transnationals. Political policy in the country seemed to be primarily responsive to the exigencies of national socio-politics rather than constrained by conditions prerequisite to the successful operation of subsidiaries of international firms.

One possible explanation for the high degree of autonomy in national economic decision-making was a near monopoly in world production of one of the country's major products – refractory grade calcined bauxite – in an industry which enjoyed low costs of mining an extremely high-grade product. Unlike the oil refining in Trinidad, which had little international significance, Guyana's was a strategic source of supply of calcined bauxite for the international market. A second explanation was that sugar production, the country's major industry until the 1960s, had been dominated by a company which was almost totally dependent upon its Guyanese operations. Moreover, international sales of sugar and its byproducts were made on the basis of bilateral intergovernmental agreements which protected and guaranteed them rather than through intracompany transfers as was the case with oil. The third largest contributor to the country's economy was rice, an industry which was totally in the hands of local producers and which depended for markets primarily upon local sales and upon sales to the Anglophone Caribbean.

The direct contribution to the GDP (at current factor costs) of sugar, bauxite, and rice ranged from 36 percent in 1968 to 47 percent in 1975. The three products normally account for between 80 and 90 percent of the country's total exports at factor costs. Bauxite's contribution to total exports averages between 40 and 50 percent and sugar between 30 and 35 percent (figures from the Statistical Bureau, Ministry of Economic Development).

Sugar: The relative insulation of regime survival in Guyana from its willingness to satisfy the accumulative claims of the sugar transnationals was partly dictated by the latter's dependence upon the state. Until the mid-1970s, the sugar industry in Guyana was owned and controlled by four companies. It was dominated, however, by a single firm, Bookers Sugar Estates Ltd, a subsidary of Booker–McConnell Ltd of London. In addition to producing 80 percent of the country's sugar, Bookers was involved in several other activities including retailing, shipping, manufacturing, and fishing. A smaller firm, the Demerara Company Holdings Ltd, also registered in the United Kingdom, owned and operated two sugar factories and was engaged in some manufacturing and retailing. But, to all intents and purposes, sugar in Guyana meant Bookers.

From the very beginning, and throughout the company's history, the Guyana holdings of Booker-McConnell had been the centerpiece of its operations. It expanded through the years by exploiting investment opportunities as they appeared in Guyana and concentrated its efforts at diversification in areas pertinent to the country's needs.

Political developments after independence began to produce a shift in Booker-McConnell's investment policy away from Guyana – even though the company's Guyanese holdings remained so important that the chairman of the company likened them in the early 1970s "to the bee's sting, pull them out and we die" (reported in *The Scotsman*, 24 March 1977). In 1974, after a great deal of international diversification, 43 percent of the company's profits still derived from its Guyanese operations. In other words, despite a general belief among the Guyanese population and administration that the country was irretrievably dependent upon Booker-McConnell, it turns out that, until the mid-1970s, the company was even more dependent than the

Guyanese economy upon its operations in the country for its economic viability.

There were factors, apart from the concentration of its assets in Guyana, which cemented Booker-McConnell's dependence upon state decision-makers. The price the company received for its sugar was negotiated on an intergovernmental level through state elites and was typically much higher and much more stable than that obtained on the free world market. These negotiated prices were tied to quotas which guaranteed sales for the company's products (see Hintzen 1981: 181–97).

The almost absolute reliance of the sugar producers upon bilateral intergovernmental negotiated prices and quotas for marketing their products cast company–government relations in Guyana in a different mold than that which normally obtained in third world countries. As a result, the state-controlling elite had much leeway in dictating conditions of operation to the sugar companies without the fear of debilitating retaliatory action severe enough to produce economic collapse. In other words, this dependence allowed a greater degree of state control of the activities in the industry. The dependence of the sugar-producing companies upon the state was reinforced even more because the country's Commonwealth status guaranteed that most of their sugar would be sold at highly preferential prices.[2]

There was also the question of alternative uses for the resources employed in the sugar industry. Unlike the situation in Trinidad where production and import of crude were the primary elements in the whole economic picture, the essential resource in the Guyanese sugar industry was agricultural land. The possibility of alternative uses could thus be entertained – should the industry collapse, all was not lost. Indeed, this formed the basis of arguments against the continued presence of sugar companies in the country by leading economists (see Thomas 1971: 51).

Another factor which determines the degree of control to be exercised by the state over the activities of foreign transnationals is the availability of the requisite skills and resources to run the industry. The mode of operation of the local sugar industry made it highly vulnerable to state takeover. It is labor intensive, employing simple technology, with relatively low capital demands, and had been run for a long time with a predominantly Guyanese senior staff. In 1975, the total assets of Bookers in the country was estimated

[2] This was the case with sugar production in both Trinidad and Guyana. The difference between the two countries, however, was that sugar was the major economic activity in Guyana until the mid-1960s, whereas Trinidad became almost totally dependent on oil. Sugar continues to be of major importance in the Guyanese economy.

154   *State control of the economy*

by the Guyanese government to be around G$450 million and by the company at around G$900 million. These assets employed close to 20,000 persons with a senior staff of which over 80 percent was Guyanese. Figures for the period between 1966 and 1971 showed an average fixed investment in the industry of around G$8 million per annum. This meant that capitalization of the industry was easily within the capabilities of the state. The importance of the sugar subsidiaries in the Guyanese economy was diluted even more by their relatively low contribution to total government revenue which, between 1960 and 1966, averaged only 7·4 percent (Thomas 1971). Thus, the picture that emerges is of an industry that was, for some time, within the range of state capabilities in terms of financing and operation.

Clearly, in Guyana the position of foreign investors in sugar was defensive. There was nothing that they could do when government nationalized the holdings of the smaller Demerara Company in May 1975. Booker-McConnell, even after an intensive program of diversification in Britain and Africa, could do little but worry with 20 percent of its business still located in Guyana. The company's local holdings of 22 subsidiaries directly employing 23,000 persons were eventually nationalized in May 1976, after the government agreed to pay close to G$500 million in compensation out of future profits.

As expected, the immediate international economic backlash from nationalization was quite minimal. The United States government, in probable retaliation against the regime, refused to exempt the country from a trebling of duties on imported sugar. That action served to cut the nationalized industry from its highest paying market in which it sold 91,000 tons of sugar (approximately 30 percent of production) before 1974. However, the resulting shortfalls in sales were made up by increased purchases by China, Algeria, and the Anglophone Caribbean. That is to say that the regime was able to call upon alternative markets to offset the negative effects of Western economic retaliation

Bauxite: It was noted in Chapter 1 that the capacity for authoritative decision-making and for acquiring eventual control over the sphere of economic activity associated with international investors is considerably enhanced when a third world state has available to it the wherewithal to run foreign-owned enterprises and when these enterprises produce large volumes of strategic resources upon which industrial economies depend. Both conditions were true of the bauxite industry in Guyana.

Until its operations were nationalized in 1971, Alcan Aluminum of Canada, through its local subsidary, Demerara Bauxite Company (Demba),

State control of the economy 155

was the local giant in bauxite production. Reynolds Metals, an American-owned bauxite producer, exploited much smaller concessions acquired in the country during 1952.

When the country became independent in 1966, the local bauxite industry had been producing over 80 percent of the world's supply of calcined ore. Thus, it was from a position of strength that the government decided, in 1970, to seek majority participation in the industry. It became clear even before negotiations were begun that Alcan absolutely opposed any form of state control of and equity participation in the industry. In response to the demands of the regime, the company tabled a set of counter proposals which would, in effect, guarantee its continued domination of the industry and a continued share of the profits while recovering the costs of all of its assets after state purchase of majority interests at highly inflated prices (see Girvan 1971: 228; and Hintzen 1981: 193–7). The proposals of the state and the company were mutually unacceptable and negotiations reached an impasse. As a result, the regime made a decision to break off talks and to nationalize the company's holdings for which it paid "reasonable compensation."

The most formidable threat posed by Alcan was its ability to use its international resources and alliances to produce economic crisis in the country. Important in this regard was its ability to increase bauxite, alumina, and calcined off-take in other countries in order to constrict market opportunities for the new company. To help offset such a possibility, the Prime Minister attempted to implement the suggestions of Caribbean politicians and academics for the formation of an International Bauxite Association, a country cartel of bauxite-exporting countries similar to OPEC. In 1970, anticipating the possibility of Alcan's attempt to play bauxite producers off against each other, Prime Minister Burnham approached government leaders with the suggestion for country cartelization. He was unsuccessful (see Girvan 1976: 143–56). The problem thus became one of finding alternative buyers outside of Alcan's structure of influence. As the major producer of calcined ore, its markets were guaranteed. Nonetheless, it had to seek to replace markets lost to its metal-grade production. The newly nationalized company also had to find alternative suppliers of inputs.

Almost immediately, the nationalized company found alternative buyers for its products by engaging the services of a New York-based firm, Philipp Brothers, with a global marketing network which included the Soviet Union and Eastern Europe. Another New York firm, Samincorp, was hired as purchasing agents to provide essential equipment, spare parts, and other inputs necessary for the company's operation. Thus, even though the newly nationalized enterprise did suffer from the loss of strategic linkages within

156   *State control of the economy*

the integrated aluminum industry, losses in markets were more than offset by increased sales of calcined ore and by the securing of alternative markets for its metal grade products in Eastern Europe. In addition alternatives were quickly and easily found to provide the inputs necessary for its successful and continued operation. The new company's viability was never in doubt despite economic sanctions applied on the intergovernmental level by Western countries.

Post-independence policy

Without a doubt, the powerful bauxite and sugar lobbies operating in Britain and in the United States had a great deal to do with the constitutional change made just prior to independence which put the coalition of the Peoples National Congress (PNC) and the pro-capitalist Portuguese-dominated United Force (UF) into power (see Chapter 2). Once independence was achieved, however, the influence of the multinationals over local decision-making became constricted, and they could rely only upon the political allegiance of the minority UF with which they had formal and indirect ties. However, they continued to have clout on the intergovernmental level through the policies of their respective home governments as they pertained to the newly independent state.

During the period immediately following the granting of independence, the regime was highly dependent upon foreign capital and developmental assistance to restore stability to a devastated economy (see Chapters 2 and 3). In exchange, it had to ensure that the accumulative claims of the foreign investors were met. Foreign producers were also able to rely on their ties with the UF to maintain their influence on state economic decision-making. The executive and legislative strength of the UF was way in excess of its proportional representation in government. The party's leader held the important and strategic portfolio of Minister of Finance, and as a result, he enjoyed considerable power. Through his ministerial post, he was able to determine how and where revenue was raised and to set government program priorities by having almost absolute control over government expenditure. Thus, for the first few years of independence, the influence of the UF steered national economic policy in a direction similar to that of Trinidad's, by emphasizing development of the local private sector, by stressing limited interference with the multinationals, and by fostering and protecting conditions favorable to their operations.

By 25 September 1967, one year after independence, the PNC had consolidated its control of the state, independently of its coalition partner

State control of the economy

(see Chapters 2 and 3). The leader of the UF had no option but to resign his powerful portfolio. This ushered in a new phase in the country's strategy for control of the economy. Without the encumberance of the conservative UF, it became clear that the policy of non-interference with the multinationals would soon be changed.

The survival of the PNC depended upon its capacity to satisfy the accumulative claims of the black middle class and the demands of its black supporters for increased job opportunities, for greater job security, and for a larger share of the country's wealth. This necessitated a program of massive state expansion financed through the reallocation of private-sector earnings to the state. Such an emphasis on public-sector expansion became evident as soon as the PNC gained full control of the state. In 1968, the first full year of PNC control of the Ministry of Finance, government investments rose by 30 percent against a decline of 16 percent in private-sector investments (*Budget Speech*, 1969: 13). The current expenditure of the state was 8 percent higher in 1968 than it was in 1967 with an additional 13 percent increase the following year (*Budget Speech*, 1970: 10). Finally, there was increased spending on defense and security as part of the party's strategy for state expansion (see Chapter 3).

In the 1968 budget, the new PNC Minister of Finance made it clear that the program of state expansion was to be financed from the private sector and through increased control of the foreign-owned sector, deprecated for its widely known practice of transfer pricing and other means employed to evade taxation: "The Government, too," he warned, "is entitled to have its share of the national income, and intends, by strict tax administration, to bring to book all persons who dodge their legitimate tax liabilities or otherwise defraud the revenue" (*Budget Speech*, 1968: 11).

The 1970 budget proposals contained specific plans for increasing national autonomy in economic decision-making. They outlined new terms of private-sector participation in the economy as well as plans for the development of a vibrant co-operative sector. As in the case of Trinidad, a program of co-operative development was aimed at the black lower class which was experiencing high levels of unemployment and underemployment. As predominantly city and semi-urban dwellers, this group had little access to the agricultural resources of the country. The co-operative was seen as an entrée to that sector (*Budget Speech* 1970: 19).

Thus, at the beginning of 1970, the ruling party had a two-pronged policy in the form of a program of public-sector expansion aimed at the accumulative interests of its middle- and lower-middle-class supporters, and a program for co-operative development which catered directly to the

158 *State control of the economy*

economic needs of its lower-class membership. All in all, the implicit intention of the policy was to deliver a larger share of state resources to the country's black population (see Greene 1972, for a similar argument).

To implement the new policy there was need for substantial increases in government revenue. It became clear that the strategy to be employed was the reallocation of the earnings of the private domestic and international sectors into the state sector. Revenues were raised by increasing the tax liabilities of the private sector through a program of fiscal reform. Changes were legislated in the structure of corporate and property taxation while tax concessions granted to new and established firms were curtailed. Banks and insurance companies were subjected to new conditions of operations which included increased licensing fees and restrictions on the transfer of funds overseas. More important, government began to seek means of ensuring greater and more meaningful participation in the activities of the large multinationals operating in the country. This was when the regime decided to seek participation in the bauxite industry.

Political and economic consequences of nationalization

The nationalization of Demba was probably the single most decisive event in determining future economic policy for post-independence Guyana. It was decisive, not because it heralded a fundamental break with the past. Much more important was the demonstration effect of the successful running of the nationalized subsidiary and of the positive economic benefits that accrued to party middle-class supporters from which the company's new managers were selected. After these benefits were realized, there emerged a climate of strong support among the black middle class for similar action by government against other multinationals.

It was within the context of growing black middle-class support for its policy of nationalization that the ruling party was able, subsequently, to push through its program of massive public penetration of the private sector as the declared basis for a "socialist transformation" of the economy. Without the demonstration of benefits that would accrue to its members in the wake of state expansion, such a radical policy shift would certainly have met with considerable opposition from a bureaucratic middle class traditionally wary of any leftist programs.

State expansion, patronage, and regime survival

In the process of performing its developmental and administrative functions, the regime was able to divert state resources to the accumulative claims of its black supporters, particularly the black middle class. It was not fettered by strategic ties to the private sector or to the predominantly East Indian peasantry, and so there was little need, to cater to their accumulative demands.

The successful nationalization of Demba was a major turning point in the state's program of expansion. It spawned a new thrust by government into the private sector. Through the Public Corporations (Amendment) Act (1971), the Guyana State Corporation (Guystac) was created to "coordinate the management, personnel and financial structures and policies of Public Corporations with a view to ensuring efficient and businesslike performance" (*Budget Speech*, 1972). After its formation in 1971, Guystac experienced phenomenal growth. In 1977, it controlled 29 public corporations and companies with assets valued at over G$500 million (see Figure 5·2). The Guystac group of companies employed at the end of that year over 18,000 persons, exclusive of the five government banks, the three bauxite corporations, and the massive sugar corporation not under its umbrella.

This sudden and extraordinary corporate expansion of the state into the private sector was matched by an equally extraordinary expansion of its administrative and public welfare sectors including the military and paramilitary. In September 1976, government took control of all private schools and instituted a policy of free education at all levels. By the end of 1977, there were 400 government-owned nursery schools (where none had existed before 1975) most of which were started after 1976. Government-owned primary schools increased from 395 in 1974 to 445 in 1977, and government secondary schools increased from 31 to 45 over the same period. Technical and vocational schools increased from one to five, and two schools for teaching home economics and domestic crafts were introduced. During the 1970s, government also introduced a co-operative college, a new teacher training school, and another agricultural college to complement one already in existence (Guyana Information Service 1977).

In October 1974, a paramilitary Guyana National Service (GNS) was created which functioned "to facilitate the total motivation of those who have endured the inadequacies of insufficient, irrelevant education and those who had had no education at all" (Guyana Information Service 1977: 67). While the justification provided for the GNS was education, hinterland development, agricultural production, and small-scale industrial activities,

160 *State control of the economy*

Figure 5.2. *List of government corporations*

Guystac corporations	Non-Guystac corporations
Public utilities and service group Guyana Electricity Corporation National Insurance Scheme Guyana Housing Corporation[b] Guyana Transport Services Ltd[a] *Trading group 1* External Trade Bureau Guyana National Trading Corporation[a] Guyana Gajraj Limited[b] Guyana Wrefords Limited[b] *Trading group 2* Guyana Stores Ltd[b] Guyana National Lithographic Co. Ltd[b] Guyana National Pharmaceutical Corporation[b] Guyana National Shipping Corporation[b] Guyana Oil Company Limited[b] *Information and communication services* Guyana Telecommunications Corporation Guyana Broadcasting Services Guyana National Newspapers Ltd[b] Guyana Printers Limited[b] *Agricultural products and food processing* Guyana Agricultural Producers Corporation[a] Guyana Marketing Corporation Guyana Marine Foods Ltd[b] Guyana Food Processors Ltd[b] *Industries group* Guyana Timbers Limited[b] Small Industries Corporation[a] Guyana Forest Industries Corporation[a] Guyana Rice Board[a] Guyana National Engineering Corporation[b] Post Office Corporation	Guyana National Co-operative Bank Guyana National Co-operative Bank Trust Company[a] Guyana Agricultural Co-operative Development Bank[a] Guyana Co-operative Mortgage and Finance Bank[a] Guyana Bauxite Company[b] Berbice Mining Enterprises[b] The Bauxite Industrial Development Company[a] Guyana Construction Company Guyana Sugar Corporation[b]

[a] Created since 1971.
[b] Acquired since 1971.

State control of the economy

its real functions were to bolster the coercive arm of the state and to expand its patronage largess. For identical reasons, military growth over the period since independence, and especially during the 1970s, was enormous. In 1967, there were 1,124 personnel in the military and police forces. By 1977, this number had reached 21,751, representing one military person for every 37 citizens as opposed to one for every 284 in 1964 (Sackey 1979: 46). Expenditure on the military and paramilitary rose from an estimated 8 percent of the national budget (G$22 million) in 1973 to 14·2 percent (G$113 million) in 1976 (Danns 1978).

The spectacular growth in education and in military and paramilitary agencies was matched by similar growth in all other areas of the civil service. The number of government ministries increased from 14 before 1970 to 21 by 1977. By then, over 80 percent of all economic activity and jobs were in the state sector and most of the remaining, such as private sector, professional, and peasant undertakings were directly dependent upon the state.

State control of almost all economic activity in the country was justified by the regime as the strategy which best assured that developmental goals would be realized. In actuality, it gave to the regime control of the lion's share of the country's economic resources to be used for the satisfaction of the patronage claims of its black and colored supporters, particularly the bureaucratic middle class, and perhaps more importantly, to support the system of coercion and control. Together, these underwrite and guarantee regime survival.

The strategy of market socialism also acted to placate members of the powerful radical wing of the ruling party thereby checking any tendencies toward outbidding. It also served to attract members of the radical opposition, many of whom switched party allegiances to the PNC. Both of these proved extremely critical for socio-political order. While in Trinidad these radicals became involved in a campaign of persistent anti-regime rebellion and opposition, in Guyana many became, for the most part, ardent supporters of the ruling party.

In 1974, a full-blown program of state takeover of the private sector began to unfold. In the two years that followed, the regime nationalized all of the major multinationals in the country. First to go was Reynolds Metals (the second of the bauxite companies) in January 1975; Demerara Company, the smaller of the two major sugar producers, was nationalized in May of the same year; and finally the massive Booker holdings were nationalized in 1976.

Nationalization of Demba had proved an unequivocal success. In 1974, the company enjoyed record sales, boosted by increased production of calcined ore the price of which was spiralling upwards on the international market, and by a favorable market for alumina (see *Annual Statistical Abstract*, 1974). This spurred the confidence of the political leaders and they made the decision to nationalize Reynolds, bringing the whole bauxite industry into the ambit of state ownership. At the same time, the world market price for sugar was climbing to unprecedented highs and producing enormous profits for the local sugar companies. Nationalization of the industry seemed extremely attractive.

Thus, in 1975, bauxite and sugar production seemed to offer unlimited profit potential, and the performance of these two industries was spearheading a period of general economic prosperity. The country's foreign reserves had increased from G$28 million at the end of 1973 to around G$120 million one year later, the result of a 37 percent growth in the country's GDP (*Budget Speech* 1975). In 1975, economic growth continued unabated as foreign reserves galloped to G$256 million and GDP increased by an impressive 22 percent. These increases, entirely due to favorable conditions for sugar and bauxite on the world market, brought the country from the depths of economic doldrums. State takeover of the foreign private sector seemed, at the time, to be a very propitious move.

The patronage benefits of state expansion were immediately evident. At the end of 1974, support for the ruling party among the group of black state workers ran high in the wake of their new prosperity. The regime had provided them with an enormous hike in salary followed by a relief in income taxes and generous subsidies on major consumer items. Through the state they now enjoyed preferential access to rapidly increasing job opportunities which brought in their wake higher salaries, increased perquisites, and quick and easy promotion. If socialism meant state expansion, then state employees were all for it, as they would be for any policy – socialist or capitalist – that served their interests as an administrative group. Thus, the socialist turn of the regime had the full backing of this same strategic middle class that was so instrumental in toppling the Marxist government of Cheddi Jagan just one short decade earlier.

Two features of the use of ideology in regime survival become evident from the strategy employed by the Guyanese regime. First, there was the use of ideology to secure the support of powerful actors who had the resources with which to neutralize the effects of retaliatory actions by regime opponents. The Guyanese government's embracing of a radical ideological position went hand-in-hand with its growing dependence upon the Eastern bloc for development assistance and for markets to counter retaliatory action by the

State control of the economy 163

West in response to its program of nationalization. Secondly, the regime needed international political and strategic support to protect itself from potential attempts by the West at intervention and destabilization. A radical and activist international posture served to guarantee the support of communist and socialist states throughout the world.

The second way in which the regime employed ideology was to justify and legitimize its program of state ownership and control of the economy in developmental terms. Such ownership and control, effected through a program of nationalization and miniaturization of the private sector, allowed the regime to satisfy the accumulative claims of the black middle class which had emerged politically as the most strategic group in the country. It also allowed the regime to meet the patronage and coercive claims, discussed in Chapters 3 and 4, that were directly related to its own survival.

In summary, by the second half of the 1970s, the regime had managed to secure for itself almost absolute control of the national economy. This provided the wherewithal to satisfy the accumulative claims of the politically strategic administrative middle class and to support a program of coercion and control. The latter was effectively used to crush political opposition and to demobilize potentially dissident groups. Like Trinidad, the political and economic costs were enormous. First, the national economy became highly vulnerable to international (Western) retaliation. Secondly, in meeting the accumulative claims of the black middle class, the massive patronage claims, and the financial demands of the system of coercion and control, the regime had virtually to abandon its developmental functions. These costs are the subject of the next chapter.

Conclusion

Regime control of the economy, normally undertaken to serve developmental, administrative, and law and order functions, became converted in Guyana and Trinidad to the satisfaction of the accumulative, patronage and coercive claims necessary for regime survival. Despite the adoption of opposing ideological positions (capitalism in the case of Trinidad and socialism in Guyana), both regimes were unable and unwilling to implement policies for undertaking the developmental functions of the state. This was so because ideology was employed in both cases for regime survival rather than to inform a self-sustaining developmental program. The end product, as will be shown in the next chapter, was continued underdevelopment. Likewise, state expansion, which has been considerable in both countries, came to serve patronage, coercive and control functions rather than development and civil administrative functions. This led to ineffective and inefficient civil administration and a breakdown of the rule of law.

Together, all of these constitute the costs of regime survival which will be discussed in Chapter 6. They also serve as explanations for the persistent episodes of civil disorder which came to characterize both countries.

6. The political and economic costs of regime survival

The state has emerged almost universally in less developed countries as the key, paramount, and oftentimes sole functional unit for the satisfaction of the collective needs of society, namely: social order and stability, self-sustaining economic development, equity in the allocation of valued ends, social security of the population, and civil and political rights. At the same time, the state has become the primary and most often the sole allocator of economic and social values, the central institution of economic accumulation for individuals and groups, and the preeminent instrument of power. It is one of the central theses of this book that, under certain conditions, regime survival can become most intricately tied to these latter set of functions in ways which jeopardize realization of the former.

If it is to ensure its own survival, a regime might find itself with little choice but to allocate resources and to satisfy the accumulative demands of powerful individuals and groups in ways which render the realization of the collective needs of society highly unlikely. To deal effectively with the consequences of this, a regime might be forced to employ the state for coercion, control, and surveillance to contain the effects of social, political, and economic crisis and to prevent destabilizing anti-regime mobilization.

Collective needs can be sacrificed without jeopardizing regime survival. This is because of the contrasting role that the state plays for different sectors of society. For the masses, the reality of the state is its preponderant function as an allocator of economic and social values. Thus the lower classes in LDCs are preeminently concerned with its output functions, i.e. with the paramount role it plays in their own economic and social survival.

Such a dependence allows the state to function as an instrument of exploitation, domination, and control for the elite over the lower classes. This small group of elites may be acting on its own behalf or representing metropolitan economic, political, and security interests either directly or indirectly. Its members may be dependent upon ties with the metropole for their positions of power, status, privilege, and wealth. The absolute dependence of the lower classes upon the state's output functions gives those who control the state the power to act exclusively for the promotion and protection of elite interests and for their economic accumulation.

The domestic elite is not the only group to have the wherewithal to control state decision-making. International actors are also in a position, independently of their domestic allies and representatives, to employ the state apparatus in the service of their own interests. They can do this by using their own formidable resources to impose their will on state decision-makers.

Appeals to collective identity can free a regime in LDCs to cater to the demands of powerful and strategic metropolitan and domestic actors while sustaining mass appeal. The regime can also employ the formidable resources of the state for patronage, coercion, and control in order to demobilize mass opposition, circumvent mass participation, and repress political dissent.

What is said above is not to deny the emergence of leaders in LDCs who have been genuinely committed to the collective needs of their populations. But elite and metropolitan actors enjoy an overwhelming and insurmountable advantage because of their exclusive access to powerful and strategic resources. When all attempts at securing the accommodation and compliance of the political leadership fail, these resources can be used to create conflict and to produce social, political, and economic collapse. Leaders who otherwise may be willing to meet the collective needs of their societies might find themselves with no option but to give way to the demands of powerful interest groups in order to survive for any appreciable period. If they do not, they might find their control of the state quite tenuous and marked by endemic political and economic trauma.

Thus regime survival can, and usually does, come at the cost of the satisfaction of the collective needs of society. For the purposes of this study the term "costs" is used to mean value foregone. In this sense, it is similar to the use by economists of the term "opportunity costs" and refers to a choice to give up the acquisition of one or a set of values for the achievement of others considered to be more desirable.

At the functional level, this study concentrates on the state as the provider and maximizer of desired values and/or as the guarantor and facilitator of their achievement. At the behavioral level, it is state-controlling elites who make the choices as to which values will be satisfied and to what end: In other words, how state resources will be allocated and to whose benefit.

Following in this vein, the state becomes the "key functional unit" in the satisfaction of the collective needs of the society as a whole (Apter 1971: 11). These needs may be subsumed under the following universally recognized values:

(i) *Social order and stability*: This has to do with the maintenance of harmony, regularity, and predictability in social relations, based on universally accepted norms and upon constitutionality and the rule of law. For order to be maintained, the goals of social institutions and their structures, in terms of organization, must be congruous with the prevailing norms and values of society (Apter 1971: 18–21).

(ii) *Self-sustaining economic development*: This refers to the acquisition, development and diffusion of information and technology and the means to allow their conversion into infrastructure to be employed in concrete production. Qualitatively and quantitatively, production has to be adequate for the satisfaction of all the material needs of all the individuals in the society either directly or through international exchange. Such needs pertain to the maintenance of a standard of living adequate for the health, well-being, livelihood, and human development of all members of society. In the process of development the options available to individuals for satisfying their material needs should be constantly expanding (see Apter 1971: 6–30).

(iii) *Equity in the allocation of valued ends*: This refers to the prevailing normative preferences of individuals, of subgroups (ethno-cultural, interest, and class/status groups), and of the society as a whole. Such preferences have both a material component relating to the distribution of resources and an "ideal" component pertaining to ultimate values, beliefs, principles, ideas, etc., not associated with material ends (see Apter 1971: 15ff.).

(iv) *The social security of all members of society*: This has to do with ensuring the availability of economic, social, and cultural resources necessary for human dignity, human development, and the development of personality.

(v) *Civil and political rights*: Under these are subsumed (a) the right to life, liberty, and security; (b) the right to a free and fair trial, freedom from arbitrary arrest, detention and exile, and the right to equal protection under the law; (c) the right to freedom of thought, conscience and religion, and the freedom to hold and express opinions without interference; (d) the right to peaceful assembly and association; (e) the right to participate in government and of equal access to public resources; (f) government based upon the will of the people through free and fair elections which are regularly held; and (g) the right to education. (These are all contained in the 30 articles of the *International Bill of Human Rights*, 1978.)

In light of the prevailing structure of political and economic organization in LDCs and the web of international relations of which they are part, attempts to satisfy these collective needs might result in socio-political disorder, endemic political instability and, ultimately, regime collapse. This constitutes one of the major dilemmas facing most LDCs and can go a long way in explaining their failed economic development and endemic and persistent socio-political crises.

The strategies employed which allowed the leaders of the PNC in Guyana and the PNM in Trinidad to gain and maintain control of the state have been discussed in the previous chapters. These strategies have resulted in a system of state organization and in economic policies that have produced a growing and cummulative inability to satisfy the collective needs of society. The costs incurred by both countries became particularly acute during the 1970s and 1980s.

Regime survival and the maintenance of social order and stability

Order and stability, as they are hereby conceived, refer not merely, or at all, to the absence of generalized conflct in society. Instead, taken together, they refer in their political dimensions to the existence of a generalized consensus on the procedures for conducting the affairs of the state. In this sense they require, as preconditions, the existence of what political scientist Claude Ake (1967: 111) calls "a political class which is solidary" and characterized by a high degree of consensus in terms of some agreement over the conduct of politics and the resolution of political conflict (Weiner 1971). A second set of preconditions is that members of this political class not only represent the genuine collective interests of all members of society, but are perceived to do so legitimately by constituents. A third precondition is that this political class, collectively, is in sole control of the state.

Without value-integration of the political elite and in the absence of a generalized belief in the legitimacy of its members, then segments of the population become committed to engage in behavior that is destabilizing and disruptive of social, political, and economic order. The regime, in turn, resorts to coercion and control to prevent disruptive mobilization. Thus, coercion and control might produce a manifest absence of conflict even though the preconditions for order and stability remain unsatisfied.

Order and stability pertain to the presence or absence of generalized system legitimacy. For such legitimacy to exist, there needs to be generalized consensus that the political process and the system of political organization is responsive to the genuine collective interests of all members of society independently of the specific decisions of those currently in power. This must be contrasted with regime legitimacy which may prove highly fragile. A political elite might enjoy overwhelming generalized support from all sectors of the population because of the actual or perceived beneficial effects of its policies. When such a perception changes, however, mechanisms must be in place to effect change either in policy or leadership. System legitimacy cannot be said to exist without such mechanisms. In their absence a resort to extra-constitutional means becomes almost inevitable. If the use of extra-constitutional measures can be preempted by state coercion and control what is left is alienation. In other words, order and stability cannot be said to exist despite a manifest absence of conflict.

Regime survival and order and stability in Guyana

Initially, the conditions for survival of the PNC regime in Guyana were inextricably tied to the satisfaction of the accumulative claims of the country's black and colored middle classes who staffed and ran the state apparatus. They were also tied to the party's ability to appeal to the country's black lower classes by employing a racial idiom and by engaging in racial patronage. The PNC assumed power by constitutional fiat. Britain forced the PPP to accept changes in the electoral system that reduced the number of seats held by representatives of the East Indian population in the country's legislature from a majority to a minority. With this, there was an immediate and widespread loss of system legitimacy among the East Indian population.

Thus, when the idiom of race came to be the basis of lower-class mobilization in the competition among local political leaders for control of the state in Guyana, it set the stage for endemic disorder and instability. Irrespective of the constitution, legitimacy came to rest, for the lower classes, upon the racial identity of the party in power. The assumption to power of the PNC/UF coalition was accomplished by anti-East Indian racial mobilization, a protracted period of communal violence, and retaliation against the PPP government by powerful international actors, including the British government. The latter used its power to change the constitution to one of proportional representation paving the way for a PNC/UF victory in 1964.

Consistent with the erosion of system legitimacy, there was a violent rejection of the constitutional change by the East Indian masses and the country's post-1964 political history became peppered with episodes of social, political, and economic disruption by the organized East Indian opposition.

170   *Political and economic costs*

At the leadership level, the PPP carried out a campaign of "non-cooperation and civil resistance" which continued up to the time of writing (1986). This campaign was accompanied by the use of extra-constitutional measures such as strikes and demonstrations to oppose the regime (see Central Committee Document, Peoples Progressive Party 1977). The policy of confrontation was abandoned only for a brief period between 1975 and 1976 when the PPP opted for critical support of the ruling regime after the latter made an unambiguous commitment to socialism.

It becomes clear, therefore, that political order and stability in Guyana has been preempted by the rejection of both system and regime legitimacy on the part of the East Indian masses. This rejection stems from exclusion of their representatives from political decision-making. For legitimacy to be restored there needs to be the adoption of constitutional measures and reformulation of party policies aimed at the equitable inclusion of the East Indian population in all areas of government. This finds itself in fundamental conflict with the terms of survival of the PNC regime, initially rooted in racial mobilization and racial patronage and later in a system of coercion, control, and regimentation.

Order and stability was also preempted by an erosion of both regime and system legitimacy among the working-class supporters of the PNC as a consequence of outbidding. This emerged as the party began to cater exclusively to the accumulative demands of the black and colored middle classes and in the face of a deepening economic crisis (see Chapter 5, as well as Premdas 1972; Hintzen 1981: 337 and 1975: 67–81). After 1976 continuing economic declines made it increasingly impossible for the political leadership to meet the demands of this very black and colored middle class. The result was a growing loss of legitimacy among its members.

Hence, by the latter part of the 1970s, there was a generalized loss of system and regime legitimacy among all segments of the population. As a consequence there was an increase in acts of open confrontation with the regime which also became more generalized.

By 1971, black lower-class outbidding was added to the continuing East Indian political confrontation. These outbidding efforts were spearheaded by an organization called the African Society for Cultural Relations with Independent Africa (ASCRIA) the leaders of which had become highly integrated into the PNC party structure and enjoyed powerful positions in government. Without question, these leaders saw their role as the promotion of the interests of lower-class blacks in the country (Premdas 1972; Hintzen 1981: 337). When the regime virtually abandoned its policy of co-operative

Political and economic costs 171

development, which was aimed at catapulting members of the black lower class into the economic mainstream of business and agriculture, ASCRIA leaders resigned their government posts and began a scathing campaign against the PNC.

Black middle-class rejection of regime and system legitimacy emerged after 1976 and became particularly evident after 1978 as the regime was forced to lay off state employees on a massive scale and to "redeploy" state workers from the bureaucratic sector to the laboring sector of the economy. These measures were accompanied by significantly increased deductions from wages for national health insurance and pension schemes. Efforts to cut state spending and increase revenue were mandated at a time when the economic crisis had produced rapidly rising costs of living and increasing shortages of essential commodities (see *Solidarity*, 4 January 1979; *Guyana Chronicle*, 5 May 1978: 1 and 5).

The loss of generalized legitimacy became very evident in political confrontation and conflict during the latter half of the 1970s. The political organizations representing the disparate segments of the population combined into an informal alliance around the Working Peoples Alliance (WPA) which was itself a coalition between ASCRIA and an East Indian group, the Indian Political Revolutionary Associates (IPRA).

The WPA began an anti-regime campaign in 1978 based on the explicit rejection of the legitimacy of the system and of the regime itself. The centerpiece of the campaign was a call for the establishment of a United Front alternative government to the PNC. Almost immediately the group was able to gain active and explicit support from most of the major politicized segments of the population. Included among these were the East Indian PPP and its two affiliated unions; the radical intellectual community, particularly the University of Guyana Staff Association; the moderate Clerical and Commercial Workers Union (CCWU), which represented urban middle-class workers; the mass membership of all the major unions in the country, including those representing state bureaucratic workers; all the country's moderate and conservative parties; the major churches; and the Compass Group, comprising a moderate alliance of professionals, leading executives in the state and private sector, trade unionists, and priests (see Hintzen 1981: 343–55). The campaign was supported by workers in the two major nationalized industries (sugar and bauxite), who began to engage in a series of anti-regime strikes.

Hence, by 1978 the very strategy adopted by the regime to ensure its own survival had managed to produce a generalized loss of system and regime legitimacy, the primary preconditions for political order and stability. At this juncture, continued regime survival came to depend upon the success of efforts to demobilize the population and to control mass organizations.

The use of coercion can buy a political elite enough time to develop and implement an effective long-term response to challenges to its power. In light of this, the PNC regime began to intensify its use of violent and non-violent coercion to buy time while restructuring the state machinery of control. Initially, regime survival had depended upon coercive deployment against the country's East Indian population, particularly during electoral campaigns. In 1971 this deployment was extended to ASCRIA, and in 1973, to dissident formerly pro-regime unions. By 1978, the use of the regime's coercive resources came to be directed at securing the generalized political demobilization of the entire population. Singled out for particular attention were members of the WPA and all activists engaged in any overt form of political dissent. Leaders of the anti-regime movement were arrested on trumped-up charges, while known political dissidents were placed under constant surveillance. The houses of anti-regime activists, and those associating with them, were constantly searched under the powers of a National Security Act which gave the police sweeping powers. Leading members of the opposition were constantly intimidated with a campaign of state-directed violence. Some, including the most important and dynamic of the WPA activists, Walter Rodney, were killed. Many more were arrested, some on charges of treason.

The coercive assault proved extremely effective. By 1980 the movement of generalized opposition was successfully demobilized and public demonstrations against the regime came to an abrupt end. By then, a loyal group of party elites had secured control of almost every sphere of state-related activity, including the running of the country's economy. At the same time, leaders co-opted by the regime had managed to gain absolute control of all the major mass organizations in the country. Control of the state by this elite cadre was formalized in a new constitution and backed by a dramatically expanded state coercive apparatus (see Chapter 3).

Because of effective demobilization, the political opposition was forced to abandon mass demonstration in the early 1980s for mass action by workers in the state sector. Such action was rendered possible because, for all its efforts, the regime had not yet managed to consolidate control of the labor movement. It finally did so by coercive legislation. In early 1984, Parliament passed a Labour (Amendment) Bill which gave the political executive power to declare any strike in the public sector illegal. The Bill also legislated the party-dominated Trades Union Council to be the sole bargaining agent for

Political and economic costs 173

the country's workers (see *Caribbean Contact*, April 1984: 1) In this manner, one of the last remaining organized vehicles for disruptive mobilization in the form of politicized industrial action was effectively stifled.

By the 1980s, therefore, regime survival had come to rest upon an ability to exclude representatives of the various segments of the population from political participation and political decision-making. This ability was sustained by the use of effective mechanisms for coercion, control, and regimentation in the face of a generalized loss of both regime and system legitimacy. The conditions of regime survival had therefore moved progressively to the point where they were in absolute violation of the prerequisites for order and stability.

Regime survival and order and stability in Trinidad

It has been pointed out that political order and stability is rooted in the existence of generalized system legitimacy. This implies a belief by all segments of the population that their interests are represented in political decision-making and that their demands are equitably met or, when this is not the case, that mechanisms are present to effect political change. When a regime enjoys generalized legitimacy, the system is hardly questioned. However, when that legitimacy is eroded and the regime is still able to retain power, commitment to the system might begin to collapse. Opponents may become increasingly willing to use extra-constitutional means to secure political change. Eventually they may be willing to consider a fundamental restructuring of the system itself.

The problem of order and stability in Trinidad is complicated because both the regime and the political system enjoyed long periods of generalized legitimacy. There were periods, however, when regime legitimacy became eroded. During such periods there were also consequent erosions of system legitimacy after the regime resorted to institutionalized mechanisms that allowed use of the state apparatus to retain power.

Generalized legitimacy was sustained in Trinidad because of East Indian lower-class commitment to the political process. Among the black and colored population regime legitimacy was sustained by racial appeal. In addition, the successful use of generalized patronage secured the commitment of the black lower classes to both the regime and the system itself. Nonetheless, there were periodic breakdowns of order and stability manifest in episodes of racial outbidding and efforts at class mobilization.

The policies of the PNM regime produced a growing inequality in the society and this hit the black lower classes the hardest. During periods of

174 *Political and economic costs*

economic crisis this sector of the population persistently backed calls for a fundamental restructuring of the system. Political mobilization of the black population in support of such calls was always met by coercive retaliation followed by legislation aimed at increasing regime control over the political activities of the black population. This was the regime's choice of response when it had to face the very first challenge to its control of the state from its own lower-class supporters. It answered this challenge by formulating the Industrial Relations Act (IRA) in 1965 after facing a serious political crisis caused by anti-regime trade union mobilization. The intention of the Act was to neutralize politically the trade union movement after using the state's coercive apparatus to secure its demobilization (see Chapter 3).

The strategy of coercion followed by legislation to control political behavior was also responsible for regime survival during the 1970–3 period which was marked by a loss of generalized system legitimacy. It was bolstered by legislation which institutionalized a system of racial patronage directed mainly at the black lower-class dissidents (see Chapter 3).

With the post-1973 oil boom, there was a restored commitment both to the system and the regime among most segments of the population. This was not the case however, for a significant proportion of the country's black youths, forced to face unemployment, poverty, and their own uncompetitiveness in an increasingly industrialized environment. These negative effects of the regime's mixed-economy capitalist policies began to open the way to racial outbidding within this group. Black youths began to articulate their own rejection of the political, social, and cultural systems in the form of Rastafarianism, a philosophy developed among black lower-class Jamaicans and rooted in the rejection of Europeanism as "evil." For the most part, its Trinidadian variant was politically benign. Nonetheless a few of its adherents turned to political violence. As a result, episodes of political terrorism began to increase after 1977 with incidents of bombing, attacks on security outposts, and attacks on government officials (*Caribbean Contact*, August 1980: 15). Enjoying generalized legitimacy, the regime was easily able to contain and overcome these violent challenges (see *Caribbean Contact*, August 1977: 1).

Breakdowns of political order and stability in Trinidad have, thus, been periodic. Generalized system legitimacy was preserved partly because the regime did not have to alter the fundamentals of the constitution, as these pertain to elections and political representation, to remain in power. It was also able to sustain majority support, except during 1970–3, because of racial appeal to the black lower classes and the support it enjoyed from the country's middle and upper classes. Episodes of erosion of system legitimacy were confined to the black lower-class segment of the population during periods of economic crisis. For the most part, therefore, conditions of regime survival, as they pertain to majoritarian support, did not conflict with the conditions for political order and stability. This is despite the existence of a constitution that virtually excluded the East Indian lower classes from political representation. At the same time, however, the regime showed itself capable of employing coercion and control to stay in power when faced with a generalized loss of both regime and system legitimacy.

Regime survival and self-sustaining development

I have dwelt extensively in the previous chapter upon the economic conditions of regime survival in Guyana and Trinidad. In Trinidad, these conditions led to an almost exclusive concentration upon the energy-based sector of the economy, which is dominated by international investors; upon the satisfaction of the accumulative demands of the local private sector; and upon the distribution of massive amounts of generalized patronage. In Guyana, these conditions came to be based upon the appropriation of the assets of the private sector by the state, and the use of state resources for the accumulative interests of the administrative middle class and to finance a program of coercion and control. In addition, in Guyana the distribution of state resources came to be rooted in an extensive clientelistic network centered around the state-controlling elite. Despite their differences, conditions of regime survival in both countries came with debilitating developmental costs.

Trinidad

In the previous chapter I discussed of the pattern of allocation of state resources which led to the development of an energy-based industrialization program, growth of an import-dependent local manufacturing sector, and a massive program of state construction. The central feature of these undertakings was their failure to develop internal linkages with the rest of the economy and their absolute dependence upon external inputs, foreign skills, and technology, and export markets (see Hintzen 1981: 147–62). Their most visible benefits were the employment and incomes generated by construction and local manufacturing.

The policies which informed such a pattern of allocation were conditioned by the commitment of the regime to a strategy of capitalist development. The argument for capitalist policies of this sort is that they generate economic growth through increased foreign investment and heightened local business activity. This provides to the local population enormous opportunities for employment with incomes high enough to guarantee social and economic betterment for the majority (see, for example, Rostow 1960; Lewis 1954; Ranis and Fei 1961). As the pool of capital resources expands, the benefits that accrue to investors are inevitably and immutably "trickled down" to the vast majority of persons on the lower rungs of the socio-economic ladder.

This was not the case in Trinidad. The benefits that were supposed to have accrued to the lower classes were hardly realized. The emphasis upon capital intensive ventures ran counter to the need for job expansion. Thus, the task of supporting and encouraging labor-creating economic activity fell upon the shoulders of the state. In this the PNM regime was hindered by economic demands created by its own policies and programs. The state's job-creating efforts remained confined, largely, to non-productive activities.

The potential for self-sustaining economic growth and for generation of productive employment rested in the development of the country's agricultural and fishing resources. It is these that offer the greatest chances for increasing domestic input into the economy and for a solution to the problem of galloping unemployment and underemployment.

Conditions of regime survival preempted the implementation of a viable agricultural and fishing policy. The East Indian population, which has an almost exclusive predomination as agricultural labor and own-account small- and medium-sized farmers, was not politically strategic for the PNM's hold on power. The regime depended for its mass support upon the racial mobilization of lower-class blacks. To survive it had to allocate resources in ways that proved most beneficial to the middle- and upper-class sectors of society while engaging in a system of racial patronage directed at this black lower-class population. This meant that spending upon agriculture had to be neglected. Such neglect was clearly evident in the pattern of developmental spending undertaken by the regime.

Of development allocations totalling TT$2·4 billion located in the 29 special funds at the beginning of 1977 (see Table 5.1, pp. 148–9), agriculture, through the Food Development Fund, got TT$42·8 million or a mere 2 percent. Only TT$6·7 million of this was actually withdrawn from the Fund to be spent on agricultural development. The rest was invested in the private sector.

The regime's neglect of agriculture is reflected in a drop in the industry's share of the GDP from 6·3 percent in 1966 to 3·6 percent in 1976. Between 1970 and 1976 the values of the contribution of export agriculture to the

Political and economic costs   177

GDP at constant prices (1970 base) fell from TT$12·9 million to TT$7·9 million – a decline of 38·8 percent. The contribution of domestic agriculture to the GDP at constant prices (1970 base) increased slightly from TT$32·2 million to TT$46·0 million, a mere 2 percent per annum as opposed to a 16 percent annual growth rate for the entire economy between 1966 and 1976 and a 20·9 percent growth between 1970 and 1976 (Central Statistical Office 1977). The industry's share of total employment dropped from 22 to 13 percent in the same seven-year period. The absolute number of pesons employed in agriculture, forestry, hunting, and fishing dropped from 71,800 in 1971 to 49,700 in 1975 (*Annual Statistical Digest*, 1974–5).

Agricultural financing from sources external to the sector was limited at best. In 1975, commercial loans for agriculture accounted for only 2·3 percent (TT$21·5 million) of all loans compared with a figure of 4·7 percent (TT$8·1 million) in 1966. When inflation is taken into account, the real absolute increase in the level of funding from commercial sources was negligible. Moreover, most of these loans went to the large cultivators of export crops rather than to the small farmer. Thus the small farmer was plagued by inadequate financing and left without the wherewithal to improve extremely low levels of productivity, estimated in 1972 to be 21·6 percent of the national average.

The demise and neglect of agriculture was also directly related to the regime's policies of capitalist development. In Chapter 5 it was shown how regime survival after 1973 came to be linked to the securing of massive transfers of oil-generated surpluses to the state without jeopardizing the interests of foreign transnationals in energy-related industries. This was done through a policy of state capitalization in the form of equity investments in foreign oil and energy-based projects and a change in the tax structure to ensure a greater proportion of surplus transfers to the state. The strategy succeeded because of the tremendous increases in profits generated in the oil industry as a result of dramatically higher oil prices on the world market.

With massive state surpluses, the regime was able to meet the domestic conditions for its own survival, namely: satisfying the accumulative claims of the country's private sector and its middle classes while securing greater control of the domestic economy and meeting the economic demands of its lower class black supporters through a massive system of patronage. As was pointed out, such a policy proved highly inflationary, driving wages and prices dramatically upwards (see Chapter 5). This proved disastrous for the labor-intensive agricultural sector.

High wages in the oil and oil-related sectors were sustained by the relatively low contribution of the wage bill to total costs of production.

Comparatively high wages in the state sector were supported by considerable increases in state revenue from petroleum. High wages in the service sector were sustained by the high price individuals and companies were able to charge for the services provide to the oil companies and to their highly paid employees. All of this had a depressing effect upon agriculture. Competition for labor with these high-paying sectors forced agricultural wages up under conditions where the wage bill was a major contributor to cost of production. Attempts at modernization within the industry were frustrated by lack of funds, whilst inflation and a spiralling wage bill acted to reduce profit margins to levels inadequate for self-financing of developmental needs. Without adequate funding from the commercial sector and from the state, there ensued continued declines in production and productivity.

Because the predominantly East Indian agricultural producers and workers did not constitute a politically strategic group, agricultural declines had no effect on regime survival. The neglect of domestic agriculture might even have proved beneficial in the short run. With massive surpluses of foreign exchange, the regime was able to embark upon importation of foreign-grown foodstuffs at prices much cheaper than would have obtained locally given the spiral of prices and wages. In other words, the availability of foreign exchange surpluses served to justify and legitimize a "cheap food" policy which proved beneficial to urban consumers by driving the price of food downwards.[1]

The net effect was an enormous increase in the importation of foodstuffs. Between 1966 and 1976 imports of meat and its by-products increased at an average annual rate of 19·1 percent. Dairy products increased at a rate of 12·3 percent, cereals at 31 percent and fruits and vegetables at 32·3 percent (see *White Paper on Agriculture*, 1978: 11). By 1981 imports of foodstuffs were valued at TT$835 million as compared with a total value of local agricultural production (including export agriculture and production for local consumption) of TT$443·4 million. Agricultural imports increased by 8·4 percent over the 1981 figure to TT$905 million in 1982 (see *Quarterly Economic Bulletin*, March 1983).

The tremendous growth in oil-generated foreign exchange surpluses rendered export agriculture redundant and economically irrelevant except

[1] Michael Lipton (1980: 67) discusses what he sees as "the systematic action by most governments in poor countries to keep down food prices." He sees this in terms of an "urban bias" in policy. "The urban employer wants food to be cheap, so that his workforce will be well fed and productive. The urban employee wants cheap food too, it makes whatever wages he can extract from the boss go further." When the conditions of regime survival rests almost exclusively with the support of the urbanized population, "cheap food" policies become imperative.

for its contribution to total employment. Thus, the production of export crops (cocoa, coffee, and citrus) began to suffer considerably from state neglect. The share of profits in the value added of output for export agriculture (the proportion of profits in the final price minus the costs of initial raw resources) which was as high as 45 percent in 1963 dropped sharply to 6 percent by 1971 (Inter-American Economic and Social Council 1974). Even more dramatic declines affected the sugar industry, 96 percent of which was acquired by the state in 1970. In this case, the general picture came to be one of an industry, which contributed 53·7 percent to the GDP of agriculture at factor costs, fighting to cover its investments as it suffered from steadily rising costs of production.

The implications of the agricultural decline for self-sustaining economic development are that Trinidad became increasingly incapable of satisfying its food needs locally, unable to sustain growth in employment generating productive activity, and incapable of creating the conditions for internally integrated economic growth.

The beginning of economic crisis

Thus, by the beginning of 1980, the economy of Trinidad and Tobago became absolutely tied to a continued ability to sustain massive amounts of oil-generated foreign exchange surpluses and massive transfers of oil revenue to the state. It also depended upon the continued availability of tremendous amounts of fiscal surpluses to be poured as liquidity into the domestic economy, upon a continuing upward spiral of state spending, upon a tremendous amount of state investment in foreign and local business ventures, and upon state underwriting of domestic capital expansion. All of these conditions were tied to a capacity for continued high earnings by the country's crude production. They proved consistent with the economic prerequisites of regime survival, tied as they were to satisfying the accumulative demands of the oil transnationals and of the country's upper and middle classes, and the patronage demands of its black lower class. Such prerequisites preempted the implementation of an internally integrated developmental program. As a result, economic performance became even more firmly tied to the performance of a single-product cluster (oil and its byproducts) on the international market.

The increasing fragility of the economy of Trinidad and Tobago soon became highly evident. In 1981 the country began to experience significant declines in oil production, declines in the price of its crude outputs, and continued declines in refinery throughout. These had begun as early as 1978.

Between that year and 1981 the real value added of the petroleum sector dropped at an annual rate of 6·6 percent (see Bobb 1983: 93). In 1978 export earnings in the petroleum sector were 15 percent below those for 1977 (see *Journal of Commerce*, 16 April 1979), and there were warnings from the International Monetary Fund that the oil-generated surplus "could disappear as quickly as it came." This was in view of projected continued declines in oil output (see *Financial Times*, 10 January 1979).

In 1982, government expenditure showed a rapid increase of 51 percent over its 1981 level despite a drop in oil revenues from TT$4,253 million to TT$3,531 million. The decline represented a drop of 17 percent and was the first since the beginning of the boom in 1973 (see Bobb 1983: 94). Such an increase was made necessary by the fact that continued economic stability was tied to expansions in state expenditure and even more so by a deep and growing recession in the non-oil sectors.

In 1982, there was a fiscal deficit, the first since 1973, which totalled TT$3,300 million, equivalent to 18·5 percent of the country's GDP (Bobb 1983: 95). Also, for the first time in nine years there was a balance of payments deficit. The twin problems of a fiscal deficit and a balance of payment deficit spelled disaster for the economy. Their real effects were delayed by a decision on the part of the government to withdraw TT$2,941 million from its accumulated savings that had accrued over the years of the oil boom and by drawing down TT$525 million from its foreign exchange reserves (Bobb 1983: 95). The latter was aimed at covering a foreign exchange deficit of TT$1·5 billion out of reserves totalling TT$7,162 million (*Trinidad and Tobago Review* 1983, vol. 6, no. 9). Despite these efforts, the figure for total public debt in June 1983 increased to TT$3·9 billion when state companies and enterprises were taken into account (*Trinidad Guardian*, 30 June 1983: 3).

The economic implications of all this were staggering. Being absolutely dependent on foreign exchange reserves and upon the accumulated savings of the state, both derived from the petroleum sector, the viability of the national economy in the immediate and short-term future became very uncertain.

The country's industrialization drive was justified in terms of the need to develop an economic alternative to offset exclusive dependence upon the export of petroleum. The lion's share of the investible surpluses of the state was poured into joint ventures with foreign firms to achieve this end. As it turned out, however, this pattern of investment spending quickly proved to be detrimental to long-term prospects for self-sustaining development. That such a pattern was followed had more to do with its consistency with the economic conditions of regime survival in the short run than with general developmental needs. It was a means of capitalizing foreign participation in energy-related industries which brought bonanza profits to foreign investors. In some cases, such profits came in the form of fees and other service charges levelled against the joint ventures by parent companies which more than offset losses suffered by the productive entities. The industrialization drive also created opportunities for earning high profits for local entrepreneurs in supportive services and for those providing facilities and supplies. Finally, it created opportunities for high earnings for the country's salaried, professional, and skilled workers.

With generous fiscal surpluses available to finance losses in the country's new industrialization drive, the non-viability of major undertakings posed few problems. However, when surpluses began to decline and foreign exchange became scarce, these highly import-dependent industries began to take a financial toll on the state.

Soon, problems began to emerge in almost every one of the ventures associated with the energy-based industrialization drive. Projected non-availability of markets for a proposed aluminum plant forced postponement in the completion of its construction. The iron and steel plant began to suffer losses, also relating to limited international demand for its products. High costs of production in the fertilizer plant resulted in a deficit between 1977 and 1982 of TT$56·8 million. An estimated price tag of TT$4,500 million to complete a liquid natural gas facility forced a cessation of construction. There was little guarantee that, once completed, international markets would be found for the latter's products. High costs of production led to a permanent reliance upon state subsidy to ensure the continued operation of a cement plant. In other words, all the major investments of state's resources in high-energy ventures, both in terms of loans and equity, were proving to be financially disastrous. With the further infusion of state resources to prop up these industries, state expenditure began to grow at a time when revenues to support such growth were declining rapidly (see *Alliance News*, November 1982: 8).

Faced with a growing crisis, the regime was forced to implement measures aimed at cutting state expenditure, saving foreign exchange, and raising revenue from the non-oil sectors of the economy. As early as 1981, it began to abandon a number of state-funded projects after considerable expenditure (see *Trinidad Guardian*, 30 June 1983). In 1983, new fiscal measures were legislated which effectively removed and reduced subsidies on basic consumer items such as fuel, building material, and foodstuffs. Tariffs were increased on various public utilities such as telephone, electricity, and transport. Plans were begun to introduce a sales tax as a means of raising additional revenue (see *Budget Speech*, 1983). In 1985, the government devalued its currency by 33 percent and placed severe restrictions on the export of funds. Finally, the state began a massive program of retrenchment which contributed to a drop in total employment from 411,000 in 1984 to 392,000 in 1985 (*Trinidad Guardian*, 17 June 1986: 4).

In sum, because of the economic conditions of survival the regime had to employ the state's massive foreign exchange surpluses and its enormous state savings to support the accumulative claims of foreign investors and the country's middle and upper classes while developing an elaborate system of patronage aimed at its black lower-class supporters. This preempted the development of a viable strategy for self-sustaining development which, to be successful, had to be rooted in the expansion and diversification of domestic and export agriculture. Such a program of state expenditure, it was shown, would have proved politically disastrous.

The problem for the regime centered around the use of the enormous reserves of natural gas, foreign exchange, and fiscal surpluses. In providing capital financing for foreign endeavors through equity participation in energy-based industries, the regime made a choice that was consistent with the conditions for its own political survival. The choice of an alternative strategy more consistent with the conditions for self-sustaining development was preempted. Such a strategy might have involved the employment of fiscal surpluses to finance a program of agricultural and fisheries development, an industrial development program employing domestic resources and geared towards domestic and regional (Caribbean) needs, and the employment of technology that was appropriate to the skills and demands of the region. Infrastructural development might have been geared towards such a program and the country's abundant energy supply might have been converted to the achievement of its goals.

The regime could have chosen to attract energy-intensive industries without providing capital financing either in the form of loans or equity participation. This would have ensured that a demand was there for the country's gas reserves. At the same time it would have avoided the risk involved in investing in non-viable industries. Foreign investors would have been forced to be much more prudent in their choice of industries were they to carry fully the burden of losses in their local subsidiaries. Sensible tax policies such as those formulated for crude production could have easily ensured the transfer of surpluses from such industries to the state. Foreign exchange surpluses might have been more prudently invested in the Caribbean region either directly through private ventures, or through regional financial institutions such as the Caribbean Development Bank. A case might even be made for capital investments in Europe and North America to ensure high returns until the necessary preconditions for capital absorption in the domestic and or regional economy were in place. The country's gas reserves might have become available to satisfy the energy needs of agriculture, fishing, and domestic industry as well as for domestic consumer consumption at cheap rates. The state's program of infrastructural development might have been directed to these ends, in addition to those undertakings necessary to attract energy-based foreign industry.

The problem with the program outlined above is that it would have threatened regime survival. The East Indian lower-class population would have found itself in the mainstream of its benefits, given the emphasis on agricultural development. This would have left the regime vulnerable to outbidding within the black population upon which its majoritarian support rested. Traditional domestic business rooted in finance, commerce, and manufacturing under licence to foreign firms would have found itself largely left out of such a program of development. Support from this sector was a strategic pivot in regime survival. Finally, foreign investors would have found themselves without the benefits of cheap domestic financing and without state participation in non-viable domestic ventures where profits were made through licencing fees and charges for services and the like that accrued to the home office. The international resources of these companies might easily have been brought to bear on the regime and decisions might have been made to contract exploration and production activities in the oil-producing sector (see Chapter 5). In other words, the program outlined above for self-sustaining development would have proved inconsistent with those conditions for regime survival related to the satisfaction of the accumulative claims of foreign investors and the domestic business class. It would also have proved detrimental to the conditions of mass support rooted in the regime's racial appeal.

Guyana

Guyana is endowed with abundant agricultural, mineral, and hydro resources. The problem, however, is that regime survival has depended upon the use of the country's economic surpluses to satisfy the accumulative demands of the most non-productive sectors of the economy: the state bureaucratic sector and the security, coercive, and surveillance branches of government. It has also depended upon a program of spending on urban services, facilities, and infrastructure to cater to the needs of the regime's middle-class urban supporters. This pattern of spending comes at the cost of rural and agricultural development and of infrastructural development for the exploitation of the country's abundant natural resources.

The regime's absolute initial dependence upon racial support preempted the choice of policies which was best suited to self-sustaining development. As with Trinidad, the major beneficiaries of such a program would have been the East Indian rural population. In fact, it was opposition to just such a program which provoked the mobilization of state workers against the PPP regime beginning in 1962 (see Chapters 2 and 3).[2]

During the 1970s the regime's program of state expansion was geared toward the satisfaction of the accumulative demands of the country's black middle classes upon which regime survival depended. Its basis was the nationalization of the assets of all of the major foreign companies in the country. This decision resulted in economic and political retaliation by powerful international actors. The consequent economic decline forced the regime to rely almost exclusively upon coercion, surveillance, and control by a small cadre of party elite to stay in power. More and more, the meagre and diminishing resources of the state had to be employed to this end.

Because of the regime's choice of economic policies there was a serious deterioration in the Guyanese economy to a point where the state became unable to guarantee even the basic necessities of life to the population. At the same time, with the system of coercion, surveillance, and control in place, regime survival became freed from conditions relating to the satisfaction of the accumulative claims of any sector of the population excluding the upper echelons of military, security, and surveillance branches of the state and the small group of party and governing elite in control of the administrative and corporate branches of the state bureaucracy. The regime thus came to be quite capable of surviving generalized economic crises.

State expansion, state ownership, and control of the assets of all the major companies in the private sector, regime control of all the agencies of mass mobilization, and the development of formidable coercive and surveillance

[2] Programs of agricultural and rural development initiated by the PPP government between 1957 and 1964 were either curtailed or dropped entirely by the PNC when it assumed power. In the early part of the 1970s, the party embarked on a Feed, Clothe and House Ourselves Programme (FCH) which involved plans to employ domestic resources to meet domestic needs. At the state level, a program of Co-operative Development was initiated to catapult blacks into agriculture, fishing, and small and mid-scale industry. At the party level, attempts were made to expand the base of support by recruiting East Indians into the PNC. The co-operative strategy was abandoned in favor of a program of state expansion. Attempts to recruit East Indian support met with such vehement hostility that party leaders quickly resorted back to racial exclusivism (see Chapters 3 and 5 above, and Hintzen 1975: Chapter 11).

capacities came to be the pillars of regime survival in Guyana. Initially these ensured the satisfaction of the accumulative demands of the black middle class through the transfer of resources from the private to the public sector. They also ensured demobilization of the political opposition including the domestic private sector and the rural East Indian population.

It was envisaged that with nationalization, the revenue available to the state would increase enormously through profits generated by the state corporate sector. However, as the new managers were soon to discover, profitable production was ultimately dependent upon conditions operative in the international market. Local industries in small third world states have little leverage upon the prices fetched for their products and these, in turn, have little relation to costs of production. Secondly, economic planners are quite impotent in controlling costs of production in the state-run enterprises since these are highly responsive to costs of inputs imported from the Western industrialized economies. Thirdly, the separation of the nationalized state-owned operations from vertically and horizontally integrated international corporate structures means that losses cannot be cancelled out by gains in other subsidiaries located in different countries. The state must sustain these losses and await more fortuitous increases in the prices of its products to offset them. So far, the surplus generated during peaks in the international market for Guyanese products have been insufficient to sustain economic parity. Finally, nationalization of the Guyanese economy called forth the need for enormous amounts of finance capital, increasing considerably the debt burden of the country. At the end of 1979 the debt servicing commitments of the state were so severe on the budget that the government was forced to refinance 80 percent of the debt installments due in 1980 and 1981 (*Journal of Commerce*, 4 February 1980).

Like Trinidad, therefore, the conditions of regime survival continued to call forth policies which tied the country's economy even more firmly to export earnings and to enormous surplus generation in industries whose products were marketed internationally. Unlike the case of Trinidadian crude, however, the international economic environment became increasingly unfavorable for the products of the Guyanese economy.

After unprecedented highs in 1974 and 1975, the price of sugar fell to a point where in 1978 local costs of production per ton was G$301 above the price fetched on the world market (*Guyana Chronicle*, 21 July 1978). While most of the country's sugar continued to be marketed under the terms of an agreement between the EEC and the ACP countries, the more favorable prices were not enough to prevent losses in the industry. At the same time a deteriorating picture in the international steel industry, the major consumer of calcined bauxite, caused a decline in markets for the country's bauxite industry. Between 1978 and 1980 sugar production averaged 40,000 tons less than the output for 1969, and bauxite and alumina outputs fell significantly below the record levels produced soon after nationalization.

All the above had visible effects upon the economy. After a high of G$250 million in 1975, the country's foreign reserves fell to minus G$175 million in 1979 and the national debt increased to G$1·8 billion from a figure of G$267 million in 1970 and G$673 million in 1974 (Thomas 1980; see also *Journal of Commerce*, 4 February 1980, and *Financial Times*, 23 February 1980).

In view of continued and persisting poor economic performance in the international sector, the regime was forced to raise revenue from direct taxes on incomes, custom duties, purchase taxes and the like, and to remove subsidies on essential consumer items. Measures were also instituted to curtail imports in efforts to minimize deficits in the balance of payments. In an economy characterized by a high propensity to import, these measures invariably cut the importation of essential items.

By the beginning of 1978 economic hardships were such as to produce severe cutbacks in capital projects. The state's current expenditure was drastically curtailed and state employees had to be retrenched. Balance-of-payments problems forced the regime to cut back even further on imports, producing severe shortages of essentials and affecting the capacity of the state to provide essential services. These combined problems produced an unemployment figure estimated to be 30 percent of the labor force of approximately 352,000 (Thomas 1980).

Economic deterioration continued to the point where the economy was incapable of meeting food, health, education, and welfare needs of the population. There was a dramatic decline in food production. Between 1968 and 1978 the supply of milk fell by 56 percent and had become almost non-existent by 1983. Between 1977 and 1983 beef production had fallen by 30 percent. Poultry production fell 64 percent in the two years between 1981 and 1983. The availability of pork fell between 1981 and 1982 by 20 percent. To these problems was added a total ban on the importation of wheaten flour in April 1982 because of balance-of-payments problems (see *Guyana Update*, January–February 1984).

The food shortage produced a nutritional crisis for the population. Results of a survey conducted by the country's Ministry of Health during the first quarter of 1983 revealed that 49 percent of the country's children below five years of age suffered from moderate to severe malnutrition. Deaths from malnutrition recorded at the country's main hospital increased 335 percent over the period 1982–3. In the population of pregnant women 74·9 percent had inadequate dietary intake while there were dramatic increases in dietary-related diseases and infective and parasitic diseases resulting from poor and inadequate diet (see *Catholic Standard*, 16 October 1983).

General economic performance was further impaired as a result of continued and increasing difficulties experienced by the state in maintaining services and facilities. This was particularly true of water, electricity, and transport.

As was the case in Trinidad, all the problems mentioned above stemmed directly from an inability to check declines in foreign-exchange earnings and, relatedly, in state revenue in an economy that was primarily export-dependent. The decline in the productive sectors for export in Guyana was particularly precipitous after 1980, particularly between 1982 and 1983 when GDP fell by 10·6 percent. In all, export earnings for sugar, rice, and bauxite fell by 12·3 percent between 1982 and 1983 in a continuing downward spiral.

Poor economic performance produced, by September 1983, an external public debt of US$700 million which required, in 1984, US$120 million in debt servicing alone – an estimated 42 percent of projected export receipts for that year. In September 1983 the built-up arrears in medium and long-term debt payment was estimated at US$32 million and arrears for payments for imported goods and services was US$250 million on 31 December, 1983. At the time, the generated public sector deficit was G$727·34 million as compared to an estimated current revenue for 1984 or G$554 million. The latter was expected to cover an estimated state current expenditure of G$789 million producing a further projected deficit of G$235 million, exclusive of an additional G$128 million to cover the funding of external debt. It was estimated that for 1984 there would be losses of G$141 million for the Guyana Sugar Corporation and G$127 million for the state bauxite operation. No surpluses were expected to be generated in the rest of the public corporate sector (all these figures were taken from the Guyana *Budget Speech*, 1984).

Clearly, the Guyanese economy was in the depths of crisis at the beginning of 1984. At the time, the country was hard pressed to meet its most minimal foreign exchange needs because of an inability to obtain short-term financing.

Thus, in Guyana the opportunities for short-term economic viability and long-term self-sustaining development were foreclosed by the prerequisites of regime survival. In Trinidad, the policy choices followed logically from the regime's adopted program of development. In Guyana, this was not the case. From the time the PNC gained full control of the state in 1967 it had in place plans for a developmental program which were consistent with the

188   *Political and economic costs*

developmental needs of the country. The problem was that the conditions for survival preempted implementation of these plans.

On the surface, the problems of the post-1974 Guyanese economy were identical to those experienced by all net oil-importing developing countries faced with a rapidly escallating oil bill, galloping inflation, and a recession in the Western economies. In addition, Guyana had to face Western hostility after its program of nationalization, its declared commitment to socialist transformation, and its increasingly anti-West foreign policy position. To a large degree, however, the problems stemmed from the regime's failure to implement developmental programs which would have substituted domestic resources for imports and which would have expanded and diversified production for export. By virtue of the resources available in the country, such a program would have gone a considerable way to insulate the economy from the effects of the post-1973 international economic crisis. At the same time, without the imperative of massive state expansion into the private sector, the regime might have been able to implement a much more viable program of economic control free from the need to nationalize companies whose long-term viability was in question and which had been spared the consequences of Western economic retaliation.

It was argued in Chapter 3 that given the character of sugar and bauxite production in Guyana, nationalization offered the best way to ensure regime survival by satisfying the accumulative demands of the country's black middle and lower-middle classes. Public takeover of the economy was undertaken to satisfy the imperative of reallocating the earnings and assets of the private sector into the state sector. It acted, however to foreclose opportunities for implementing policies towards the country's multinationals that were consistent with long-term developmental needs. The state acquired the assets of the bauxite and sugar companies at a time when the prospects for future earnings were diminishing. The need to finance the costs of acquiring these foreign assets as well as to operate them subsequent to their nationalization considerably increased the debt burden of the country. This tied the regime even more firmly to an inflexible policy aimed at continued and exclusive dependence upon the products of these industries.[3]

---

[3] This is not to deny that, when the decision to nationalize was being made, the regime *believed* in the rectitude of its policies. Nonetheless, the decision was made more for its *political* implications (the exemption being the nationalization of Demba which was made more out of an issue of national sovereignty). It was politically strategic for the regime to nationalize in view of the benefits that would accrue to its middle-class supporters. Internationally, the decision was critical in placing Guyana firmly in the ranks of the socialist and third world radical regimes. This might explain why much more effort was not placed in examining the long-term economic implications of nationalization.

Given the dominant role of Guyanese calcined production in the world market, the regime might have used its leverage derived therefrom to change the tax structure of the industry ensuring a greater transfer of surpluses to the state. This would have come without the burden of purchasing and financing an industry soon to be faced with problems of declining international demand and increasing international competition. Similarly, the growing noncompetitiveness of sugar on the international market should have forestalled nationalization. Instead, a program of agricultural diversification for export and domestic production should have been undertaken.

The country's resources were abundantly suited to a massive program of agricultural diversification, the fundamentals of which were already in place when the PNC inherited power in 1964. The PPP government had made far-reaching plans for agricultural development involving the drainage and irrigation of hundreds of thousands of acres of high-quality unused land. This program was abandoned by the coalition government only to be resuscitated by the PNC regime during the 1970s when the means for its implementation were no longer available. Had it been undertaken before the nationalization of sugar, the state might have been in a position to incorporate the lands of the sugar companies into its program of agricultural diversification as they began to suffer from the inevitable production declines that became characteristic of the late 1970s.

The potential for agricultural development and diversification is enormous. Less than 50 miles from the capital city, and located on the costal plain, 433,000 acres of land are available and suited for production of rice, food crops, corn, cattle, and other livestock. To these can be added hundreds of thousands of acres of additional land along the coast and in the hinterland. The development of these lands would allow a vastly expanded rice production as well as production of numerous food and vegetable crops, chickens, eggs, sheep, goats, and dairy and beef cattle.

The country also enjoys an undeveloped potential for a vastly expanded freshwater and saltwater fishing and shrimping industry and for significant increases in the country's output of forest products. Were these potentials to be converted into actual production, the country's export earnings would increase significantly while its import bill would be dramatically cut. This is in addition to the tremendous increases in employment opportunities and in the opportunity for development of downstream and upstream linkage industries as a consequence of these projects.

The most devastating effect upon the country's economy after 1973 stemmed from the phenomenal increase in the cost of energy. Again, domestic alternatives to imported energy could have been available if a

190 *Political and economic costs*

sound developmental policy was implemented. Guyana has abundant potential for small-, medium-, and large-scale hydro-electric production. The country also has potential for the development of charcoal and the production of biogas. In addition, known reserves of oil and gas have been discovered yet were left wanting from the absence of funds for exploration and development.

The existence of all the resources detailed above and their potential for development were well established when the PNC took office in 1964. However, the conditions of regime survival dictated a program of state expansion in the traditional sectors of the economy, allocation of state surpluses in the urban sectors of the country, and massive growth in the state bureaucratic and security apparatus. This was so because a program of agricultural and hinterland development would have proved most beneficial for the East Indian agricultural population and for small- and medium-scale business engaged in local commerce and industry. The latter comprised a significant number of Portuguese and Chinese. Current expenditure would have had to be kept to a minimum, placing severe limits on growth in the state bureaucratic and security apparatus. At the same time, urban growth would have had to be curtailed, urban expenditure cut to a minimum and a program of rural relocation of the population encouraged. Those most affected by such a program would have been the regime's black middle- and lower-class supporters. This would have left the regime open to outbidding at a time when its apparatus of coercion and control was not in place.

If the program of development was implemented there was the real possibility of strengthening the political opposition by putting resources in the hands of the East Indian, Portuguese and Chinese populations. In other words, to have embarked upon a program that was consistent with self-sustaining development would have been tantamount to political suicide.

It was only in 1978, when regime power became firmly rooted in coercion and control, that the political directorate was free to embark on a program consistent with self-sustaining development. By then, the foreign and domestic private sector had been virtually eliminated or, in the case of the latter, co-opted; the institutions of mass mobilization were firmly under state control; and the regime's coercive capacity was such as to prevent political dissent, organized or otherwise, from affecting its own survival. That year the regime unfolded a four-year developmental program centered around infrastructural development to bring several thousand acres of agricultural land into production; a massive forestry program; phenomenal expansion in fishing and shrimping; a program of alternative energy development in the form of charcoal and biogas; a massive hydro-electric project involving the construction of a 3,000 megawatt generating plant surrounded by an industrial complex; the upgrading of another hydro-electric generating station; mineral exploration; and the production of oil, gas, kaolin, and manganese (see *Budget Speech*, 1978).

At the time of the plan's formulation, however, the country was already deep in the economic crisis that was affecting every aspect of economic performance. Economic growth rates were experiencing declines, which continued up to the time of writing in 1986; spiralling budget deficits were forcing drastic cutbacks in both current and capital expenditure; and declining export earnings, increasing costs of imports, and high interest rates were combining to produce a rapidly escalating external debt. In other words, the country was incapable of financing its planned developmental program either from internal or external sources.

Given the regime's recent history of nationalization, socialism, and anti-Western policies, private foreign investors had written off the country long before. Moreover, after a decade of tremendous inflation, the cost of financing the program of development had risen to a level way above that which, even under the best of circumstances, could have been funded from all available sources. The regime had waited until too late, especially in view of the international financial crisis that was producing escalating indebtedness in most LDCs. The plan's implementation was further hindered by the need to divert a tremendous amount of resources into the state apparatus of coercion, control, and regimentation since these had become the new bases of regime survival (see Chapters 3 and 5).

In view of its ideological shift away from a more radical foreign policy in 1978 (see Chapter 3) the regime was able to attract some bilateral funding from the United States and Canada and some multilateral funding from the World Bank mostly for its agricultural, forestry and hydro-electric projects. It was also able to get an IMF loan to ease the burden of its external debt. All of these, however, proved vastly inadequate and the country continued on its downward economic spiral. None of the planned projects came on-stream and, by the early 1980s, the country moved into a state of virtual bankruptcy, unable to obtain even short-term financing for its normal international transactions.

In summary, the economic and political imperatives for regime survival in Guyana led to a pattern of state expansion which preempted the choice of policies that would have guaranteed self-sustaining development. In the process, the private sector was virtually eliminated and access to international resources was foreclosed. Faced with the economic and political backlash of its choices, the regime had to pour an increasing amount of the state's resources into its own survival. This served to exacerbate the conflict between development and survival during a period of deepening economic crisis. In the end, the regime found itself without the wherewithal to pursue any program of self-sustaining development because of opportunities foreclosed in the process of guaranteeing its own survival.

Regime survival and self-sustaining development in Guyana and Trinidad

The comparison between Guyana and Trinidad serves to highlight the political dimension of the problem of development. The failure to achieve developmental transformation in LDCs may be not merely the result of inadequate access to resources for financing development programs or of a deficiency in natural resources and developmental infrastructure. Regimes may be forced to allocate resources in keeping with their own survival needs. In doing so they may have to undertake measures that preempt choices which are consistent with developmental prerequisites.

Despite tremendous capital and foreign exchange surpluses in post-1973 Trinidad, the regime was unable to implement a program of self-sustaining development. Political imperatives prevented use of such surpluses for developmental transformation. Resources had to be channeled into sectors of the economy where growth exacerbated the problems of underdevelopment. Similarly, an abundance of agricultural, mineral, and hydro resources in Guyana did not raise the country from the depth of endemic underdevelopment. These resources had to remain undeveloped and unutilized if regime survival was to be guaranteed.

Undoubtedly, there are economic prerequisites for self-sustaining development: (i) the availability of surpluses for investment and/or access to finance capital; (ii) the availability of abundant domestic resources to cater to domestic demand and which can be advantageously employed, given their comparative advantage, for external trade, and; (iii) the existence of a developmental infrastructure which allows the optimum exploitation of the country's resources. At the same time, however, development cannot occur in an environment of political instability given its consequent social disorder. A rapid turnover of regimes constitutes a symptom of this instability. Self-sustaining development is, therefore, best guaranteed when its conditions are consistent with those of regime survival. When they are not, development may be achieved only to the extent that the conditions of survival can be freed from the need to cater to the demands of those domestic and international actors whose interests conflict with the generalized economic interests of the society as a whole. The task for leaders of LDCs is devising strategies which free them from dependence upon these actors without affecting the survival of their own regimes.

Regime survival versus equity and social security functions

In the performance of its equity functions, the state has to guarantee that there is no discrimination against individuals, groups, and members of social and economic categories in the satisfaction of their normative preferences. It has to ensure that the opportunities to acquire these preferences are not diminished or foreclosed in order that the demands of preferred segments of the population are satisfied. Closely related to this is the state's social security function through which every individual is guaranteed the economic, social, and cultural resources necessary for maintaining human dignity and promoting human development and the development of personality.

It becomes clear from the preceeding discussions that performance of equity and social security functions in Guyana and Trinidad conflicted with the conditions of regime survival. Both regimes had to depend upon racial mobilization for gaining and maintaining control of the state under conditions in which the strategic significance of the respective East Indian populations was limited. Racial patronage and black domination of the state apparatus – necessary conditions of regime survival – ruled out any commitment to equity. Indeed, the state apparatus became the instrument for the preservation of an inequitous order upon which political power was based. In both countries regime survival came to rest upon the denial of equitable representation to the East Indian masses and upon a discriminatory pattern of resource allocation away from the rural, lower-class members of that population.

To this is added a class dimension: regime power in Guyana was rooted in the reallocation of the country's resources in a manner where the primary beneficiaries were the country's black and colored middle classes. This came at the expense of members of the country's upper classes, who were virtually eliminated, and of the country's lower classes who became progressively impoverished. In Trinidad, regime survival rested in satisfying the accumulative claims of the country's upper and middle classes. Apart from the beneficiaries of racial patronage, poverty among the lower classes increased in absolute and relative terms.

Naturally, therefore, the state functioned differentially, relative to the race and class position of the individual, in guaranteeing social security in both Guyana and Trinidad. Despite the post-1973 boom in Trinidad, members of the rural East Indian and lower-class black populations still found themselves without fundamental guarantees that their social security needs would be met. In Guyana, the economic crisis eroded the state's capacity to meet its social security functions except to all but a very few who had become pivotal in the system of oligarchic control.

Poverty, unemployment, and skewed income distribution in Trinidad

Differential performance of equity and social security functions in Trinidad can best be measured by focusing on poverty, unemployment, and income distribution. This is because of the almost exclusive role of the state in determining economic prosperity for members of all sectors of society. Such determinations were made through the decisions of state controlling elites in allocating the enormous resources which became available to the state particularly between 1973 and 1980.

It has already been established (see Chapter 5) that the survival of the PNM regime in Trinidad rested upon the development of a mixed economy system of capitalism. This involved state expansion into the private sector, the pouring of state capital and state resources into energy-based capital intensive ventures, and tremendous financial and legislative support for the group of domestic entrepreneurs. Such a choice of strategy acted to preclude spending on a developmental program that would have guaranteed increased income earning and upward mobility opportunities for the country's lower classes.

Thus the exceptionally high growth rate of the GDP following 1973 was not matched by comparative declines in unemployment. From 17 percent in 1973, unemployment decreased only slightly to 14 percent in 1977 – this after enormous efforts to increase public-sector employment by the state. The unemployment problem was most severe among those under 25 years of age. In 1973, for example 39 percent of the labor force between 15 and 19 years, and 26 percent of the 20 to 24 age group were unemployed. Later trends in employment suggested no change in this pattern. During 1977, it was estimated by the Ministry of Education that only 20 percent of high school graduates were employable (*Liberation*, August 1977).

This problem of unemployment had to do with the choice by the regime to pour the lion's share of the state's fiscal surpluses into energy-intensive industrialization. As a result, there was very little relationship "between the growth in total output and the growth of total employment" (Central Statistical Office 1978: 14). At the beginning of 1978, the major problem was still one of absorption of the over 50,000 unemployed and of providing incomes adequate to the estimated 82,000 households representing 350,000 persons – a full 34·1 percent of the population – living below the poverty line (*Trinidad and Tobago Review*, June 1978).

There were some efforts at job creation especially in the form of direct state employment. The government sector grew steadily in the proportion of the labor force it employed. In 1965, government workers comprised 15·2 percent of the total labor force while in 1976 this figure had increased to 20·2 percent, making the state the biggest sectoral employer even though it contributed only 7 percent to the GDP. However, growth in state employment was linked to the development of the system of racial patronage. Increases in state employment were sustained by the Special Works Programme (which later became DEWD) that was aimed specifically at providing jobs for the black unemployed in areas of community works, housing, and urban rehabilitation.

At the beginning of 1980, the unemployment picture continued to be extremely bad. While the government estimated that 53,600 persons were officially out of work (12 percent of the work force) it was suggested that the true unemployment figures were closer to 85,000–90,000 (16–17 percent) (see *Caribbean Contact*, September 1980). At the same time, state policies had produced tremendous inflation. For example the cost of buying and renting dwellings was growing astronomically. Rents of TT$4,000 per month for family houses and between TT$1,000–2,000 per month for apartments were normal under conditions where most unskilled laborers in the private sector earned around TT$120 per month. An average family home in the suburbs cost TT$250,000 to buy.

As the economic crisis deepened, the regime was forced to make even more concessions to the private sector while cutting back on efforts to alleviate poverty, unemployment and underemployment and to provide for the welfare needs of the population. The state's ability to provide health services, water, and electricity to the general population deteriorated considerably even as the rates charged for the latter two were increasing. Educational performance declined because of the failure of the country's educational development program. At the same time, the unemployment picture increased dramatically. One estimate was that between 1982 and 1983, 50,000 workers had been retrenched with 10,000 coming from the oil sector alone (see *Trinidad and Tobago Review* 1983: vol. 6, no. 10). This came at a time of dramatic declines in state subsidies on essential consumer items.

Meanwhile, the emphasis in state policy on industrialization and upon the development of manufacturing was paying large dividends to the long-established local business class, and to the group of professionals in the

196   *Political and economic costs*

country who stood to benefit from lucrative business ventures and from expanding opportunities created by the economic surge. These two groups are disproportionately white and contain a rapidly growing number of East Indians within them. The policy of public-sector expansion also provided increased opportunities and higher incomes for members of the black and colored middle classes employed in government and in parastatal organizations. Thus, all the sectors of the middle and upper classes, irrespective of racial background, benefited enormously from the regime's policies. These benefits created the conditions for the consolidated support by members of these groups and upon which regime survival rested.

The easy availability of cheap capital for local business was responsible for the progressive development of large conglomerates which forced small- and medium-sized businesses out of the economy. The former, about 10 in number, recorded enormous profits, primarily the result of legislative protection and indirect subsidies from the state (see *Vanguard*, 8 July 1983: 2). Because of the liquidity pumped into the economy by the fiscal surpluses of the state, and because of the extraordinary demand for capital by business and for consumer credit, the country's banking industry also recorded extraordinary levels of profit (see *Vanguard*, 8 July 1983: 2).

The response of the state to the economic crisis of the 1980s was to increase the tax burden on the general population; cut back subsidies on essential consumer items, state utilities and services; cut back on employment; and decrease the level of social security and welfare provided to the population. At the same time, the regime began to engage in economic bail-outs for the multinational corporations while continuing its measures directed at sustaining the high profitability of local conglomerates (see *Trinidad and Tobago Review* 1983: vol. 6, no. 6: 12). It quickly became clear that the paramount function of the state was to serve the accumulative interests of the multinational corporations, the large conglomerates, and the country's middle- and upper-class populations. This preempted considerations of equity and came at the expense of the social security of the lower-class population.

Economic collapse, equity, and social security in Guyana

In Trinidad the problem of equity and social security had to do with how the country's abundant surpluses were allocated. The choice was to do so in such a way that regime survival would be guaranteed. In Guyana, policies undertaken to ensure regime survival acted to produce endemic economic crisis. The organization of a system of control insulated the regime from the

Political and economic costs

effects of this crisis. The generalized social security functions of the state could then have been sacrificed without placing regime survival in jeopardy. The regime was thus free to guarantee to those who directed the system of control and those who headed the security apparatus an inordinate share of the country's wealth.

Since the system of control was rooted in oligarchic domination, the gap between the elite and the rest of the population became quite significant. In 1978, these top leaders in the country earned about G$25,000 annually and senior bureaucrats about G$12,000 to G$15,000. By contrast, unskilled and semiskilled full-time workers in the state sector earned G$3,000. In that year, 75 percent of the work force held these lower-class occupations while unemployment had soared to 30 percent (Hintzen 1981: chapters 2 and 5). The regime did everything to protect the interests of the privileged group. After a devaluation of the dollar in 1981 it increased the salaries of the military and senior bureaucrats to protect them from the invariably higher costs while denying similar increases to all other employees of the state.

Because of declining economic performances, considerations of equity and social security, as defined at the beginning of this chapter could have had no place in regime policy. After 1976, there was no recorded real growth in the economy. Partly as a result, external debt reached US$1 billion by May 1983. The real per capita income for the Guyanese population in 1981 was lower than that of 1970 and 30 percent below that of 1975. During 1981, estimated unemployment exceeded 30 percent (see *Caribbean Contact*, May 1983). To offset the destabilizing consequences of growing impoverishment and inequities all efforts had to be directed towards maintaining the system of coercion and control and sustaining the loyalty of the country's strategic elite.

Regime survival and civil and political rights in Guyana and Trinidad

It becomes clear that any attempt to guarantee the civil and political rights of the Guyanese population would result in regime collapse. Because of its absolute reliance upon coercion, regimentation, control, electoral fraud, patronage, and the absolute loyalty of a small group of political elite, regime survival in Guyana came to depend upon a continued ability to deny civil and political rights to the general population.

The situation is much more complex in Trinidad. Human rights violations in that country came to be covered by a mantle of legitimacy. This was particularly true of the right to participate equally in government. Because of the electoral constitution, the East Indian rural lower classes cannot be said to enjoy fully this right despite the existence of generalized system legitimacy. Were the constitution changed to reflect the numerical strength of the East Indian population, the regime would have found itself unable to maintain an electoral majority.

The absence of full representation for the East Indian population led directly to its relative exclusion from the benefits of state expenditure. Regime neglect of agriculture had a great deal to do with the fact that the East Indian rural population was neither politically strategic nor did it play any significant part in the power equation of the country, at least not until 1986.

The problem of equal access to public resources extended beyond a racially skewed pattern of resource distribution. A party-centered system of patronage and a massive system of elite patronage acted to exclude from the benefits of the state those who were neither elite nor party supporters. Moreover, the series of constitutional amendments discussed in Chapter 3 which strengthened state powers of arrest, search, seizure, and surveillance, when combined with a generalized acceptance of arbitrary violence and brutality by the armed branches of the state, placed in severe jeopardy the civil rights of the population at large as they related to equal protection under the law.

The country managed to maintain a judiciary that was relatively independent of the political elite. But because this judiciary was part of the core of ruling elite of the country, with a firm commitment to the status quo, it functioned to protect elite interests against potential violations by the regime. At the same time, this Trinidadian judiciary exhibited little sympathy for issues of human rights as they pertained to the population at large.

Regime survival in Trinidad came to be rooted in an ability to satisfy the accumulative claims of the country's middle and upper classes and continued ability to deny full and equal political participation to the country's rural East Indian population. Black lower-class political dissent, the result of outbidding, was contained through coercion and control and lower-class political movements were demobilized. By contrast, the country's middle and upper classes managed to guarantee constitutionally the civil and political rights of their own members through the establishment of an independent judiciary.

Regime survival and collective needs in Guyana and Trinidad

Any attempt by the Guyanese and Trinidadian regimes to commit state resources fully to the satisfaction of the collective needs of the two societies (namely social order and stability; self-sustaining economic development; equity; social security; and civil and political rights) would have created conditions where neither could have maintained control of the state apparatus. The dilemma for many third world countries is that any attempt to ensure that these functions are performed brings with it the distinct possibility of an overt manifestation of social, economic, and political conflict and instability. This has to do with (i) the concentration of the resources of power in the hands of a small local elite, (ii) the extreme economic and political vulnerability of the state to international actors and events, and (iii) the mutually reinforcing pattern of relationships between the two.

What the Guyanese and Trinidadian regimes managed to do was to satisfy the terms under which the most strategic local elites and the most powerful international actors continued, however reluctantly, to refrain from behaving in a destabilizing way. In the process, both regimes had to acquiesce to the latter's demands and to become subject to their influence. Such acquiescence acted to foreclose policy choices aimed at the satisfaction of the collective needs of society. As a result, both regimes had to engage in perpetual campaigns of reactive crisis management to prevent mass dissatisfaction from spreading into generalized conflict of the sort which threatened their own survival. It was the success of these campaigns that explained the perpetuation of the two regimes in power.

7. Collective needs versus the demands of powerful actors in less developed countries

The approach that has been employed in the foregoing analysis of Guyana and Trinidad and Tobago is similar to what Samuel P. Huntington (1971: 319–21) calls the "crisis" model of political change. It emphasizes the choices made by a political leadership in the quest to gain and maintain control of the state. It subscribes to the notion, argued by Rustow (1970: 337–63), that the conditions for conquest of power are different from those necessary to ensure political tenure.

Political leaders in LDCs can come to power by directly representing the interests of powerful and strategic actors who are dissatisfied with the existing state of affairs and/or by making alliances with them. In this manner, they can assure themselves of access to resources for use against the political incumbents. These resources vary and can include sheer numbers, financial power, economic control, coercive resources, propaganda, and the like. They can be located in both the domestic and international environments.

To remain in power, the incumbent regime must seek to accommodate dissident actors, either by giving them direct control of political decision-making or by formulating policy to meet their demands, or it must seek to neutralize them. The object of neutralization is to insulate the political, social, and economic systems from the effects of negative and destabilizing actions or to insulate the regime itself from the consequences of such actions.

International actors

International actors can pose the most formidable threat to the stability of regimes in LDCs. The economic, strategic and political demands of these actors can, and normally do, conflict with prerequisites for the satisfaction of collective needs. Regimes might, therefore, be forced to choose between one and the other or to choose to align themselves with those international actors whose agenda are more consistent with the collective needs of their own societies.

Collective needs vs demands of actors in LDCs 201

International actors are aware of the conflict between their own interests and the collective needs of less developed countries. Their willingness to intervene and their manner of intervention are conditioned by their assessment of this conflict and by their perception of the consequences for themselves and the interests they represent were they not to do everything in their power to ensure regime acquiescence to their demands.

Governmental actors

The most powerful and strategic of these international actors are Western governments and Western economic agencies and institutions. This is so for a number of reasons. The economies of almost all LDCs are highly integrated with and highly dependent upon the West as far as imports, markets, and financing are concerned. In addition, the legacy of colonialism and quasi-colonialism has meant a high degree of penetration of Western beliefs, values, and institutional arrangements in the social, political, cultural, and economic systems of the LDCs. This has produced considerable generalized legitimacy for the Western way of doing things, particularly among the middle classes. Such legitimacy has contributed greatly to the enormous influence enjoyed by Western agencies and institutions, both governmental and non-governmental, over domestic actors.

The freedom to pursue collective needs without facing the prospects of retaliation by Western governments has to do with (i) the importance the latter attach to their strategic and economic interests in a particular LDC, and (ii) the prevailing ideology of those in control of foreign policy. The greater its perceived strategic and economic stakes in a particular LDC, the more a Western government would seek to ensure that the regime in power is one that is prepared to acquiesce to its demands, whatever the consequences for the domestic population. Countries where such interests are perceived to be minimal find themselves much more free to adopt programs and policies that might conflict with the interests of Western agencies and organizations. This is illustrated by the enormous post-war efforts to install, protect, and prop up pro-Western regimes in South East Asia, the Middle East, and Latin America because of the perceived political, strategic, and economic stakes. Such efforts were not matched by similar actions in Africa south of the Sahara. The two possible exceptions to this were the Portuguese struggle to maintain its colonial hegemony in its Southern African colonies and Western support for the South African regime.

The nature and pattern of Western intervention and, to a certain extent, its definition of interests, are conditioned by the ideology which informs the foreign policies of a particular Western government. At one extreme is the conservative position associated with the foreign policy "hawk." In the middle is the moderate liberal position of the foreign policy "dove." At the other extreme is the progressive position of the democratic socialist governments of Western Europe.

Under the influence of both doves and hawks, the foreign policies of Western governments tend to embrace active intervention in favor of those political elites advocating a capitalist, free enterprise economic agenda in LDCs. Doves, however, see economic liberalism, social equity, and political moderation as absolute and indispensable elements to the process of third world modernization to which they are firmly committed. This can lead to intervention in favor of political leaders committed to "human rights", mass democratic participation, and economic reform involving redistribution of income. In other words, when doves inform the foreign policy of Western nations, intervention may be such as to promote actively policies aimed at the satisfaction of the collective needs of the LDCs. The major exception to this is in the economic sphere where there is an insistence upon capitalist policies and programs (see Huntington 1971: 285–90; Feinberg 1983: 14–30).

When conservatives direct and dictate the foreign policies of Western nations, LDCs are viewed as battlegrounds in the confrontation against communist, and particularly Soviet, expansionism. All countries become strategically and economically important because of the real threat of them falling, in a domino-like manner, under the Soviet-dominated communist umbrella. Foreign policy is therefore one of aggressive and active intervention in all LDCs to install, support, and prop-up leaders who are unequivocally anti-communist, pro-capitalist, and pro-West. The collective needs discussed in the last chapter are seen to be pertinent only to Western industrialized societies. They are the result of a long history of development and modernization not experienced by LDCs. Attempts to base support for political elites on the latter's commitment to ensure that such needs are satisfied are therefore misinformed, at the least, and invariably dangerous to Western security and economic interests. Since LDCs do not have the wherewithal for the satisfaction of these collective needs, such policies can only result in the overthrow of "moderate autocrats" friendly to Western interests. They can create socio-political chaos which is then exploited by the agents of communist subversion to establish pro-Soviet totalitarian left-wing dictatorships (see, for example, Kirkpatrick 1979; Feinberg 1983: 14–30).

The hawk–dove distinction is quite characteristic of the foreign policy of the United States of America where it is manifest as a tendency toward one or the other position rather than an absolute commitment to either. Moreover, the more the perceived security and economic interests in a particular LDC, the more has been the tendency of the various US governments to pursue hawkish policies toward it.

At the more general level, the administration of President Carter most exemplified a dovish position as opposed to that of President Reagan which has exhibited a distinctly hawkish bent. For the former, civil and human rights became the yardstick upon which much of the support for a regime was based. To this was added attempts at *rapprochement* with radical and progressive LDCs and an unwillingness to intervene to destabilize their governments. To a certain extent, these policies led to the abandonment of President Somoza in Nicaragua and the Shah of Iran in favor of support – tacit or otherwise – for their moderate opponents. It was partly as a result of this that both regimes collapsed.

Dovish policies can considerably diminish the imperative to resolve the conflict between the demands of international actors and the collective needs of society in favor of the former. Regimes in LDCs become free to take action against international interests with a greater certainty that the resources of Western governments will not be employed for the purposes of destabilization.

This is not true when hawks advise the foreign policies of powerful Western governments, for then there is an increased willingness to employ economic, military, and covert action whenever narrowly defined Western interests or the interests of Western actors appear to be jeopardized by the policies and programs of regimes in LDCs. During the administration of President Reagan, for example, the US military was employed in Grenada, Lebanon, and Libya and there was covert military support for groups opposed to radical regimes throughout the world. There was also increased militarization throughout the third world both in terms of an escallated US military presence and of the beefing up of the military arsenals of pro-American governments and groups. The United States also increased economic support for pro-American regimes while employing economic retaliation against progressive regimes. The Reagan administration also actively sought to impose its will upon the economic policies of LDCs to ensure implementation of pro-capitalist, free enterprise programs highly favorable to US investors. While such activism was not enough to save the staunchly pro-American regimes of President Ferdinand Marcos of the Philippines and President Jean-Claude Duvalier of Haiti, it was enough to ensure that Western economic and security interests were not jeopardized by their successors.

Regimes in LDCs might attempt to protect themselves against the intervention of powerful Western states by forging strong alliances with progressive regimes and groups that support their "right of self determination" and their efforts to act in their own national interest. In the West, these groups and regimes usually adhere to the principles of democratic socialism. Such principles lead to foreign policy positions which support a regime's right to pursue the collective needs of its citizens, even at the expense of the perceived economic and security interests of the West. Democratic socialists advocate and support anti-capitalist policies and the right of LDCs to establish relations with communist nations. They strongly reject Western interventionism and any effort at destabilization. At the same time they propose a pattern of economic relations where the beneficiaries are the LDCs themselves.

At the government level, alliances with Western democratic socialist states might offer an LDC regime the chance to pursue alternatives to economic and political relations with the more hawkish countries. Democratic socialist states together with non-governmental groups throughout the West might act to forestall or minimize intervention while providing some degree of freedom to pursue relations with the communist bloc. Such relations may prove important in countering economic, political, and military retaliation by countries pursuing hawkish policies.

International organizations

Because of their multi-nation membership, international organizations are much less interventionist in ways that can affect regime survival. Likewise, their agenda for LDCs are much more likely to be consistent with collective interests than obtains at the bilateral level. The exception to this are the agencies dominated and influenced by Western nations which provide to LDCs resources that are critical for economic stability. These agencies can and do (usually implicitly) serve the interests of Western actors if only because of the particular philosophy which informs their activities. Most important in this regard are the International Monetary Fund (IMF) and (to a lesser degree) the International Bank for Reconstruction and Development (World Bank) and its affiliates. State-controlling leaders of LDCs have been forced to adopt policies and programs dictated by these agencies to stave off or meliorate economic crisis with the full knowledge that the collective needs of their societies would have to be further compromised. The consequences of doing without aid and assistance from these agencies can be economic crisis and political collapse. This has been particularly true of the IMF which has a mandate for maintaining equilibrium in the international monetary system and for the mitigation of disequilibrium in balance of payments at the country-level (see Dell 1984). Powerful Western governments in positions to influence the policies of these agencies can secure their intervention in support of a regime in an LDC or to destabilize it politically. The critical role these agencies play in providing economic and developmental assistance explains why they can be so easily converted into agencies of destabilization.

The more genuinely multinational the *de facto* decision-making process in international agencies, the less are the chances for a hidden agenda in their behavior towards LDCs. This is true even of agencies representing exclusive Western interests. As an example, the European Economic Community (EEC) has implemented a program of association, based on developmental assistance and trade with LDCs, with an agenda that is relatively neutral politically.

It is possible, therefore for an LDC to counteract the destabilization efforts of international actors, including powerful governments. They can do so by appealing to international agencies for direct assistance, by demanding implementation of measures to restrain the offending actors, or by seeking some form of punitive action against them. International agencies and organizations can also act as mediators between LDC regimes and these international actors. The chances for international support for an LDC, however, normally rests upon the argument that the regime-threatening actions of international actors also prevent or make difficult the satisfaction of collective needs. The strategy of securing assistance and support from international agencies might ensure that alternatives to the resources of offending international actors are provided and that the latter are pressured to restrain and check their destabilizing behavior. If the strategy proves successful it might also free a regime to pursue even more independent policies in keeping with its self-interests and to develop alternative international alliances which might have been preempted by its former association. For example, strong international support in the face of retaliation against a regime by a powerful Western government usually frees the regime to pursue relations with Eastern bloc countries. Such relations would have been ruled entirely out of the question when the regime was dependent upon resources transferred as a result of its former alliances with the particular Western government and with its agencies, institutions and companies.

Naturally, the international agencies that are most likely to support LDCs in their conflict with powerful international actors are those where the LDCs themselves have the greatest influence. The various branches of the United Nations, with the exception of its financial bodies and including its General Assembly, have become particularly strategic for LDCs under attack from powerful international actors. So have the Non-Aligned Movement, the group of Commonwealth Nations, and the several regional economic and political associations, organizations, alliances, and *ad hoc* bodies not dominated by the West.

In some instances, however, as has been the case with the Organization of American States (OAS) and the Association of South East Asian Nations (ASEAN), the interests of Western international actors have, at times, been paramount in programs, policies, and actions. The OAS and ASEAN have been employed to support Western, and particularly US, intervention in Asia and Latin America, to support retaliatory actions against governments in the respective regions, to ensure and enforce Western preeminence in the face of East–West confrontation, to protect the security interests of the West, and to legitimize, promote, and encourage policies of member states that are supportive of the interests of Western investors and businesses. This has had to do with the inordinate influence of the United States over these two organizations and, particularly, because of its status as a member of the OAS – exercising at one-time a near hegemony over its policies and actions. Increasingly, however, regional organizations among LDCs are becoming directed towards the promotion and protection of the collective and individual interests of their member states, particularly when these conflict with those of powerful international actors (see Feinberg 1983: 33–61).

International business

International business constitutes a third set of international actors whose interests can conflict with the satisfaction of collective needs. Transnational corporations can control enough resources to determine which sets of leaders run an LDC and which sets of policies these leaders adopt. Invariably, however, irrespective of developmental strategy emphasized, there is bound to be a conflict between regimes in LDCs and foreign investors. Regimes choosing capitalist strategies of development usually have as their ultimate goal the development of a local entrepreneurial and manufacturing sector. Regimes pursuing non-capitalist strategies de-emphasize the private sector in favor of state ownership and state control of the economy. The conflict becomes exacerbated by the efforts of regimes to wrest control of the economy away from the foreign sector following an increasingly nationalist definition of developmental prerequisites. When developmental policy becomes directed to exclusively national goals it can conflict with the conditions for profit maximization of international investments.

Many international investors attempt to accommodate the demands of host governments in the organization of their operating strategies so that these come to be consistent with a country's developmental needs. But there soon comes a time when governmental demands begin to conflict with their own conditions of profitability. When this occurs these companies may use their resources to change state policy or to secure a change in the regime itself. This is particularly true of the larger and more powerful international corporations in countries where the stakes are high. Of course, such companies seek to influence the political process from the inception to place in power those leaders already committed to the protection of their own particular interests.

The strategies employed by international investors include commiting their home governments, with their formidable array of resources, to intervene in the affairs of their hosts; influencing the policies of international agencies, organizations and companies upon which host governments depend; divesting themselves of holdings in the host country, or threatening to do so; refusing to increase their investment holdings; direct economic retaliation such as denying the country markets for its products; charging exorbitant fees and interests for services; denying a country access to skills and technology; and, of course, direct and indirect support for political opponents who are much more favorably disposed to serving their interests. When effectively employed, any of these might result in political and socioeconomic chaos.

On their part, host governments may successfully employ an array of counter-strategies including nationalization, securing majority participation, legislating measures to ensure domestic control, and seeking international support to offset and neutralize the negative effects of retaliatory measures employed by foreign companies and their supporters in the international community (see Feinberg 1983: 93–8).

International actors and collective needs

In summary, given the prevailing structure of international relations, third world regimes must seek alliances with, support from, and the protection of powerful international actors if they are to survive. Whether or not they could do these things and still retain the freedom to satisfy the collective needs of their own societies depends upon the prevailing ideology which informs the behavior of their international allies, the perceived interest of these allies, and whether such interests are compatible with the collective needs of the population. When a conflict develops, their freedom to pursue collective needs may depend upon their ability to enter into alternative alliances with international actors who have the resources at their disposal to counteract the effect of those whom they are trying to neutralize. More often than not, they are forced to settle for trade-offs and compromises given the limits to the resources of international actors who are most likely to support satisfaction of collective needs in comparison to those whose specific interests override such concerns. Regimes making a stand in support of the collective interests of their countries are therefore the ones least likely to survive. If they do, they may eventually be forced into international alliances with those Eastern bloc countries that are in positions to underwrite their political survival. At the same time, because of historical patterns of relationships and a generalized resource inadequacy, such alliances might prove economically detrimental.

Part of the explanation for the persistent failure of LDCs to satisfy the collective needs of their own populations rests with the imperative of international alliances for regime survival. These alliances prove detrimental because of the formidable resources in the hands of those international actors whose interests conflict with national interests. National leaders willing to protect and promote the interests of these international actors are the ones more likely to gain and retain control of an LDC despite the existence of generalized dissatisfaction. This is because of the resources made available to them in exchange for their acquiescence to foreign interests. Regimes in LDCs are, therefore, highly likely to concentrate on satisfying the demands of powerful international actors at the expense of catering to the needs of their own domestic populations.

Domestic actors

There are two domestic conditions which cause a regime to lose power in an LDC: mass anti-regime mobilization by a significant segment of the population, and the political mobilization of strategic sectors of the state bureaucracy, particularly the military and security forces. These conditions apply whether a regime loses an election or is ousted from power. At the domestic level, therefore, it is the sensitivity of these two phenomena to the collective needs of the population that will determine whether these needs are satisfied in regime policy.

Many problems facing LDCs pertain to the overdeveloped character of the state. The latter has emerged, even more so than in the developed countries, as the key, paramount, and oftentimes sole functional unit in the satisfaction of the collective needs of society. At the same time, the state has become the primary and most often the sole allocator of economic and social values, the central institution for economic accumulation for individuals and groups, and the preeminent instrument of power.

In most LDCs, there is a historical colonial legacy of state function geared almost exclusively to the protection and promotion of the interests of a small group of elites. From the inception, therefore, there has been a conflict between the functioning of the state for the satisfaction of the collective needs of society and its role as an instrument of power, exploitation, and accumulation.

The erosion of direct and indirect metropolitan control of the state in LDCs went hand-in-hand with the growth of a group of domestic bureaucrats who staffed and ran the state bureaucracy. This growth was part of a process evident among the entire group of salaried middle class functionaries as localization of the public and private sectors proceeded apace.

Middle-class actors

Given the role of the state as the paramount instrument of power, those who staffed and ran the state bureaucracies became potentially the most powerful and strategic set of domestic political actors in many LDCs. The potential is realized when their members become politicized. Normally, however, such politicization is aimed at the protection and promotion of their own interests as a salaried middle class against accumulative claims made by other segments of society. In its wake, the capacity of the state to satisfy collective needs becomes restricted.

The influence of a politicized group of state bureaucrats generally leads to policies of statist control over a wide range of political, economic, and even social activities. In the economic sphere, such policies are directed at serving the economic and status interests of the salaried middle class rather than the promotion of economic development. They can include state control of economic activities and state ownership of productive assets. There might emerge an exclusive "urban bias" in the allocation of resources in efforts to keep urban costs of living down, to increase the benefits enjoyed by the urban middle classes, and to improve vastly the services and facilities available to them. All these must, necessarily, come at the expense of rural development, which is indispensable to an effective program of self-sustaining economic development in most LDCs. They must come also at the expense of policies aimed at the betterment of the country's urban lower classes. Statist policies directed toward middle-class interests can therefore contribute significantly to the growing impoverishment of the country's rural and urban lower classes.

Statist expansion based upon the aspirations of the salaried middle class might also provoke enormous political dissatisfaction within the private sector. The policies informed by such expansion can easily result in the curtailment of and control over the latter's economic activities. Hence, political animosities can develop when a country's policies are driven by the need to satisfy the demands of the salaried middle class. The effects of these policies can produce growing lower- and upper-class dissatisfaction. The normal response to this dissatisfaction by a regime bent on protecting middle-class privilege is a curtailment of political and civil rights.

Thus, when the survival of a regime becomes linked to its willingness to acquiesce to the accumulative claims of the country's salaried middle class through a program of statist expansion and urban spending, the consequences can be highly detrimental to the satisfaction of collective needs. The vulnerability of regimes in LDCs to political mobilization by the state bureaucratic sector nonetheless renders the implementation of such policies much more likely than those directed towards collective needs.

Lower-class actors

In the typical LDC, the constituencies represented by influential elites are extremely narrow and privileged. At the same time representatives of lower-class interests are, for the most part excluded from the corridors of power. This is why state decision-making becomes concentrated upon serving the interests of international actors and those of the most powerful and strategic sectors of the middle and upper classes. Efforts aimed at satisfying the welfare and social security needs of the lower classes are fiercely resisted when they conflict with the interests of the latter. The domestic upper and middle classes and powerful international actors view the state as an instrument of political control and economic accumulation and use their formidable resources to fashion state decision-making to suit their own economic, political, and security agenda.

The relative weakness of the lower classes stems from their inability to convert their own resources, apart from their sheer numbers, into ones that are politically strategic. It also stems from the preponderant role of the state as an allocator of economic and social values and the reliance of the lower classes upon the state's output functions: i.e. with the paramount role the state plays in their own economic survival. Under such conditions, the lower classes are forced to rely upon the patronage of leaders with access to state resources in exchange for providing mass support to bolster the latter's political aspirations.

Leaders who gain control of the state by popular mandate are usually those who are able to separate conditions of support from any commitment to satisfy the collective needs of their mass constituents. They are the ones most able to employ successfully subjective appeals to communal or nationalist sentiment. Because mass support comes to be rooted in collective identity rather than need satisfaction, these leaders become free to cater to the interests of powerful middle-class, upper-class and international actors.

Moreover, after gaining control of the state, a regime has available to it a whole array of resources to be employed for coercion and control. These resources may be employed to demobilize the mass movements upon which the leadership depended to gain power. In addition, with state resources, such movements can be easily converted into institutions of regimentation in which absolute control of their members are guaranteed and which can be used to bolster regime power.

In the final analysis, the most the mass majority of the populations of LDCs may hope for is "top down populism" where a leader sympathetic to their interests is committed to provide them with elemental social and economic guarantees. Because of "marked inequalities in the control of wealth, status, and power," these populist leaders are forced to employ patronage to distribute benefits in exchange for the loyalty and support of the latter (see Scott 1972: 181ff.).

Regime survival and the link between domestic and international actors

In no LDC can a regime run the state without access to international resources. This is so because almost every element in the state bureaucratic sector is derived internationally. These include the skills of the state personnel, technology, equipment, state infrastructure, communication facilities, weaponry, energy, and most other things necessary for state function. What is critical in this regard is not merely access to the international sources that provide these elements, but also access to foreign exchange and developmental assistance to afford their acquisition. Both become imperative since an effective state bureaucracy constitutes the key to regime survival in LDCs.

The transfer of the above resources to the state is conditioned by the existing relationship between a regime on the one hand and the domestic representatives, allies, and supporters of international actors who provide them on the other. The terms of the transfer are linked directly to the willingness of state-controlling elites to meet the demands of both the international actors and their domestic allies. In the process, international actors become assured that their interests are articulated to the regime within a domestic political framework and are put on the domestic political agenda. At the same time, domestic actors, by virtue of their control of the transfer of international resources to the state, are able to influence national policy, and ultimately to determine who runs the state.

There are a number of implications which stem from this particular formulation of the relationships between international actors, national actors, and regimes in LDCs. First, there is a class implication; since the lower classes, which constitute the large majority of the populations of most LDCs, have the least ties with international actors, they are in by far the least favorable position to exploit the transfer of international resources in support of their own interests. The upper classes, on the other hand, by virtue of such ties become extremely powerful. So do certain sectors of the middle classes.

A second implication has to do with autonomy and self-determination in LDCs. If domestic actors are rendered powerful by virtue of their international ties, then there is the perpetual danger of international interests superseding domestic concerns in the local political arena. Important in this regard are the demands of the managers and technical staff of foreign companies. Such demands are usually supported by many locals who depend directly upon the activities of these transnational firms. A regime might find itself unable to reject such demands because of the foreign-exchange earnings and revenue transfers generated by these companies and upon which the state depends. Yet these demands typically have more to do with the interests of the international firms than with domestic needs.[1]

Autonomy and self-determination are also affected by the international affiliations of domestic voluntary organizations. These span the gamut from political parties, trade unions, religious organizations, and Chambers of Commerce to the local chapter of Amnesty International, various service clubs such as The Lions, fraternal lodges and the like. Such organizations can adopt, wholesale, the agenda of their parent or affiliated international bodies and insist upon making these part of their own domestic agenda. In exchange they are provided with resources which make them politically formidable. At the same time, they serve as local representatives to the international bodies in a way which dictates how the resources of the latter are committed to their

[1] The relationship between a regime and transnational corporations is complex and scholars have widely divergent views concerning its effect on national policy. For a discussion of this complexity and such divergences with regard to non-oil mineral industries in the third world, see Stephens 1987.

Collective needs vs demands of actors in LDCs   213

own countries or how these resources are used to influence the policies of powerful governments and international agencies. It goes without saying that determinations about which group of political leaders run an LDC and the types of policies they pursue can be profoundly affected by the behavior of the international affiliates of these voluntary organizations. This is quite self-evident with political parties and labor unions which have a more political agenda and, in the case of the former, which normally call directly upon international support to further the political aspirations of their leaders.

Voluntary organizations may be provided with resources to support mass mobilization against unsympathetic regimes, they may influence the allocation of international resources to prop up and support sympathetic governments, or they might successfully appeal for international intervention. More often, they influence the allocation of resources which are necessary for maintaining state function. This can determine whether or not a particular regime can maintain its control of the state in an LDC.

Because of the pivotal and strategic role played by international resources in the political economy, powerful domestic actors with no direct ties to international or metropolitan bodies can also base their behavior on agenda pertaining to the interests of international actors. This is particularly true of members of the state bureaucracy and of the salaried middle classes as a whole. The satisfaction of their own accumulative interests is dependent upon the ability of the state to attract international resources. Such a dependence is not merely confined to their jobs, wages, and salaries, but extends to their very life styles given consumption habits which are highly import-dependent.

Unlike other powerful actors, however, state-sector workers can be quite ambivalent in their choice as to which international alliances to support. This is because their interests lie in statist policies which can invariably come into conflict with the interests of the international business community. At the same time, they are fully cognizant of the link between economic stability and the international transactions in which these companies participate. Their interests can be most severely affected by any economically destabilizing actions undertaken by these foreign businesses or their home governments.

State workers are highly likely to support a regime that undertakes statist expansion. This support is likely to diminish, however, when such expansion begins to affect the ability of the state to maintain the requisite level of international transfers necessary to meet their own accumulative and prestige claims. This is the dilemma that has led to the adoption of a mixed-economy approach in many LDCs. Such an approach constitutes an attempt to reconcile a capitalist developmental policy with the need for state ownership and control of domestic economic assets and domestic production. Another approach to the problem has been the development of some form of state socialism and the exploitation of ties with progressive actors in the West to preempt or offset economic retaliation by international business faced with nationalization and increasing state control. A third approach has been the adoption of a pattern of realignment with the Eastern bloc as a strategy for maintaining transfers of critical international resources after statist policies are implemented. Each of these strategies can gain the overwhelming support of members of the civil, security and corporate branches of the state in LDCs. This is so despite the fact that each engenders a fundamentally different pattern of international alliances.

Urban and rural workers and agricultural producers not endangered by state appropriation might also be ambivalent to the pattern of international ties pursued by a regime. Nonetheless, lower-class groups are not free from manipulation by international actors. Leaders of mass organizations can be provided with international support to mount mass mobilization campaigns against a regime. Such support comes out of the recognition of the profoundly destabilizing effect of mass protest.

Conclusion

A number of prerequisites must be in place if the collective needs of the populations of LDCs are to have any chance of being met. At the domestic level, forms of genuine democratic representation (not necessarily based on the Western competitive party-political model) must be developed. These must be combined with new patterns of lower-class political organization which constitute a shift from subjective identities to collective needs as the basis of mobilization. Ways have to be found to neutralize politically the upper classes. Finally, measures have to be undertaken to prevent the politicization of the salaried middle class, particularly state-sector workers, which has a tradition of organization to promote its own exclusive interests.

At the international level, alliances need to be made with international actors who can provide LDCs with the greatest degrees of freedom to formulate and implement national policy in keeping with collective needs. At the same time, LDCs need to pursue the means of freeing themselves from absolute dependence upon resources provided by international actors whose interests conflict with the generalized interests of their populations.

The dilemma for a typical LDC is that the bureaucracies of the state and national organizations (such as political parties and trade unions) have become instruments for elite domination. In turn, these bureaucracies are absolutely dependent upon a formidable array of internationally derived economic, political, coercive, technological, and cultural resources. This was not the case in the development of the Western democratic states. While absolutism and elitism existed, it was in the context of weak states that were quite vulnerable to mass mobilization. As the state bureaucratic apparatus grew stronger, there was in these societies a parallel development of democratic representative government. Quite the opposite occurred in LDCs where powerful states emerged as the instrument of elite hegemony and became so well ensconced as to make ineffective any attempt at mass mobilization for democratic representative government. At the same time, those who controlled these states found themselves exclusively reliant for their survival upon the support of international and domestic actors whose demands conflicted with the collective needs of their populations. Escape from the consequences of this condition rests with the chances for equitable mass participation in the domestic political process and for the development of alternative international alliances with politically neutral actors whose paramount concern is the satisfaction of collective needs.

Appendix. Interview schedule

Study of leaders in Guyana and Trinidad

1 Looking back over everything that has happened since Guyana/Trinidad became independent, what do you now think about political independence for the country?
2 What do you consider to be the three most significant policies or pieces of legislation enacted since the country gained its political independence?
What is/was your personal position on these issues?
3 What, in your opinion, is the greatest single problem facing the people of this country?
4 Since independence, have you ever had any doubts about the economic viability of this country?
What were these doubts?
5 What are your opinions on the following:

(i) A national insurance scheme which provides money to all those out of work?
(ii) Free education at all levels provided entirely by government (including university)?
(iii) The elimination of all private medical practice in favor of free government-provided health care?
(iv) Increased old-age pension on a totally government-run basis?
(v) A national service in which everyone is required to serve on a conscription basis?
(vi) Free meals and free books provided to schoolchildren?

6 Do you think that foreign-owned enterprises should be nationalized, brought under stringent local control by the government, or neither of these?
7 What do you think about a policy stipulating that all employees of all business concerns should be Guyanese/Trinidadian (except when employment needs cannot be satisfied locally)?
8 In your opinion, how much importance should be placed upon foreign investment for the economic development of Guyana/Trinidad?
9 What do you think should be the nature of economic relations with other countries if this country is to achieve the greatest level of economic self-determination? For example, should the country increase or decrease economic relations with any particular country or set of countries?

Appendix 217

10 What are your personal opinions concerning the Caribbean Common Market (CARICOM)?
What benefits do you think have accrued to the country as a result of CARICOM?
What major criticisms do you have of CARICOM?
11 Do you think that this country should join a West Indian federation involving a central West Indian government now or in the future?
12 What do you see as the ideal relationship between Guyana/Trinidad and the rest of the Caribbean?
13 What do you perceive to be the major groups in this country and do you see any problems in their relationships with each other?
Do you think that there is any or enough effort being made to reduce these problems?
Do you think that these problems will be significantly reduced in the future?
14 What do you see as the more serious problem in this country, race or poverty?
15 Do you think that there is any one country or group of countries with which this country needs to make a special effort to improve its relations?
16 Why do people in Guyana/Trinidad vote the way they do?
17 Looking at the world situation today with respect to international relations, with which group of countries do you think Guyana/Trinidad should be associating itself: the Western nations, the Communist nations, the neutralist nations, or any other group?
18 Do you think that the Western democratic form of government is best suited for this country?
(If NO) What kind of government would be best?
19 (If NOT a politician) How active a role do you play personally in politics?
Which party or political group do you support?
Why?
20 What changes would you make, given the opportunity, to ensure a more fair system of representation in this country?
21 What groups in this country have benefited most from the policies of the present government?
How have they benefited?
What groups have benefited the least?
Why?
22 Have there been any cases of the systematic violation of human rights in Guyana/Trinidad?
23 Do you think that the conditions of life for the average man have improved since independence?
What about the poorest groups such as the plantation worker, the village dweller, and the urban lower classes? Have their conditions of life improved?
24 Do you think that the gap between the rich and the poor in this country has widened, remained the same, or diminished since independence?
25 What do you think are the country's prospects for the future, say 20 years from now?

26 In general, do you think that this country has qualities which are uniquely Guyanese/Trinidadian, or do you think its culture is similar to that of the West Indies in general?
(If UNIQUE) What, specifically, is unique about the culture of this country?
27 Regarding your own personal tastes:
   (i) What are your favorite foods?
   (ii) What type of music do you like?
   (iii) What type of movies interest you?
   (iv) What type of books do you like?
28 What language, other than English, do you think should be emphasized in this country?
Why?
29 What would you like to see emphasized in the cultural development of this country?
Why?
Are there any cultural aspects that are being stressed too much?
What specific objection do you have to this?
30 If there was just one change you could help bring about in this country over the next 15 years, what would it be?
31 Considering all aspects of Guyanese/Trinidadian life, who would you say are the most important influential individuals in the entire country? (See Updated List of Guyanese/Trinidadian Leaders.)
Is there anyone you would like to add to this list?
32 What is your age?
33 What is the highest level, or degree of formal education you have?
34 Where was it obtained?
35 What is your average annual income?
36 What is your net worth?
37 What is your major occupation?
38 (By observation) Sex.
39 (By observation) Color or race.
40 (Ask of political and labor leaders) What was your occupation prior to entering politics or union work?
41 In what area of the country were you born?
42 What was/is your father's occupation?
43 What was/is your mother's occupation?
44 How many times have you moved since you were 15 years' old?
45 What is your religion?
46 How often do you go to church?
47 Would you describe yourself as a religious person?

Bibliography

Adam, H. 1971. *Modernizing Racial Domination.* Berkeley, Cal., University of California Press
Ake, Claude 1967. *A Theory of Political Integration.* Homewood, Ill., Dorsey Press
Alavi, H. 1972. The state in post-colonial societies. *New Left Review* 74, July–August: 59–81
Allum, Desmond 1975. Legality vs. morality: a plea. In *The Aftermath of Sovereignty: West Indian perspectives,* ed. David Lowenthal and Lambros Comitas: 330–4. New York, NY, Anchor Books
Amin, S. 1976. *Unequal Development.* New York, NY, Monthly Review Press
Apter, D. 1971. *Choice and the Politics of Allocation.* New Haven, Conn., Yale University Press
Bahadoorsingh, Krishna 1968. *Trinidad Ethnic Politics: The persistence of the race factor.* London, Institute of Race Relations
 1971. The racial factor in Trinidad's politics. In *Readings in Government and Politics of the West Indies,* ed. Trevor Munroe and Rupert Lewis. Mona, Jamaica: University of the West Indies, Department of Government
Bairoch, Paul 1975. *The Economic Development of the Third World.* Berkeley and Los Angeles, Cal., University of California Press
Barkan, J. D. 1979. Legislators, elections, and political change. In *Politics and Public Policy in Kenya and Tanzania,* ed. J. D. Barkan and J. Okumu. New York, NY, Praeger
Beckford, George L. 1972. *Persistent Poverty.* New York, NY, Oxford University Press
Bell, Wendell 1964. *Jamaican Leaders: Political attitudes in a new state.* Berkeley and Los Angeles, Cal., University of California Press
 (Ed.) 1967 *The Democratic Revolution in the West Indies.* Cambridge, Mass., Schenkman Publishing Co.
Bell, Wendell and J. William Gibson, Jr. 1978. Independent Jamaica faces the outside world. *International Studies Quarterly,* vol. 22, no. 1, March
Bendix, Reinhard and Guenther Roth 1971. *Scholarship and Partisanship: Essays on Max Weber.* Berkeley, Los Angeles and London, University of California Press
Best, Lloyd 1968. Outlines of a model of pure plantation economy. *Social and Economic Studies,* September

219

220 Bibliography

1969. Doctor politics in the Caribbean. *Express*, parts 1, 2 and 3. Port-of-Spain, Trinidad, 30 May; 1, 4 and 6 June

1971. Size and survival. In *Readings in the Political Economy of the Caribbean*, ed. Norman Girvan and Owen Jefferson. Kingston, Jamaica, New World

Bobb, Euric 1983. The oil industry: impact on the local economy review 1982/ forecast 1983. In *Quarterly Economic Bulletin*, Central Bank of Trinidad and Tobago, vol. viii, no. 1, March

Bodenheimer, S. 1971. Dependency and imperialism; the roots of Latin American underdevelopment. In *Readings in U.S. Imperialism*, ed. K. T. Fann and D. C. Hodges: 155–81. Boston, Mass., Peter Sargent

Braithwaite, Lloyd 1953. Social stratification in Trinidad. *Social and Economic Studies*, vol. 2

Brewster, H. 1971. Planning and economic development in Guyana. *Readings in the Political Economy of the Caribbean*. Mona, Jamaica, Institute of Social and Economic Research, University of the West Indies

Burnham, L. F. S. 1955. Our party – its tasks. *Thunder* (Guyana), part I, 19 November: 4

1968. Address to the PNC Congress. 14 April, Georgetown

1970. *A Destiny to Mould*. London, Longman Caribbean

1974. Address at Vesting Day Rally. Linden, Guyana, 14 July (mimeo)

Carrington, Edwin 1971. Industrialization in Trinidad and Tobago since 1950. In *Readings in the Political Economy of the Caribbean*, ed. Norman Girvan and Owen Jefferson. Kingston, Jamaica, New World

Chaliand, G. 1978. *Revolution in the Third World*. New York, NY, Penguin

Chase, A. 1964. *A History of Trade Unionism in Guyana*. Georgetown, Guyana, New Guiana Co.

Chernick, Sidney E. 1978. *The Commonwealth Caribbean: The Integration Experience*. Baltimore and London, Johns Hopkins University Press

Cockroft, J., A. G. Frank, and D. J. Johnson (eds.) 1970. *Dependence and Underdevelopment*. Garden City, NY, Doubleday and Co.

Cohen, A. 1969. *Custom and Politics in Urban Africa*. Berkeley, Cal. University of California Press

Craig, H. 1953. *The Legislative Council of Trinidad and Tobago*. London, Faber and Faber

Danns, G. 1984. *Domination and Power in Guyana*. New Brunswick, NJ, Transaction Books

DeCaries 1979. Intense political pressures on Guyana's judicial system. *Caribbean Contact*, June

Dell, Sidney 1984. Stabilization: the political economy of overkill. In *The Political Economy of Development and Underdevelopment*, 3rd edn, ed. Charles K. Wilber. New York, NY. Random House

Demas, W. 1978. The Caribbean and the new international economic order. *Journal of Inter-American Studies and World Affairs*, vol. 20, no. 3, August

Despres, Leo A. 1966. *Cultural Pluralism and Nationalist Politics in British Guiana*. Chicago, Ill., Rand McNally

1967. Differential adaptation and micro-cultural evolution in Guyana. In *Afro-American Anthropology*, ed. Norman F. Witteh and John F. Szwed. New York, NY, The Free Press

1968. The implications of nationalist politics in British Guiana for the development of cultural theory. In *State and Society*, ed. Reinhard Bendix, *et al.*: 502–28. Berkeley and Los Angeles, Cal., University of California Press. Reprinted from *The American Anthropologist*, vol. 66, no. 5, October 1964: 1050–77

1975. Ethnicity and resource competition in Guyanese society. In *Ethnicity and Resource Competition in Plural Societies*, ed. Leo A. Despres. The Hague and Paris, Mouton Press

De Vos, George 1975. Ethnic pluralism: conflict and accommodation. In *Ethnic Identity*, ed. George De Vos and Lola Romanucci-Ross. Palo Alto, Cal., Mayfield Publishing Company

De Vos, George and Lola Romanucci-Ross 1975. Ethnicity: vessel of meaning and emblem of contrast. In *Ethnic Identity*, ed. George De Vos and Lola Romanucci-Ross. Palo Alto, Cal., Mayfield Publishing Company

Dookan, Isaac 1975. *A Post-Emancipation History of the West Indies*. London, Collins

Dos Santos, T. 1970. The structure of dependence. *American Economic Review*, 60, May: 231–6

Enloe, Cynthia 1973. *Ethnic Conflict and Political Development*. Boston, Mass., Little, Brown and Company

1976. Civilian control of the military: implications in the plural societies of Guyana and Malaysia. In *Civilian Control of the Military*, ed. Claude Welch. Albany, NY, State University of New York Press

1980a. *Ethnic Soldiers: State Security in Divided Societies*. Athens, Ga., University of Georgia Press, and London, Penguin Books

1980b. *Police, Military and Ethnicity: Foundations of State Power*. New Brunswick, NJ, Transaction Books

1984. Security blankets, civil–military relations, "national security", and human rights. Unpublished paper, Clark University, Worcester, Mass.

Farrell, Trevor M. 1978. The unemployment crisis in Trinidad and Tobago: its current dimensions and some projections to 1985. *Social and Economic Studies*, vol. 27, no. 2, June 1978

Feinberg, R. E. 1983. *The Intemperate Zone*. New York, NY, W. W. Norton and Co.

Frank, A. G. 1969. *Capitalism and Underdevelopment in Latin America*. New York, NY, Monthly Review Press

Fried, M. 1956. The Chinese in British Guiana. *Social and Economic Studies*, vol. 5: 54–73

Furtado, C. 1964, *Development and Underdevelopment*. Berkeley, Cal., University of California Press

Girvan, Norman 1971. The Guyanese–Alcan conflict and nationalization of Demba. In *Readings in Government and Politics of the West Indies*, ed. Trevor Munroe

Bibliography

and Rupert Lewis. Mona, Jamaica, University of the West Indies, Department of Government

Glasgow, R. A. 1970. *Guyana: Race and Politics Among Africans and East Indians*. Hague, Martinus Nijhoff

Gomes, A. 1954. *Hansard*, 10 December

Greenberg, S. B. 1980. *Race and State in Capitalist Development*. New Haven, Conn., Yale University Press

Greene, J. E. 1971. An analysis of the general election in Trinidad and Tobago, 1971. In *Readings in Government and Politics of the West Indies*, ed. Trevor Monroe and Rupert Lewis. Mona, Jamaica, University of the West Indies, Department of Government

1972. Participation, integration and legitimacy as indicators of developmental change in the politics of Guyana. *Social and Economic Studies*, vol. 21, no. 3

1974. *Race vs. Politics in Guyana*. Mona, Jamaica, Institute of Social and Economic Research, University of the West Indies

Greene, Reginald H. 1974. Tanzania. In *Redistribution with Growth*, ed. Hollis B. Chenery. New York, NY, Oxford University Press

Hammarskjold, Dag 1975. What now: another development. *Development Dialogue*, nos. 1 and 2

Haq, Mahbub ul 1976. The third world and international economic order. Development Paper no. 22. Washington, DC, Overseas Development Council

Hintzen, Percy C. 1975. Problems of national integration in Guyana: a study of four urban areas. Unpublished Master's thesis, Clark University, Worcester, Mass.

1977. The colonial foundations of race relations and ethnic politics in Guyana. *The Guyana Journal of Sociology*, vol. 1, no. 3, April

1981. Capitalism, socialism, and socio-political confrontation in multi-racial developing states: a comparison of Guyana and Trinidad. Ph.D. dissertation, Yale University

1983. Bases of elite support for a regime: race ideology and clientelism as bases for leaders in Guyana and Trinidad. *Comparative Political Studies*, vol. 16, no. 3, October

1984. Elite integration and political stability. Unpublished paper, University of California, Berkeley

Hintzen, Percy C. and R. Premdas 1982. Coercion and control in political change. *Journal of Inter-American Studies and World Affairs*, vol. 24, no. 3, August: 337–54

1983. Race, ideology and power in Guyana. *Journal of Commonwealth and Comparative Politics*, vol. 21, no. 2, July

Holmquist, F. 1979. Class structure, peasant participation and rural self help. In *Politics and Public Policy in Kenya and Tanzania*, ed. J. D. Barkan with J. J. Okumu: 129–53. New York, NY, Praeger

Hope, Kemp and Wilfred David 1974. Planning for development in Guyana: the experience from 1945 to 1973. *Inter-American Economic Affairs*, vol. 27, no. 4, Spring

Huntington, S. P. 1971. The change to change. *Comparative Politics*, April

James, C. L. R. 1962. *Party Politics in the West Indies*. San Juan, Trinidad, Vedic Enterprises
Jagan, Janet 1968. Election fraud. *The Mirror* (Guyana), 29 December
1973. The army take-over in the Guyana elections. *Thunder* (Guyana), April–July: 36–44
Kasfir, N. 1979. Explaining ethnic political participation. *World Politics*, vol. 21, no. 3, April: 365–88.
Kirkpatrick, J. 1979. Dictatorships and double standards. *Commentary*, vol. 68. no. 5, November
Kuper, L. 1971. Plural societies: perspectives and problems. In *Pluralism in Africa*, ed. L. Kuper and M. G. Smith. Berkeley, Cal., University of California Press
Langdon, Steve 1977. The state and capitalism in Kenya. *Review of African Political Economy*, January–April
Lens, Sidney 1965. American labor abroad. *The Nation*, 5 July
Lernoux, Penny 1980. Jonestown Nation. *The Nation*, 15 November: 510–12.
Lewis, G. K. 1968. *The Growth of Modern West Indies*. New York, NY Monthly Review Press
Lewis, W. Arthur 1954. Economic development with unlimited supply of labor. *The Manchester School*, May
Leys, C. 1976. The "overdeveloped" post-colonial state: a reevaluation. *Review of African Political Economy*, 5, January–April: 39–48
Lipton, M. 1980. *Why Poor People Stay Poor*. Cambridge, Mass., Harvard University Press
Lustick, I. 1979. Stability in deeply divided societies: consocialionalism vs. control. *World Politics*, vol. 31, no. 3, April: 321–44
Lutchman, H. A. 1970. *The Crown Colony System of Government*. Georgetown, Guyana, Chritchlow Labor College
Mafeje, A. 1971. The ideology of tribalism. *Journal of Modern African Studies*, 9, August
Magubane, B. 1979 *The Political Economy of Race and Class in South Africa*. New York: NY, Monthly Review Press
Mandle, Jay R. 1976. Continuity and change in Guyanese underdevelopment. *Monthly Review*, vol. 28, no. 4, September
Manley, Robert H. 1979. *Guyana Emergent: The post-independence struggle for non-dependent development*. Boston, Mass., G. K. Hall and Schenkman Publishing Co.
McArthur, J. Sydney 1912. Our people, *Timehri*, vol. 2, no. 1
Milne, R. S. 1977. Politics, ethnicity and class in Guyana and Malaysia. *Social and Economic Studies*, vol. 26, no. 1, March
1981. *Politics in Ethnically Bipolar States: Guyana, Malaysia, Fiji*. Vancouver, University of British Columbia Press
Mitchell, Adrian 1968. Jagan and Burnham: It's polling day tomorrow. Has Guyana's election already been decided in Britain? *The Sunday Times* (London), 15 December
Monroe, C. 1980. Burnham given broader powers. *Guardian* (USA), 15 October: 6

224 Bibliography

Moran, T. N. 1974. *Multinational Corporations and the Politics of Dependence: Copper in Chile.* Princeton, NJ, Princeton University Press

Moskos, Charles C. 1967. *The Sociology of Political Independence.* Cambridge, Mass., G. K. Hall and Schenkman Publishing Co.

Moskos, Charles C. and Wendell Bell 1967. Emerging nations and ideologies of American social scientists. *American Sociologist*, vol. 2, May

Muller, Ronald 1979. The multinational corporations and the underdevelopment of the third world. *The Political Economy of Development and Underdevelopment*, 2nd edn, ed. Charles K. Wilber. New York, NY, Random House

Murray, Roger 1967. Second thought on Ghana. *New Left Review*, 42

Newman, P. 1964 *British Guiana: Problems of Cohesion in an Immigrant Society.* London, Oxford University Press

Omag, J. 1976. U.S. blamed for campaign to destabilize Guyana. *Guardian* (London), 21 March: 1

Oxaal, I. 1968. *Black Intellectuals Come to Power.* Cambridge, Mass., G. K. Hall and Schenkman Publishing Co.

1971. *Race and Revolutionary Consciousness.* Cambridge, Mass., Schenkman Publishing Co.

Pearson, Drew 1964 U.S. faces line holding decision. *Washington Post*, 31 May

Post, K. 1972. Peasantization and rural political movements in Western Africa. *Archives Européenes de Sociologie*, vol. 13, no. 2

Premdas, Ralph R. 1972. *Voluntary Associations and Political Parties in a Racially Fragmented State.* Georgetown, Department of Political Science, University of Guyana

1975. The rise of the first mass-based multi-racial party in Guyana. *Caribbean Quarterly*, vol. 20, nos. 3 and 4, January: 5–20

1977. Guyana: communal conflict, socialism and political reconciliation. *Inter-American Economic Affairs*, vol. 30, no. 4

1978. Guyana: Socialist reconstruction and political opportunism. *Journal of Inter-American Studies and World Affairs*, vol. 20, no. 2

1980. Guyana, socialism and destabilization in the Western Hemisphere. *Caribbean Quarterly*, vol. 25, no. 3

Ramlogan, Vishnu 1980. The sugar industry in Trinidad and Tobago: management challenges and responses. *Inter-American Economic Affairs*, vol. 33, no. 4, Spring

Ranis, Gustav and J. C. H. Fei 1961. A theory of economic management. *American Economic Review*, September

Richardson, E. C. 1957. Significance of history in West Indian Affairs. *PNM Weekly*, 4 March

Robinson, Rob and Wendell Bell 1978. Attitudes towards political independence in Jamaica after twelve years of nationhood. *British Journal of Sociology*, vol. 29, no. 2, June

Roopnerain, Rupert 1980. WPA tells you the way forward. *Caribbean Contact*, July: 8–9

Rostow, W. W. 1960. *The Stages of Economic Growth: A non-Communist Manifesto.* Cambridge, Cambridge University Press

Bibliography

Rustow, D. A. 1970. Transitions to democracy: toward a dynamic model. *Comparative Politics*, 2, April

Ryan, Selwyn 1971. Restructuring the Trinidad economy. In *Readings in the Political Economy of the Caribbean*, ed. Norman Girvan and Owen Jefferson. Kingston, Jamaica, New World

1972. *Race and Nationalism in Trinidad and Tobago*. Toronto, University of Toronto Press

Sackey, James A. 1979. Dependence, underdevelopment and socialist-oriented transformation in Guyana. *Inter-American Economic Affairs*, vol. 33, no. 1

Saul, J. 1973. Frelimo and the Mozambique revolution. In *Essays on the Political Economy of Africa*, ed. G. Arrighi and J. S. Saul. New York, NY, Monthly Review Press

1976. The unsteady state, Uganda, Obote, and General Amin. *Review of African Political Economy*, 5, January–April: 12–38

Schlesinger, Arthur, Jr 1965. *A Thousand Days*. New York, NY, Houghton Mifflin

Schurmann, F. 1968. *Ideology and Organization in Communist China*. Berkeley, Cal., University of California Press

Scott, J. C. 1972. Patron–client politics and political change in Southeast Asia. *American Political Science Review*, 66, March: 91–113

Sheehan, Neil 1967. C.I.A. men and strikers in Guiana against Dr. Jagan. *New York Times*, 22 February

Sims, P. 1966. *Trouble in Guyana*. London, Allen and Unwin

Smith, R. T. 1962. *British Guiana*. London, Oxford University Press

Smooha, Sammy 1980. Control of minorities in Israel and Northern Ireland. *Comparative Studies in Society and History*, vol. 22, no. 2, April

Spinner, T. J. 1984. *A Political and Social History of Guyana, 1945–1983*. Boulder, Col., Westview Press

Stephens, E. N. 1987. Mineral strategies and development: international political economy, state, class and the role of the bauxite/aluminium and copper industries in Jamaica and Peru. *Studies in Comparative International Development*, vol. 22, no. 3, Fall

Stone, Carl 1972. *Stratification and Political Change in Trinidad and Jamaica*. Beverley Hills, Cal., Sage Publications

1973. *Class, Race and Political Behavior in Urban Jamaica*. Kingston, Jamaica, Institute for Social and Economic Research, University of the West Indies

1980. *Democracy and Clientelism in Jamaica*. New Brunswick, NJ, Transaction Books

Thivolet, Pierre-Michel 1979. Food shortages and ethnic divisions. *Manchester Guardian Weekly*, 23 December

Thomas, C. Y. 1971. *Sugar Economics in a Colonial Situation*. Georgetown, Guyana, Ratoon

1974. *Dependence and Transformation: The economics of transition to socialism*. New York, NY, and London, Monthly Review Press

1980. Inside Burnham's cooperative republic. *Caribbean Contact*, February

Von Frehold, Michaela 1977. The post-colonial state and its Tanzanian version. *Review of African Political Economy*, January–April

Weber, M. 1964. *From Max Weber: Essays in Sociology*, trans. and ed. H. H. Gerth and C. Wright Mills. New York, NY, Oxford University Press
Weiner, Myron 1971. Political integration and political development. In *Political Development and Social Change*, ed. Jason L. Finkle and Richard W. Gable. New York, NY, John Wiley and Sons
Williams, Eric 1962. *History of the People of Trinidad and Tobago*. Port-of-Spain, Trinidad, PNM Publishing Co.
  1970. *The Chaquaramas Declaration – Perspectives for a new society*. An Address at the Special Party Convention in November 1970. PNM Publishing Co.
  1974. *Economic Transformation and the Role and Vision of the PNM*. An address to the PNM Annual Convention, Trinidad.
Young, C. 1976. *The Politics of Cultural Pluralism*. Madison, Wis., University of Wisconsin Press
Zolberg, Aristede 1971. The structure of political conflict in the new states of tropical Africa. In *Political Development and Social Change*, ed. Jason L. Finkle and Richard W. Gable. New York, NY, John Wiley and Sons

Reports, documents, pamphlets, and magazines
Guyana
ASCRIA 1973. Statement on the negative direction in Guyana. ASCRIA Pamphlet, 1 April
ASCRIA 1974. The race question and the suffering of the people. ASCRIA Pamphlet, 11 January
Bank of Guyana 1978. *Bulletin*, no. 8 Georgetown, Guyana, October
Budget Speech 1968. Sessional Paper no. 4/67. First Parliaments of Guyana, 2nd session, 24 December 1967
  1969. Sessional Paper no. 2/69. Second Parliament of Guyana, 1st Session, 28 February 1969
  1970. Sessional Paper no. 4/69. Second Parliament of Guyana, 1st Session, 28 February 1969
  1972. Sessional Paper no. 2/71. Second Parliament of Guyana, 3rd Session, 7 December 1971
  1975. Sessional Paper no. 1/74. Third Parliament of Guyana, 4th Session, 9 December 1974
  1976. Sessional Paper no. 1/76. Third Parliament of Guyana, 1st Session, 24 November 1975
  1977. Sessional Paper no. 2/76. Third Parliament of Guyana, 1st Session, 30 December 1976
  1978. Sessional Paper, Parliament of Guyana
  1981. Sessional Paper, Parliament of Guyana
  1982. Sessional Paper, Parliament of Guyana
  1983. Sessional Paper, Parliament of Guyana
  1984. Sessional Paper, Parliament of Guyana
Central Committee Document, Peoples Progressive Party 1977. *For a National Front Government*.

Bibliography 227

Colonial Annual Report on British Guiana 1953. London, HMSO
1957. London, HMSO
Guyana, A Decade of Progress. 1974. Georgetown, Guyana, PNC, December
Guyana Chronicle (daily) 1974, 1977, 1978, 1979, 1980
Guyana Information Service 1977. Guyana in Brief. Georgetown, December
Guyana Update (London) January–February 1984
International Commission of Jurists 1966. Racial Problems in the Public Service. Report of the British Guiana Commission of Inquiry, October 1965
Ministry of Economic Development 1974. Annual Statistical Abstract, 1974. Georgetown, Guyana
Newsletter 1974. Embassy of the Republic of Guyana. Washington, DC, September–December, no. 4/1974.
Parliamentary debate. 12 December 1973
Peoples Progressive Party, 21 Years 1950–1971 1971. Georgetown, New Guyana Company
Report of the British Guiana Commission of Inquiry into Disturbances in British Guiana 1965. International Commission of Jurists, Geneva, Switzerland, October
Statistical Bureau 1974. Annual Statistical Abstract. Georgetown, Guyana
1976. Quarterly Statistical Digest. Georgetown, Guyana, December

Trinidad and Tobago
Budget Speech 1964–5. Trinidad and Tobago Parliament
1978. Trinidad and Tobago Parliament
1982. Trinidad and Tobago Parliament
1983. Trinidad and Tobago Parliament
Central Statistical Office 1969. Annual Statistical Digest. Port-of-Spain, Trinidad
1975. Annual Statistical Digest, 1974–5
1973. Continuous Sample of the Population
1977. The Gross Domestic Product of Trinidad and Tobago, 1966–1976
1978. Review of the Economy, 1977
1983 Review of the Economy, 1982
Commission of Enquiry into the Oil Industry 1963–64. Report of the Commission. Port-of-Spain, Trinidad
Economic Commission for Latin America 1982. Economic Activity 1981 in Caribbean Countries. Trinidad and Tobago. United Nations, New York
Industrial Stabilization Act 1965. Laws of Trinidad and Tobago, Act no. 8
Info vol. 4, April 1977; no. 12, December 1977
Inter-American Economic and Social Council, Permanent Executive Committee 1974. The Economic and social development of Trinidad and Tobago. (Unrevised version.) CEPECIES Subcommittee of Trinidad and Tobago
1975. The economic and social development of Trinidad and Tobago. CEPECIES Subcommittee of Trinidad and Tobago. OAS, 20 October
National Security Act 1970 Government Printery, Port-of-Spain, Trinidad
Oilfield Workers Trade Union (OWTU) 1968. Speeches by Georges Weeks at the

228 *Bibliography*

Tripartite Conference on Employment and Retrenchment. Port-of-Spain, Trinidad, July
Quarterly Economic Bulletin 1983. Central Bank of Trinidad and Tobago. Vol. 8, no. 1, March
Report on the General Elections 1961, 1965 Port-of-Spain, Trinidad
The peoples charter: A statement of principles 1966. *Major Party Document*, vol. 1, Port-of-Spain, Trinidad
Third Five-Year Development Plan 1969–73 1971. Port-of-Spain, Trinidad, Government of Trinidad and Tobago
White Paper on Agriculture 1978. Trinidad and Tobago, Ministry of Agriculture, Lands and Fisheries, December

Other Countries
Catholic Institute for International Relations (London) 1980. *Special Report on the Politics of Guyana*, pamphlet, May
International Bill of Human Rights 1978. Office of Public Information, United Nations, New York

Parliamentary debates, House of Commons, Great Britain 1937–8. *Hansard*, vol. 332
Population Census of the Commonwealth Caribbean 1970 1973. Kingston, Jamaica, Census Research Programme, University of the West Indies
Race Today, April 1975
West India Royal Commission 1938–9 1939. Statement of Action on the Recommendations. Cmd 6656 (London)

Newspapers
Issues of the following newspapers have been cited throughout the text.

Guyana
Catholic Standard
Guyana Chronicle
Guyana Graphic
Guyana Times
Solidarity
Sunday Graphic
The Mirror

Trinidad and Tobago
Alliance News
The Bomb
Guardian Weekly
Liberation
Nation

Bibliography 229

Sunday Guardian
Sunday Express
Tapia
Trinidad Express
Trinidad Guardian
Trinidad and Tobago Review
Vanguard

Other Countries
Caribbean Contact (Barbados)
Christian Science Monitor (USA)
Covert Action (USA)
Financial Times (London)
Guardian (USA)
Journal of Commerce (USA)
Los Angeles Times
Manchester Guardian Weekly (United Kingdom)
Miami Herald
Nation (USA)
New York Times
The Guardian (United Kingdom)
The Scotsman (United Kingdom)
The Sunday Times (London)
The Times (London)
Washington Post

Further Reading
Ahluwalia, Montes S. 1974. Income inequality: some dimensions of the problem. *Finance and Development*, September
Apter, D. 1965. *The Politics of Modernization.* Chicago, Ill., University of Chicago Press
1966. *Ghana in Transition.* New York, NY, Atheneum
Balogh, Thomas 1972. The mechanics of neo-imperialism. In *Economic Imperialism*, ed. Kenneth Boulding and Tapan Mukerjee, Ann Arbor, Ill., University of Michigan Press
Beckford, George L. 1980. Socioeconomic change and political continuity in the Anglophone Caribbean. *Studies in Comparitive International Development*, vol. 51, no. 1, Spring
Bhagwhati, Jagdish N. 1967, *The Trying of Aid.* Prepared for UNCTAD Secretariat. TD/7/Supplement 4, 1 November
Caves, Richard E. 1974. International trade, international markets and imperfect markets. Princeton University, Special Papers in International Economics, no. 10, November
Chenery, H. B. and A. M. Strout 1966. Foreign assistance and economic development. *American Economic Review*, September

230 Bibliography

Danns, George K. 1978. Militarization and development: an experiment in nation building. *Transition*, Journal of the Faculty of Social Sciences and the Institute of Development, University of Guyana, vol. 1, no. 1: 23–44

Demas, William 1965. *The Economics of Development in Small Countries with Special Reference to the Caribbean*. Montreal, McGill University Press

Dorner, Peter 1972. Needed redirection in economic analysis for agricultural development policy. *American Journal of Agricultural Economics*, February

Frey, F. W. 1963. Political development, power, and communication in Turkey. In *Communication and Political Development*, ed. Lucian W. Pye, Princeton, NJ, Princeton University Press

Girvan, Norman 1976. *Corporate Imperialism: Conflict and expropriation*. New York, NY, Monthly Review Press

Grant, James P. 1973. Growth from below: a people-oriented strategy. Development Paper 16, Washington DC, Overseas Development Council, December

Haq, Mahbub ul, 1973. The crisis of development strategies. In *The Political Economy of Development and Underdevelopment*, ed. Charles K. Wilber, New York, NY, Random House

Hintzen, Percy C. 1985. The dynamics of ethnicity, class, and international capitalist penetration of political economy. *Social and Economic Studies*, vol. 34, no. 3, September

Hunter G. (ed.) 1965. *Industrialization and Race Relations*. London, Oxford University Press

Huntingdon, S. P. 1968. *Political Order in Changing Society*. New Haven, Conn., Yale University Press

Ilchman, W. F. and Ravindra C. Bhargava 1966. Balanced thought and economic growth. *Economic Development and Cultural Change*, vol. 14, no. 4, July

Johnson, Harry G. 1971. The ideology of economic policy in new states. In *Political Development and Social Change*, 2nd edn, ed. Jason L. Finkle and Richard W. Gable, New York, NY, John Wiley and Sons. Reprinted from *Economic Nationalism in Old and New States*, ed. Harry G. Johnson, Chicago, Ill., University of Chicago Press

Lewis, W. Arthur 1949. Industrial development in Puerto Rico. *Caribbean Economic Review*, May

1950. Industrialization of the British West Indies. *Caribbean Economic Review*, May

Maurier, R. 1949 *The Sociology of Colonies*. London, Routledge and Kegan Paul

Meier, Gerald M. 1976. *Leading Issues in Economic Development*, 3rd edn, New York, NY, Oxford University Press

Morgan, T. N. 1974. *Multinational Corporations and the Politics of Dependence: Copper in Chile*. Princeton, NJ, Princeton University Press

Payer, Cherly 1974. *The Debt Trap: IMF and the third world*. New York, NY, Monthly Review Press

Pearson, Lester B. 1969. Report of the Commission International Development. In *Partners in Development*, New York, NY, Praegar

Pearlmutter, Amos 1971. The Praetorian state and the Praetorian army: towards a

Bibliography

theory of civil-military relations in developing countries. In *Political Development and Social Change*, ed. Jason L. Finkle and Richard W. Gable, New York, NY, John Wiley and Sons

Poulantzas, N. 1975. *Classes in Contemporary Capitalism*. London, New Left Books

Rothchild, D. 1984. Hegemonial exchange: state-ethnic relations in Middle Africa. In *Twenty-Five Years of Independence, 1957–1982*: An assessment, ed. G. Carter and P. O'Meara (forthcoming)

Ruiz, R. E. 1968. *Cuba: The making of a revolution*. New York, NY, W. W. Norton and Co.

Sauvant, Karl P. and Hajo Hasenpflug (eds.) 1977. *The New International Economic Order: Competition or cooperation between North and South?* Boulder, Col., Westview Press

Scott, R. E. 1967. Political elites and political modernization. In *Elites in Latin America*, ed. S. M. Lipset and A. Solari, New York, NY, Oxford University Press

Seers, Dudley 1963. The limitations of the special case. *Bulletin of the Oxford Institute of Economic and Statistics*, vol. 25, no. 2, May

1969. The meaning of development. *International Development Review*, vol. 11, no. 4. Reprinted in *The Political Economy of Development*, ed. Norman T. Uphoff and Warren F. Ilchman. Berkeley, Cal., University of California Press, 1972

Seligman, Lester G. 1971. Elite recruitment and political development. In *Political Development and Social Change*, 2nd edn, ed. Jason L. Finkle and Richard W. Gable, New York, NY, John Wiley and Sons

Shils, Edward 1971. The intellectuals in the political development of new states. *Political Development and Social Change*, 2nd edn, ed. Jason L. Finkle and Richard W. Gable. New York, NY, John Wiley and Sons

Singham, A. W. 1968. *The Hero and the Crowd in a Colonial Polity*. New Haven, Conn, Yale University Press

Smith, M. G. 1965. *The Plural Society in the British West Indies*. Berkeley and Los Angeles, Cal., University of California Press

1971. Institutional and political conditions of pluralism. In *Pluralism in Africa*, ed. Leo Kuper and M. G. Smith, Berkeley and Los Angeles, Cal., University of California Press

Smock, D. R. and A. C. Smock 1975. *The Politics of Pluralism*. New York, NY, Elsevier

Thomas, C. Y. 1976. Bread and justice: the struggle for socialism in Guyana. *Monthly Review*, vol. 28, no. 4 September

Van Den Berghe, Pierre 1969. Pluralism and the polity: a theoretical exploration. In *Pluralism and Africa*, ed. Leo Kuper and M. G. Smith, Berkeley, Cal., University of California Press

Williams, Eric 1964. *Capitalism and Slavery*. London, Andre Deutsch

1976. New Year message to the nation. 1 January

Index

African, Caribbean, and Pacific Countries (ACP), 185
African Society for Cultural Relations with Independent Africa (ASCRIA), 170–1, 172
Agriculture: development in Guyana, 189–90; development funding in Trinidad 74, 176–7; development program in Trinidad 137, 177–9
Ake, Claude, 168
Alcan Aluminum Co., 154
Algeria, 154
All Trinidad Sugar Estates and Factory Workers, 38
Amerindians: in Guyana, 3, 26
Amoco, 145
Association of South-East Asian Nations (ASEAN), 206
Autonomy, political: in economic decisionmaking, conditions for, 16–17, 212–15
Avebury, Lord, 100

Bauxite production, in Guyana, 151, 154–6, 185–6, 188–9
Best, Lloyd, 14
Black intellectuals in formation of PNM, 44
Black population: Guyana, 2, 23–5; in security forces, 92; Trinidad, 2, 23–5
Bookers Sugar Estates Limited/Booker McConnell Ltd, 152, 153–4, 161
British Guiana Labour Union (BGLU), 32, 38
British Labour Party: influence on politics of Guyana and Trinidad, 31–3, opposition to PPP, 49
British Petroleum Company (BP), 137, 140
British West Indian Airways, 76
British West Indies, 30, 105, 182
Bureaucracy: colonial, 4–5; function of, 4; state, 8
Burnham, Forbes, 34, 94, 100; and formation of the PNC, 50; and metropolitan interests, 52; political ideology of, 63–4; and racial politics, 63–4
Butler Party, 43–4; and East Indians, 43–4; and elections in 1956, 45
Butler, Uriah, 43

Cadet Corps (Guyana), 92
Cambodia, 94n3
Canada, 191
Capitalist leaders, in Guyana and Trinidad, 113–14
Caribbean Development Bank (CDB), 183
Caribbean Socialist Party, 43
Carnival Development Committee, 74
Carter administration (USA), 203; and Guyana 69–70, 99
Central Intelligence Agency (CIA), 52
Chinese, in Guyana and Trinidad, 3, 27
Churchill, Winston, 49
Civil administrative functions of state: and regime survival, 127–8
Civil and political rights: and regime survival 197–8
Class: definition of, 17; organization and composition in Guyana and Trinidad, 17–20
lower classes, and collective needs, 210–11; in Guyana and Trinidad, 18; politics of, in Guyana, 50; politics of, and the PNM, 78, 90, 140–1, 173–5
lower middle class, in Guyana and Trinidad 18–19;
middle class, and collective needs, 209–10; and politics, 41–2; politics and the PNC, 55–6, 64–7, 159, 162–3, 171, 193; politics and the PNM, 44–5, 63, 78
upper middle class, in Guyana and Trinidad, 19
upper class, in Guyana and Trinidad, 19–20
Class mobilization: colonialism and, 28–9; impediments to, 20; nationalism and, 29–32, 37; Guyana, 32–7

233

234 Index

Clerical and Commercial Workers Union (CCWU), 171
Clientelism, see Patronage
Coercion: by Britain in Guyana, 33–4, 36; by state 12; and regime survival, 57, 77–8, 128; and regime survival in Guyana, 90–100, 172–3; and regime survival in Trinidad, 79–90, 100, 146
Collective needs: 2, 165, 167–8; and elite demands, 200; and international actors, 207–8; and regime survival, 198–9
Colonial bureaucracy, 4–5
Colonial government: in Guyana and Trinidad, 30–1, 33–4; and suspension of constitution in Guyana, 36–7;
Colonial Office, 29, 31, 32
Colonial state: role of, 8
Coloreds: in Guyana and Trinidad, 26
Commission of Inquiry into the Oil Industry of Trinidad and Tobago (1964), 132
Commonwealth of Nations, 206; support for PPP, 49
Communal Politics: and elite support, 104; and support for political leaders, 38; Guyana, 37–9, 92–100, and trade union organization, 37; Trinidad, 37–9, shift to communal politics, 43–5, 87, and trade union organization, 87; see also Racial politics
Communalism/communal organization: and social segmentation, 6, 7; and political organization, 6, 7, 9, 37, 87, 94n3
Communist bloc: Guyana's relations with, 98–9
Compass Group, 69, 171
Constituencies, see Electoral boundaries
Constitutional change: in Guyana (1961), 51–2; in Guyana (1964) 54, 96–7, 172; in Trinidad (1950), 39–40; PNM demand for, 62
Constitutional suspension (Guyana 1953), 36–7
Control: of economy in regime survival, 126–31, 151; by the political executive, 11; and regime survival, 57, 77–8; by the state, 11, 126–131; Guyana, 90–100, 197, of the economy, 151–63; Trinidad, 78–90, of the economy, 132–150
Cooperative development in Guyana, 184n2
Cooptation: of elites, 11, 13, 57, 71; of elites in Guyana, 70–3, 121–3

D'Aguiar, Peter: as Minister of Finance, 65; and the United Force 50
Defence functions of state, 128

Demerara Bauxite Company (Demba), 154–5, 158–9
Demerara Company Holdings Ltd., 152–4, 161
Democratic Action Congress (DAC), 119
Destabilization, 13–16; of PNC government, 68–9; of PPP government, 35–7, 52–4
Development and Environmental Works Division (DEWD), 73–4, 195
Development Funds (Trinidad), see Special Funds
Development functions of state, 127
Domestic actors, 208–11
Dominican Republic, 135
Duvalier, Jean-Claude, 203

Eastern Europe, 99, 155, 156, 162
East Indians: Guyana, 3, 25–6, and literacy, 48, and population growth, 47, and security forces, 92, and urbanization, 47–8; Trinidad, 3, 25–6
Economic crisis: in Guyana, 68–9, 170–3, 185–93, 196–7; in Trinidad, 79, 139–41, 179–83, 195–6
Elections, see General elections; Local government elections
Electoral boundaries in Trinidad, 61, 62, 90
Electoral fraud in Guyana, 56, 72, 96–7
Elites: colonial, 5; local, 5, 7, 165–6; state controlling, 9; and claims upon the state, 128; control of the state, 103–5, 125
composition of, and party support in Guyana, 119–123; and party support in Trinidad, 116–19; and PNC policies 107; and PNM policies, 107; and regime survival 104–5
Guyana, and ideology, 111–15; and party support, 114–15, 119–23; sectoral and institutional background of, 106–9; wealth of, 106–9
Trinidad, ideology of, 111–14; and party support, 114–15, 116–19; and patronage, 75–6; sectoral and institutional background, 106–9; wealth of, 109–11
Emigration, from Guyana, 111
Employment and unemployment: in Guyana, 197; in Trinidad, 136, 194–5
Enloe, Cynthia, 130
European Economic Community (EEC), 185
Executive Council (Guyana) 33, 34, 35

Fabian socialism: impact on Guyana and Trinidad, 31–2; of Forbes Burnham, 63; and middle class, 42

Index

Federation, *see* West Indian Federation
Feed, Clothe, and House Ourselves Programme (FCH), 184
Flying Squad, 84

Gandhi, Mahatma, 31
Gandhi, Youth Organization (Guyana), 71
General elections:
  Guyana, in 1953, 34–6; in 1957, 49; in 1961, 51; in 1964, 54, 65; in 1968, 56
  Trinidad, in 1955, postpostment of, 44; in 1956, 45; in 1961, 45; in 1971, 84; in 1976, 87–8; in 1981, 88; in 1986, 101
Governmental actors, and regime survival, 201–4
Grace, W. R. and Co., 145
Gradualism, *see* Political gradualism
Great Britain: efforts against PPP, 64; parliamentary deliberations, 30; policy and practice in Guyana, 46, 48–9, 51, 63–6; policy and practice in Trinidad, 39–40, 51, 58–63
Grenada, 203
Guerrilla movement in Trinidad, 85
Guiana Industrial Workers Union (GIWU), 33
Guiana Volunteer Force, 91
Guyana Administration of Justice Bill (1978), 98
Guyana Defence Force (GDF), 91–4
Guyana National Service (GNS), 92, 159
Guyana State Corporation (Guystac), 159
Guyana Sugar Corporation, 187

Haiti, 203
Hindus: in Guyana, 26, 71; in Trinidad, 26; and politics in Trinidad, 88
Hoechst and Kaiser Aluminum Co., 60
House of Israel, 94
Hoyte, Desmond, 94
Hudson-Phillips, Karl, 89, 90
Human rights, *see* Civil and political rights

Ideology: capitalism, 94n3, 129, 138; socialism 94n3, 129; socialism in Guyana, 158
Incrementalism, and nationalist politics, 37
Independence, for Guyana and Trinidad, 3
India, 31
Indian Political Revolutionary Associates (IPRA), 171
Industrial Court, 75, 79
Industrial Development Corporation (IDC), 138
Industrial Relations Act, 1965 (IRA), 174
Industrial Stabilization Act (ISA), 75, 79

Industrialization program in Trinidad, 101, 110–11, 145, 150, 177, 180–3, 195
International actors, 7, 13, 200–1; and collective needs, 207–8
International Bank for Reconstruction and Development (World Bank), 204; and Guyana, 99
International Bauxite Association (IBA), 155
International business, and collective needs, 206–7
International Confederation of Trade Unions (ICFTU), 52
International Monetary Fund (IMF), and aid to Guyana, 99, 204
International organizations, and collective needs, 204–6
International realignment as a regime strategy, 12

Jagan, Cheddi, 33, 34, 162; policies of, 49–51
Jamaica, 121n12
James, C. L. R., in the PNM, 60
Jews, in Trinidad, 27
Job creation, by the state in Trinidad, 74–5
Judicial Service Commission, 98
Judiciary; in Guyana, and control by regime, 97–8; in Trinidad, 77, 198

Kenya, 122

Labor mobilization: in Guyana, 29–36; in Guyana against the PPP, 53–4; in Trinidad, 29–32, 37–9, 43–4, 78–81, 86–8
Labor riots, in Anglophone Caribbean (1930s) 29–30; in Trinidad 29–30
Labour (Amendment) Bill (1984), 172
Laos, 94n3
Law and order, as functions of the state, 128
Leaders, *see* Elites
Lebanese in Trinidad, 27
Lebanon, 203
Legislative Council, in Guyana, 32, 34, in Trinidad, 39–41
Liberator Party, 120
Libya, 203
Local government elections, in Trinidad (1982), 101
Localization, process of, 5
Lockheed, 76

Maha Saba: and the PNC in Guyana, 71; and politics in Trinidad, 44, and ULF, 90

236   Index

Majoritarianism: and political power in Guyana, 96–100; and political power in Trinidad, 39
Man Power Citizens Association (MPCA), 38
Management Development Centre (Trinidad), 138
Marcos, Ferdinand, 203
Marxism/Marxism–Leninism, 7; of Guyana's leaders, 38; in PNC, 69; in PPP, 47, 48, 120
Mass mobilization: and race and class in Guyana and Trinidad, 20–7; role of, 5
McDonnell-Douglas, 76
Middle East War (1973), and impact on Trinidad, 85, 141
Military: and state function, 130 Guyana, defence budget, 92, 161; intervention in politics, 91–100; and politics, 161
Trinidad, American military presence, 60–1; intervention in politics, 80–3
Mini-states, 14–16
Ministry of Labour (Trinidad), 75, 79
Mitsui Chemicals, 145
Mixed population in Guyana and Trinidad, 2
Moskos, Charles, 105, 110n3, 111n5
Muslims, in Guyana and Trinidad, 26

National Economic Advisory Council, 62–3, 110n3
National Joint Action Committee (NJAC), 80, 88, 119
National Petroleum Company, 136, 140, 141
National Reconstruction, Program of (1971), 85, 140
National Security Act (1978), in Guyana, 172
National Security Act (1970), in Trinidad, 83
National United Freedom Fighters (NUFF), 84–6
Nationalism/nationalist mobilization, 5–6; and mass mobilization under colonialism, 28–9; in Guyana and Trinidad 37–9, 29–32; in Guyana, 32–7
Nationalist ideology, role of, 5, 29
Nationalist politics, and progressive ideology 42; in Guyana 3, 29–37; in Trinidad, 3, 29–32, 35
Nationalization: effects of, 188; program in Guyana, 67–8, 111, 154, 158, 161–3; problems of, 185
New Investment Code (Guyana), 69

Non-Aligned Movement, 206
North Korea, 99

Oil industry/oil production, *see* Petroleum production
Oilfield Workers Trade Union (OWTU), 37–8, 43, 86
Organization for National Reconstruction (ONR), 88, 90
Organization of American States (OAS), 206
Organization of Commonwealth Caribbean Bar Association (OCCBA), 98
Organization of Petroleum Exporting Countries (OPEC), 17, 155
Outbidding, 78; definition of, 118; and the PNC, 170; and the PNM, 78–90, 100, 135
Overdeveloped state, 103nl

Patronage, 11, 122n13; and control of the state, 70; elites, 104; and regime survival, 57, 72, 76–7, 100, 128, 144, 198
Guyana, and regime survival, 70–3; and state employment, 95
Trinidad, direct patronage, 73–4; elite patronage, 75–6, 119; indirect patronage, 74–5; financing of, 146
People's Charter, 45
Peoples Democratic Party (PDP), formation of, 44; in 1956 elections, 45
Peoples Militia, 92
Peoples National Congress (PNC): formation, 50; ideology, 55; anti-PPP campaign, 52–4; in coalition government, 54–6, 65, 91, 169; and coercion, 90–100; economic policies, 68, 156–64; and elections of 1964, 54; and elections of 1968, 56; and electoral fraud, 56; elite support, 114, 120–4; and order and stability, 169–77; and racial support, 55, 90–1
Peoples National Movement (PNM): formation, 44–5, 59; and ideology, 58–63, 138; ideological conflict in, 69; platform 45; policies of, 132–50, 173–9; black opposition to, 78–90; and 1956 elections, 45; and 1961 elections, 45; and 1981 elections, 88, 101; and 1982 local government elections, 101; and elite support, 116–19; and federation, 59; and international interests, 60; and international interests, 60; and the judiciary, 77; and outbidding, 78; patronage, 73–7; and unions, 75
Peoples National Party (PNP), 121n12

Index

Peoples Progressive Party (PPP): 34; and racial and class support, 47; and 1953 elections, 35–6; and 1961 elections, 51; and elite support, 114; as government in 1953, 36–7, 46; as government in 1957–64, 49–51; and Great Britain, 64; ideology and ideological conflict, 48–9, 52; in opposition, 170; and the United States, 99
Peoples Republic of China, 154
Petit bourgeois: and the PPP, 47; and the PNM, 44
Petroleum production/petroleum industry in Trinidad, 101, 132, 142–50
Petroleum Taxes Act (1974), 142–3
Philippines, 203
Phillip Brothers, 155
Point Lisas Industrial Estate, 145
Political Affairs Committee (PAC), 33, 34
Political conflict: in Guyana, 32–4, 46–51, 53–4, 93–4, 169–73; in Trinidad, 80–4, 174; and military in Trinidad, 81–2, 100
Political ethnicity, 6, 7
Political gradualism, 30, 58
Political Progress Group (PPG), 39, 40
Port Authority, 75
Positional-reputational method, 105–6
Poverty, in Trinidad, 194–6
Premdas, Ralph, 34
Private investment in LDCs, 14n10
Proportional representation in Guyana, 64–5
Public Corporations (Amendment) Act (1971), 159
Public Order Bill (1970), 83
Public sector, growth in Guyana, 67

Race and class in Guyana and Trinidad, 20–7
Racial composition in Guyana and Trinidad, 2–3, 20–7
Racial politics: in Guyana 3, 37–9, 46–51; and class interests in Guyana, 46–51; and constituency system in Guyana, 38; in Trinidad, 3, 37–9, 100; and class interests in Trinidad, 39–46
Reagan, Ronald, 203
Regime survival: conditions of, 10, 13, 57; costs of, 2, 166; strategies for, 10–13, 57–8, and coercion, patronage, and control 57; and collective needs 198–9; and elite support, 103–5, 124, 200; and economic conditions, 175, 192–3; and equity and social security, 193–4; and external support, 98; and order and stability, 168–9
Guyana, 84–5, and economic conditions, 183–93; and order and stability, 168–73

Trinidad, and economic conditions, 175–83; and economic policy 132–50; and order and stability, 173–5
Reynolds Metal Co., 161
Rhodesia, 94n3
Robinson, A. N. R., 89
Rodney, Walter, 172

Sam P. Wallace Construction Co., 76
Samincorp, 155
Seamen and Waterfront Workers Trade Union (SWWTU), 75
Self rule, in Guyana, 34; in Trinidad, 62
Shell Oil, 143
Small Business Unit (Trinidad), 138
Social, Political, and Economic Council (SPEC), 93
Socialist leaders, in Guyana and Trinidad, 113–14
South Africa, 94n3, 201
South East Asia, 201
Soviet Union/Soviet bloc, 155, 203, see also Eastern Europe
Special Funds (Trinidad), 147–50, 176–7
Special Works Program, 195
State, functions of, 175, 166–8
State Council (Guyana) (1953), 35
State expansion: in Guyana, 157–63, 184; and benefits for state workers, 66, 121–2, 196;
State of Emergency, in Trindad (1970), 80–2
State workers: and political power, 41, 65–6 Guyana, and anti-PPP campaign, 53–4, 184; and patronage, 71–2, 121–2, 197 Trinidad, 195; salaries and benefits, 146
Sugar production, in Guyana, 151–4
Sugar workers, in Guyana, 34
Syrians in Trinidad, 27

Tapia, 119
Terminal economy, 14, 15
Tesoro Petroleum Company, 76, 137, 145
Texaco, 145
Third Five Year Plan (1973), 137
Trades Union Council (TUC), 33, 95, 172
Transport and Industrial Workers Union (TIWU), 80
Trinidad and Tobago Regiment, in 1970 conflict, 81

Unemployment, see Employment and unemployment
Unemployment Levy (1970), 73, 141, 142
Unions, and political power in Guyana, 66; and political confrontation in Trinidad 80; and political support in Trinidad, 77

238 Index

United Force (UF): and anti-PPP campaign, 53–4; coalition with PNC, 54–6, 65–6, 156–7; in 1964 elections, 54; and elite support, 120; formation, 50
United Kingdom Human Rights Group, 100
United Labour Front, 86, 87–8, 118, 119
United Nations, 205–6
United Sad'r Islamic Anjuman, 71
United States of America, 202; aid to Guyana, 99; efforts against PNC, 68, 154; efforts against PPP, 52–4, 64; policy to Guyana, 69, 181–2; and threat of military intervention in Trinidad, 83
Universal adult sufferage, in Guyana and Trinidad, 31, 33, 34
University of Guyana Staff Association (UGSA), 171

Viet Nam, 94n3, 135

Wages, in Trinidad, 75
Washington, Rabbi, 94
Weber, Max, 4
West India Royal Commission (1939), 30
West Indian Federation, East Indian rejection in Guyana, 48; East Indian opposition in Trinidad, 48
West Indian National Party, 43
Whites, in Guyana and Trinidad, 3, 21–23; and the PNM, 59; and politics in Trinidad, 39–41
Williams, Dr. Eric, death of, 88; as founder of the PNM, 44; and PNM policy, 61
Working Peoples Alliance (WPA), 171, 172
World Federation of Trade Unions, 52
World War Two, 30, 31

Zimbabwe, 94n3

Other books in the series

J. Milton Yinger, Kiyoshi Ikeda, Frank Laycock, and Stephen J. Cutler: *Middle Start: An Experiment in the Educational Enrichment of Young Adolescents*
James A. Geschwender: *Class, Race, and Worker Insurgency: The League of Revolutionary Black Workers*
Paul Ritterband: *Education, Employment, and Migration: Israel in Comparative Perspective*
John Low-Beer: *Protest and Participation: The New Working Class in Italy*
Orrin E. Klapp: *Opening and Closing: Strategies of Information Adaptation in Society*
Rita James Simon: *Continuity and Change: A Study of Two Ethnic Communities in Israel*
Marshall B. Clinard: *Cities with Little Crime: The Case of Switzerland**
Steven T. Bossert: *Tasks and Social Relationships in Classrooms: A Study of Instructional Organization and Its Consequences**
Richard E. Johnson: *Juvenile Delinquency and Its Origins: An Integrated Theoretical Approach**
David R. Heise: *Understanding Events: Affect and the Construction of Social Action*
Ida Harper Simpson: *From Student to Nurse: A Longitudinal Study of Socialization*
Stephen P. Turner: *Sociological Explanation as Translation*
Janet W. Salaff: *Working Daughters of Hong Kong: Filial Piety or Power in the Family?*
Joseph Chamie: *Religion and Fertility: Arab Christian-Muslim Differentials*
William Friedland, Amy Barton, Robert Thomas: *Manufacturing Green Gold: Capital, Labor, and Technology in the Lettuce Industry*
Richard N. Adams: *Paradoxical Harvest: Energy and Explanation in British History, 1870-1914*
Mary F. Rogers: *Sociology, Ethnomethodology, and Experience: A Phenomenological Critique*
James R. Beniger: *Trafficking in Drug Users: Professional Exchange Networks in the Control of Deviance*
Andrew J. Weigert, J. Smith Teitge, and Dennis W. Teitge: *Society and Identity: Toward a Sociological Psychology*

* Available from the American Sociological Association, 1722 N Street, NW, Washington, DC 20036.

Jon Miller: *Pathways in the Workplace: The Effects of Race and Gender on Access to Organizational Resources*
Michael A. Faia: *Dynamic functionalism: Strategy and Tactics*
Joyce Rothschild and J. Allen Whitt: *The Co-operative Workplace: Potentials and Dilemmas of Organizational Democracy*
Russell Thornton: *We Shall Live Again: The 1870 and 1890 Ghost Dance Movements as Demographic Revitalization*
Severyn T. Bruyn: *The Field of Social Investment*
Guy E. Swanson: *Ego Defenses and the Legitimation of Behaviour*
Liah Greenfeld: *Different Worlds: A Sociological Study of Taste, Choice and Success in Art*
Thomas K. Rudel: *Situations and Strategies in American Land-Use Planning*

For EU product safety concerns, contact us at Calle de José Abascal, 56–1°, 28003 Madrid, Spain or eugpsr@cambridge.org.

www.ingramcontent.com/pod-product-compliance
Ingram Content Group UK Ltd.
Pitfield, Milton Keynes, MK11 3LW, UK
UKHW011317060825
461487UK00005B/146